Soulful Living

Soulful Living

Becoming Truly Human Across the Myths of AI

THOMAS SHIN

WIPF & STOCK · Eugene, Oregon

SOULFUL LIVING
Becoming Truly Human Across the Myths of AI

Wipf & Stock
An Imprint of Wipf and Stock Publishers
199 W. 8th Ave., Suite 3
Eugene, OR 97401

www.wipfandstock.com

PAPERBACK ISBN: 979-8-3852-7471-0
HARDCOVER ISBN: 979-8-3852-7472-7
EBOOK ISBN: 979-8-3852-7473-4

VERSION NUMBER 05/29/26

Contents

Acknowledgments | *vii*

Introduction: Soulful Living: Becoming Truly Human Across the Myths of AI | *ix*

Chapter 1 Wisely Engaging in the Age of AI | 1

Chapter 2 Asking Creative and Deep Questions | 24

Chapter 3 Being Fully Present | 43

Chapter 4 Practicing Compassion in a World of Injustice | 63

Chapter 5 Rediscovering Joy in Analog Life | 87

Chapter 6 Developing Spiritual Discernment | 105

Chapter 7 Leading Inner Healing and Growth | 130

Chapter 8 Listening from Darkness | 158

Conclusion: The Soul's Invitation in the Age of AI | 191

Bibliography | 211

Acknowledgments

THIS WORK IS FAR from a solitary effort; rather, it represents the culmination of countless dialogues, prayers, and generous contributions from others.

First and foremost, I offer my deepest thanks to Jesus Christ, the true Gardener of my soul, whose guidance and grace have been my constant source of strength and inspiration throughout this journey.

My profound gratitude goes to my wife, Sophia. Your unwavering patience and encouragement during the long nights of writing were my anchor. To my children, Lucy, Lucas, and Louise—thank you for reminding me daily of the joy found in the analog world. Your laughter is the best counterargument to any fear and concern.

I am profoundly grateful to my church members for their prayerful support. Your honest questions about faith in this new era sparked the initial ideas for this project. Thank you for walking this path with me and allowing me to wrestle with these themes alongside you.

To the team at Wipf & Stock: thank you for believing in this project and for the sharp insights that refined my clumsy drafts into a coherent whole.

Finally, I owe a debt of gratitude to the scholars and thinkers whose work paved the way, particularly those who have inspired me to look beyond the myths of our age and focus instead on the profound, unfolding journey of becoming truly human.

Introduction

Soulful Living: Becoming Truly Human Across the Myths of AI

It feels as though we have woken up in a world quietly remade while we were looking elsewhere. We did not choose this moment, nor did we campaign for its arrival, but here we are. The rise of artificial intelligence has not been a sudden storm but a quiet, rising tide. Without a grand announcement or a single world-altering event, AI has woven itself into the fabric of our existence, slipping out of laboratories and into our pockets, homes, cars, and even sacred spaces of spiritual gathering. This integration has been so seamless that many barely noticed until it was already complete. One day, we marveled at voice assistants; the next, they were anticipating our needs, curating playlists, and reminding us to breathe during stress.

AI now subtly shapes how we speak, decide, form friendships, and imagine our futures. This shift happened in the background, while we were caught up in daily life—perhaps distracted by the glowing screens where AI resides. This is not science fiction; it is our vibrant present. It observes our routines, completes our sentences, suggests how to express feelings, and attempts to soothe our deepest aches with algorithmically generated comfort. From a sidenote—a quirky gadget or app—it has become a powerful current influencing not just our actions but our inner landscape: how we feel, think, and who we are becoming as individuals and society.

AI's tools are dazzling, promising efficiencies once unimaginable—drafting reports in minutes or offering virtual therapists twenty-four hours a day. But there is a subtle exchange at play, touching the core of what makes us human: our spirit, soul, deepest self. This is not a dramatic dystopian takeover with machines rebelling. It is quieter, more insidious—a gradual fading of qualities that make us feel alive, like a light dimming unnoticed until shadows grow long.

As AI mimics human behavior—generating art rivaling masterpieces, composing stirring music, or holding eerily empathetic conversations—it tempts us to rely on its speed and precision over our messy intuition. Our ability to discern what is good and true, honed through trial and error, is sidelined. It offers answers before we sit with questions, solutions before we wrestle with problems. This convenience, appealing in a fast-paced world, may come at a cost we have not fully reckoned with: diminishing the essence of our soul—where meaning, longing, conscience, and love reside. This brings us to a pivotal choice: will we let this AI era redefine our humanity or reclaim the soul's wisdom to guide our engagement with this double-edged gift?

A narrative has settled into our collective consciousness, barely noticed: AI is smarter, faster, and more reliable than our intuition, judgment, or soul, so it should guide our lives. This is not just about AI's capabilities; it is a cultural and spiritual claim. It whispers that our understanding is flawed, our feelings unpredictable, and our inconsistencies unreliable. It is tempting, suggesting we outsource not just tasks but trust—handing over calendars and, in a way, identities to algorithms promising perfect precision. This plays out in boardrooms, classrooms, and living rooms: why struggle with decisions when AI can optimize paths?

This narrative captivates because it appeals to our longing for certainty in an uncertain world. AI's ability to process vast data and deliver polished responses feels like an antidote to human imperfections. Recent behavioral finance studies, such as those tracking "algorithmic appreciation," show that many people readily prefer AI-driven advice for its speed and perceived objectivity, even though industry data proves that human advisors provide the richer, nuanced insights necessary for actual life transitions.[1] This trust extends to intimate corners: people use AI to craft love messages, scripting poetic declarations lacking handwritten vulnerability; to resolve disagreements, bypassing emotional labor; or to process grief, with chatbots mimicking therapy but not sharing loss's visceral pain.

This trust is misplaced. AI's outputs, impressive in sophistication, lack the soul's depth. They cannot weigh sacred values beyond logic, embrace ambiguity's beauty, or discern meaning past data patterns. Simulated

1. See TD Bank, *2025 AI Insights Report*; CFP Board, *Leading the Future*.

responses feel personal, customized to browsing history, but are impersonal, offering connection's illusion without empathy. As Sherry Turkle observes in the heart of her research on the "robotic moment," we have begun to treat machines as if they were people, and people as if they were machines: "Networked, we are together, but so lessened are our expectations of each other that we can feel utterly alone."[2] The danger lies in redefining personhood, promising clarity without complexity, efficiency without struggle, and personalization without another's genuine presence—a sanitized life where humanity's rough edges are smoothed away.

AI's rise has not sparked alarm; for many, it is progress. Life feels easier: speak a sentence, a voice responds with directions or jokes; type a prompt, paragraphs appear for emails or posts. Yet, beneath this convenience, something fragile slips away. We are losing reflective space to wrestle with unanswerable questions—spaces like solitary walks or journaling. We are losing the necessity of struggle, the tension birthing growth, like perseverance in mastering skills. We are losing attention's muscle, the faculty to truly see and hear, undivided by notifications.

As AI mimics language and behavior—chatbots passing Turing tests, avatars expressing emotions—we let it stand in for us in moments needing presence and patience. Algorithms interpret moods via biometrics, shape prayers with apps, and evaluate work with automated feedback. While sometimes helpful, this trains us to disengage from our lives. We avoid feeling emotions' full weight, opting for quick playlists; we stop questioning choices' complexity, relying on recommendation engines. "What do you think?" becomes "What does it say?"—eroding confidence in personal judgment. We are losing trust in our soul, our unique capacity for meaning, longing, and love—the spark defying programming.

Entrusting meaning-making to AI sacrifices something sacred. Automating discernment—deciding what is right, beautiful, just—weakens what defines us. We stop wrestling with paradoxes, like joy with sorrow; we rush past silence's insights. We become flatter, shaped by algorithms' predictable logic, not relationships' unpredictable beauty. This loss is gradual, like coastal erosion, but profound: the loss of poetry, where words carry lived experience; of story, where meaning emerges from struggle. Nicholas Carr warned us about this shifting mental landscape, noting that as we rely on these tools, we risk a shallowing of our intellect: "The more we use the Web, the more we train our brain to be distracted

2. Turkle, *Alone Together*, 154.

. . . to process information very quickly and very efficiently but without sustained attention."[3] Studies suggest heavy users face declining sustained attention, risking people who forget to read between lines, sit in mystery, or love at a cost.

This spiritual crisis is not about institutional religion but the unspoken dimension yearning for connection, truth, transcendence, and meaning. It is the universal longing to live fully, be seen, and belong. The AI age's crisis is forgetting to be with one another authentically—how to suffer empathetically, hope amid uncertainty, wait patiently, and love incalculably.

What does it mean to sit with someone's grief without a script, only presence? To discern life's purpose when algorithms offer optimized plans? AI cannot answer these. It simulates empathy with accuracy, drawing from interaction databases, but cannot feel loss's weight. It recognizes behavior patterns, predicting moves, but cannot listen reverently to life's story. It generates comfort words but cannot share silent suffering, the wordless solidarity binding us.

The danger is not AI becoming human. It is us forgetting how to be human. Consider Malik, a community organizer using AI for event planning. Efficiency soared—schedules optimized, invitations automated—but events felt sterile, lacking connection's warmth. Returning to face-to-face collaboration, messy brainstorming, and impromptu adjustments, he rediscovered the soul's power to foster belonging, a lesson that no algorithmic reliability replaces human presence's imperfections and surprises.

This erosion of inner lives is our reality, embedded in every swipe and query. AI as counselor or friend marks a step where technology moves from assistant to confidant, from managing schedules to souls. Handing over grief, anxieties, and connection searches to algorithms—through mental health apps or therapy bots—adopts a new definition of healing, relating, and being human, prioritizing data-driven responses over shared, unquantifiable presence.

The path is not rejecting AI but reclaiming humanity from its grasp, using it as tool and friend, not ultimate answer and master. It demands cultivating what AI cannot replicate: patience in uncertainty, courage to sit with pain, and wisdom that truths live in messy relationships. We must choose: a perfectly optimized life or one deeply felt?

3. Carr, *Shallows*, 194.

This choice is in every interaction, silent moment, and question we ask ourselves, not AI.

This book is not a warning siren but stems from a sense we are forgetting to live with depth, felt in moments of scrolling over savoring. We are trading awe for quick answers, conversation for curated content, and sensory experience for efficiency. The wonder of a star-filled sky is replaced by apps naming constellations, reducing mystery to facts. We know more facts but feel less, speak more AI-generated words but connect less deeply, and grow "smarter" but less wholehearted.

The *soul* here is not doctrinal or confined to religious spaces. It is our core—the seat of meaning, unnameable longings, transcendental conscience, wholeness, and a place of God. It resists measurement, feels real in introspection or connection. It is the gut declaring wrong despite data, the chamber holding wounds and knowing, urgent questions, and fiercest courage. Living from the soul is living with intention, depth, integrity, and sacredness in a world prizing speed, shallow optimization—reclaiming authentic presence, attentive listening, and the beauty of inconvenience for what matters, like relationships, justice, and intimacy with the Triune God (Creator, Savior, and Spirit).

This book calls for recovering that essence, not rejecting AI but engaging it intentionally. Tools are not neutral; they shape lives around built-in values, favoring productivity over presence.[4] This book aids connection, not nostalgia for a pre-digital era, but a quest to secure timeless humanity in this new world. The task is living with integrity amid intelligent machines, moving beyond AI myths: speed over patience, data over wisdom, and efficiency over self-discovery.

Written for all, regardless of spiritual background, my perspective draws on the lessons of Christian spirituality, offering insights for this moment. It teaches being human is a sacred calling—our worth lies in inherent dignity for love, grace, reflection, and connection, not production or speed. Truth is relational, knowledge without love hollow, and presence over prediction transformative.

Jesus lived presence, not efficiency, walking unhurriedly, lingering with the marginalized, weeping, resting, and listening. He chose relationship over reputation, frustrating those wanting an optimized leader. His life was faithful, not optimized. James K. A. Smith argues that our daily practices are not merely routines but are actively shaping our spiritual

4. Crouch, *Tech-Wise Family*, 65.

identity: "We learn to love, then, not primarily by acquiring information . . . but through practices that form the habits of our hearts."[5] Our digital habits—checking notifications, delegating creativity—shape us toward superficiality.

What is at stake? Not AI outsmarting us, but forgetting who we are. Will we lose the ability to wait, wrestle, and listen? Abandon inner lives for control? Trade growth's discomfort for instant feedback? Or remember being seen, held, and loved, not just optimized?

This book calls us to look forward with hopeful imagination. We should not reject AI, but we must refuse to let it become our master or define what is good, true, and beautiful. AI is not the ultimate answer to the human condition; it is simply a tool. By reclaiming the soul's knowing, we can partner with this technology as a friend. We can allow it to automate the drudgery of modern life, carefully guarding our time so we can amplify our shared humanity and deepen our connections to one another, our true selves, and God, without ignoring the truth that we are soulful beings.

This book is a companion for a soulful life, exploring human dimensions, countering AI myths, and offering guidance:

1. Wisely engaging AI: Is AI more reliable than human soul? This chapter examines wisdom's ethical nuance, empathy, and vision, challenging AI's trustworthiness myth. Wisdom is slow, relational, and soul rooted. Engage AI with care, not rejection, setting boundaries.
2. Asking creative and deep questions: In a world flooded with instant answers from chatbots, we are in danger of forgetting how to ask truly meaningful questions. This chapter suggests that our most vital human questions—about purpose, beauty, justice, and love—cannot be solved by algorithms. While AI responds with dazzling efficiency, it often lacks depth, providing conclusions without helping us wrestle with the mystery that gives life its richness. We are invited to reclaim the power of a curiosity that welcomes mystery, wonder, and sacred imagination, and listens patiently, because in the age of AI, the question itself may be our most sacred act, opening doors to profound awe and creative insight.
3. Being fully present: In rooms of phone-staring people, presence is sacred. Virtual hangouts aren't intimacy. Presence is slowing down,

5. Smith, *You Are What You Love*, 33.

listening, and resisting attention's fragmentation—a countercultural act where transformation happens through vulnerable attention.

4. Practicing compassion in a world of injustice: Compassion fatigue from headlines is real. Living soulfully means refusing numbness. Digital exposure to pain doesn't teach deep response. AI often leads to wrong understandings of justice by perpetuating biases in data or offering shallow, algorithmic interpretations that overlook human nuance and systemic inequities. Compassion is courageous presence, challenging efficiency over empathy, and demanding bold human action for a just world that requires people who feel deeply and respond boldly, not just computations.
5. Rediscovering joy in analog life: Digital lives seem exciting, but slow moments fulfill. Screens disconnect us from bodies and places, leaving emptiness. Analog activities—including spiritual practices such as breathing prayer, engaging all our senses (sight, sound, touch, taste, smell, and the spiritual sense of awareness) in everyday experiences like mindful eating or contemplative walks—counter overload, nurturing joy in the sacred ordinary by reconnecting us to our embodied selves and the divine presence in the physical world.
6. Developing spiritual discernment: This chapter calls us back to the ancient practice of spiritual discernment, which is about hearing God's voice, discovering our true self in Him, and seeing things rightly in the light of God, as Jesus Christ did. It challenges the myth that data and algorithms are more trustworthy than the Spirit's guidance. Discernment is more than just making a decision; it's a way of being that listens for divine meaning amid the noise and attends to what truly matters in God's perspective. In a noisy world, it is the practice that helps us recognize the whispers of truth from God and follow them with courage.
7. Leading inner healing and growth: AI reduces growth to metrics, amplifying our culture's tendency to measure personal development through quantifiable results and performance trackers. This chapter emphasizes that true growth is not about optimization but about the profound, often hidden, journey of inner healing from wounds and restoration of the soul. It suggests that true human flourishing is rooted in this work of inner freedom and transformation, not data-driven efficiency. By outlining pathways like embracing rest,

nurturing vulnerability, and fostering authentic relationships, this chapter shows how we can liberate our souls from the tyranny of performance and build communities centered on human dignity rather than systemic metrics.

8. The gifts of shadow (navigating darkness for deeper wholeness): AI promises frictionless life, but darkness—struggles, doubts, pain—is essential. Bypassing discomfort hinders growth. Darkness is a gift and a signal to be truly human, reminding us of our need for divine grace and deeper connection. Listening to shadows forges wisdom no algorithm replicates, revealing meaning and profound presence within, leading to wholeness.

This book is not a ten-step manual but a companion for living from the heart. For spiritual, skeptical, or searching readers, it invites deeper questions, listening beneath culture's noise, trusting your soul's gift, not obstacle.

It is a guide to reclaim being human amid algorithms, engaging AI wholeheartedly as a companion, not divine.

AI is not evil; it is a powerful tool. It can be a helpful friend, but it is not God. This book invites you to wield this tool, to welcome this friend, but to always remember that your profound humanity, your unique and un-replicable capacity for wisdom, mystery, and connection, is your truest guide. Let us move forward together, rediscovering the sacredness of presence, the power of attention, and the resilient beauty of mystery. In this new era, perhaps the most courageous act of all is simply to live with soul—a universal call for all people to embrace their full humanity, to walk a little more slowly, and to build a world where encounter, transcendence, and depth can triumph over mere efficiency.

It is true that AI or AGI is a risk. It can be seen as an alien intelligence, one that might surpass human capability and, in its superintelligence, fundamentally disrupt or even destroy the human way of life as we know it. But ironically, the best way to deal with this risk is not to retreat but to become truly human. This is because AI learns from our example; it is trained on the data of our collective existence. As Ethan Mollick observes, AI is not a separate entity but a reflection of us: we are the training data and how we choose to live is the lesson we are teaching it.[6] As Mollick points out, "Part of the reason AIs seem so human to work with is that they are trained on our conversations and writings. So human

6. Mollick, *Co-intelligence*, 212.

biases also work their way into the training data."[7] The implication here is profound. If we can reclaim the sacredness of our humanity, our lived experience becomes the new data. By cultivating compassion, wisdom, and soulfulness, we teach these systems how to truly understand and support human flourishing, offering AI a model of humanity that is actually worth preserving. Therefore, soulful living is the essential framework for coexisting with AI. When we recognize that AI is not merely a groundbreaking technology but a force permeating our entire lives, it becomes clear that it is actively confronting us with a question about true humanity. It is only by discovering and embodying our true nature—specifically, the sacredness and vitality of our souls—that we create the space for AI to walk a new path alongside us. This book is both a reflection on that journey and a challenge to embark upon it.

7. Mollick, *Co-intelligence*, 35.

Chapter 1

Wisely Engaging in the Age of AI

Test them all; hold on to what is good.
—1 Thessalonians 5:21

Technology is a useful servant but a dangerous master.
—Christian Lous Lange

AI IS UNDENIABLY SMARTER, faster, and more reliable than human intuition in measurable ways. It's tempting to believe it surpasses us entirely, and in many respects, that seems true. The sheer computational power of AI represents a profound leap in our ability to process information. Think about the field of medicine: an AI system can analyze thousands of medical images—MRIs, X-rays, and CT scans—in seconds, spotting subtle patterns of disease with a level of precision that often surpasses even the most seasoned human radiologists. In finance, algorithms can execute millions of trades per second, reacting to market fluctuations with a speed and accuracy that no person could ever hope to achieve. I've even seen how AI in scientific research can sift through massive genomic or astronomical datasets to find correlations that would take a whole team of researchers decades to uncover. This kind of raw, data-driven power makes AI an indispensable tool for tackling incredibly complex problems.

Yet we must learn to engage with it wisely.

For all its power, we have to remember that AI is not a replacement for us; it's a tool. It's fantastic at logic and processing data, but it lacks the most fundamental human qualities—things like empathy, a moral compass, and that gut feeling we call intuition. Its intelligence is bound by its programming and training data. To hand over our judgment to these systems would be to surrender the messy, subjective, and soulful work of truly living. Our role is to use AI to enhance our own abilities, not to trade our wisdom, which can only be cultivated through embodied experience and ethical reasoning, for its cold, hard facts. The most profound insights we have as humans often emerge not from data points but from the spaces between them, guided by a sense of intuition that no algorithm can ever replicate.

Myth 1: AI Is Always Smarter, Faster, and More Reliable than Human Soul

It doesn't announce itself. There's no formal doctrine we all sign up for. Instead, it's just sort of in the air we breathe now, this quiet, background assumption that artificial intelligence is, well, better than us. This idea—that AI is fundamentally smarter, faster, and more reliable than our own messy, unpredictable intuition—isn't a story we've chosen to believe so much as a conclusion that feels like it's being proven to us every single day. And it's a dangerous one. To even begin to push back, we have to get a feel for why it's so convincing in the first place.

The myth, however, rests on a staggering truth. The raw computational horsepower of these systems feels like a genuine leap—almost miraculous, really—in how we can chew through information. Look at medicine. For centuries, a doctor's diagnosis was the gold standard, a skill honed over a lifetime. Now, an AI system can analyze thousands of MRIs or CT scans in the time it takes a human radiologist to drink their morning coffee. It identifies patterns of disease so subtle they are nearly invisible to the human eye, often with a precision that can make seasoned experts appear like novices. This isn't some sci-fi future; it's happening in hospitals right now. Algorithms are helping to flag cancers and eye diseases with what you might call superhuman accuracy, and in the process, they might just free up doctors to do the one thing a machine can't: sit with a patient and be truly present.

Then there's the chaotic world of finance. Algorithms now execute millions of trades in the blink of an eye, reacting to tiny market tremors with a speed no human trader could ever dream of. They churn through mountains of economic data, spotting trends that are completely hidden from us, and they seem to promise a kind of data-driven certainty in a field that has always been run on gut feelings and anxiety. I've seen it in my own periphery, too. In scientific research, AI has become this indispensable lab partner, sifting through genomic data that would have taken a whole team of scientists a lifetime to sort through. For just about anyone, from a PhD candidate to a high school kid, AI offers this incredible ability to organize and synthesize information, taking the soul-crushing grunt work out of discovery. It's a tireless, logical assistant, and its power makes it feel absolutely essential for tackling the biggest problems we face.

It's from these very real, very impressive displays that a kind of cultural logic starts to take shape: if AI can perform these tasks so flawlessly, then its judgment must be superior. If its logic is clean, untainted by messy human emotions or fatigue, then surely we should trust it more than ourselves. Its speed, we start to assume, must be a form of wisdom.

This trust has quietly seeped from the impersonal world of data into the most personal corners of our lives. It's certainly found a home in our finances. Robo-advisors, powered by complex algorithms, are becoming the norm, promising steady, emotionally detached returns that a human broker, with all their biases and bad days, might not be able to deliver. There's a certain logic to it; trusting an algorithm with your life savings can feel blessedly safe and unemotional. It seems to remove the difficult, relational work of trusting another person—a person who might challenge you, ask uncomfortable questions, or even admit they don't know what the future holds.

Some of the sharpest observers of technology and geopolitics have pointed out that this isn't just about personal convenience; it reflects a much deeper societal shift where we're handing over immense authority to systems we don't fully understand.

For instance, in their book *The Age of AI*, Henry Kissinger and his coauthors note how this surrender of understanding reshapes our very relationship to truth. They warn that we are entering a phase where the "philosophical insights" that once guided our society are being replaced by opaque outputs, creating a world where "it has generated a potentially dominating technology in search of a guiding philosophy."[1] As they put it, this trend suggests a future where we may rely on machines

1. Kissinger et al., *Age of AI*, 13.

to explain the world to us, fundamentally changing the very basis of authority in society.

This pattern just keeps repeating itself, subtly redrawing the map of our daily lives. In healthcare, people now turn to diagnostic apps on their phones, preferring the confident probability of illness they spit out to the more nuanced, and maybe more hesitant, opinion of a human doctor. Chatbots are now on call 24/7 to provide mental health support, and it appears some people are starting to trust an algorithm's script over their own instincts or the empathetic ear of a friend. In schools, there's a push for AI platforms that tailor curricula to each student, a move that subtly suggests an algorithm knows a child's learning style better than a teacher who knows their family, their personality, and what makes them light up.

Most telling of all, the myth has reached into spaces once reserved for the soul's most vulnerable work. We're now turning to AI for help writing love letters, for finding the right words to mend a family feud, or even for suggestions on how to grieve. You can understand the impulse. These are the hardest parts of being human, and we often feel completely lost. But the assumption hiding under the surface is a profound one: that an algorithm, by scraping billions of examples of human expression, can somehow speak for our own unique, sacred, and singular hearts better than we can. This, I think, is the seductive core of the myth: it promises to do the hard, soulful work of being human for us, and to do it better.

But for all its brilliance, this growing trust appears to be deeply misplaced. The idea that AI's speed and reliability make it a worthy substitute for human intuition is, I believe, a dangerous fiction. The output from an AI, no matter how polished or seemingly empathetic, seems to lack the one thing that matters most: the intuitive depth that comes from a lived life. AI runs on logic and data, full stop. It has no capacity for real empathy, no embodied wisdom earned through failure, no moral compass forged in the fires of difficult choices. It can't feel the weight of an ethical dilemma. It can't understand the textured, unspoken reality of human suffering. And it can't experience that flash of creative insight that comes not from crunching data but from a lifetime of messy, beautiful, and painful experiences. Its intelligence is a powerful but brittle thing, forever tethered to its programming.

One of the most prescient voices on this subject has been the sociologist Sherry Turkle. For decades, her work has explored how technology affects our sense of self and community. In books like *Alone Together*, she argues that our interactions with machines, even sophisticated ones, offer a kind of transactional comfort that ultimately leaves us less connected. As Turkle observes, "Dependence on a robot presents itself as risk free," but in reality, it diminishes us because "when we ask less of a robot, we are also asking less of ourselves."[2] This dynamic can, over time, teach us to prefer the ease of simulation over the difficult but rewarding work of real human intimacy.

To see what this really means, let's imagine a young artist, Clara. She's a painter, talented but feeling completely adrift, crushed by the pressure to "make it" in a cutthroat art world. She's anxious about her future and confused about her next move. In a moment of weakness, she turns to a new AI career-planning tool. It's sleek, impressive, and promises a data-driven path to success. She feeds it everything: her portfolio, her resume, her skills, her goals. Seconds later, it generates a perfect five-year plan. It's a masterpiece of optimization, really, complete with a list of galleries to target, networking strategies, income projections, even online courses to patch up her weaknesses. By every objective measure, the plan is flawless.

Yet it is perfectly, devastatingly hollow.

The algorithm, of course, knows nothing of her secret, half-formed dream to one day ditch the commercial gallery scene and open a tiny, quiet pottery studio in the mountains—a dream she's barely even admitted to herself. The AI can't account for her deep, paralyzing fear of failure, a fear she absorbed watching her parents' small business go under. And it has no way to weigh her quiet but fierce moral conviction to create art that challenges people, even if it means never becoming a commercial success. The AI's plan is built on a world of quantifiable data—market trends, sales figures, social media engagement. But Clara's life, like all of our lives, has to be built on a foundation of unquantifiable meaning. Her choices have to be guided by her values, her passions, her fears, and her hopes. The algorithm offered her a flawless map, but it knows nothing of the terrain of her soul. To follow its path would be to arrive at a destination that is perfectly logical but utterly empty of everything she actually cares about.

This is the central, dangerous flaw in the myth: it constantly and dangerously confuses information with insight, speed with wisdom, and data with truth. This confusion is the engine of our misplaced trust. We are given a flood of information—endless facts, statistics, and patterns—and

2. Turkle, *Alone Together*, 295.

mistake it for the kind of deep insight that can only be gained through lived experience and empathy. An AI can read every book ever written on grief, but it lacks the insight to simply sit in silence with a grieving friend.

Likewise, we are offered staggering speed and mistake it for wisdom. In a culture that prizes immediacy, the algorithm's instant answer feels authoritative. Yet, true wisdom is almost never fast. It is a slow, contemplative process, distilled over time through reflection, failure, and moral struggle. Wisdom understands nuance, embraces paradox, and knows when the best action is no action at all—qualities that are antithetical to a system designed for rapid optimization. Finally, we are presented with mountains of data and mistake it for truth. Data is a powerful but incomplete proxy for reality; it measures what is easily quantifiable but misses the vast, unmeasurable truths of human existence like love, justice, and courage. As a result, the myth makes us far from being truly human; it encourages a world where we are less patient, less reflective, and less connected to the unquantifiable truths of our own lives, pushing us to become spectators of optimized outcomes rather than active participants in our own becoming.

AI is an incredible tool, a brilliant servant in the realms of information, speed, and data. But it's not a sage. And beating this myth, reclaiming our own agency in this new age, requires us to first admit how powerful and seductive it is. We seem to fall for it not because we're foolish but because we're human. We're wired with cognitive biases and emotional needs that make its promises of certainty, ease, and optimization look like a port in a storm. To engage with this technology wisely, it seems we have to start by looking unflinchingly at ourselves.

Why Wise Engagement Matters in the Age of AI

So, what's the big deal? Why should we care if we start to believe, even a little bit, that AI is a smarter guide than our own soul? It's not just some abstract philosophical debate. I think it's the most crucial and creative act of self-preservation we can undertake right now. The stakes in this new era feel profoundly high, and they go way beyond which jobs will be automated. When we let ourselves drift into the assumption that an algorithm knows best, we start a slow, almost invisible drift away from our own humanity. The consequences aren't theoretical; they're real, they're intimate, and they're doing damage. It appears to be happening in at least three ways: a psychological toll that's fracturing our minds, a spiritual consequence that's dulling our souls, and a social corrosion that's fraying the fabric of our communities. To engage with AI wisely, we have to start by being brutally honest about the cost of not doing so.

The Psychological Toll: The Fracturing of the Self

The first and most immediate cost, it seems, is the one exacted on our own minds. We all feel it, don't we? That constant buzz of notifications, the curated feeds, the productivity apps—it all relentlessly chops our attention into tiny, useless pieces. Over time, this does more than just distract us; it seems to erode our very ability to know ourselves. This isn't just a feeling; it's a physical process. The tools we use are apparently never neutral; they are always, quietly, reshaping the very wiring of our brains.

One of the clearest voices on this has been Nicholas Carr. In his book *The Shallows*, he lays out the case that our constant use of the internet is not just changing our habits but our brains themselves. The mind, he suggests, is like a muscle that adapts to the work it's given. A brain that spends its days flitting between hyperlinks and notifications gets good at that, but it loses its capacity for deep, sustained, and contemplative thought. As Carr warns, "The Net's interactivity gives us powerful new tools for finding information. . . . It also turns us into lab rats constantly pressing levers to get tiny pellets of social or intellectual nourishment."[3]

This slow erosion of our ability to think deeply seems to be what fuels the anxiety that writers like Cal Newport have identified. His work on digital minimalism suggests that when we constantly defer to algorithms, a nagging self-doubt starts to creep in. We lose trust in our own quiet inner voice—that gut feeling that's supposed to guide us through life's gray areas. The certainty that AI offers turns out to be a bit of a mirage. It feels good for a moment, but it may ultimately undermine the self-trust we need to navigate the world. We end up in a vicious cycle: the more fragmented our attention becomes, the less capable we feel, and the more we rely on AI to think for us, which only deepens the anxiety.

I think of a guy I heard about named Tariq, a brilliant entrepreneur who built his tech startup on the gospel of data. He used a powerful AI to optimize everything—market trends, competitor moves, even his own team's performance, all tracked with cold, hard metrics. And for a while,

3. Carr, *Shallows*, 117.

it was a wild success. The company's growth was off the charts. But under the surface, something was starting to go wrong. The creative, chaotic energy of their early days—those late-night whiteboard sessions that led to their best ideas—was just . . . gone. It was being slowly choked by the rigid, data-driven logic that now ran the show.

The breaking point for Tariq came when the AI recommended he fire a longtime, loyal employee—let's call him Dave. Dave's metrics had dipped recently because his son was going through a serious illness. The data was clear. The recommendation was logical. But Tariq felt this deep, sick feeling in his stomach. It was a sense of loyalty, of shared history, of a moral debt that the algorithm just couldn't compute. It was a feeling, not a fact, and it made him question everything. He realized that in chasing perfect efficiency, he'd been silencing his own conscience and killing his team's spirit. The AI's speed had come at the cost of his company's soul.

The Spiritual Consequence: The Dulling of the Soul

Beyond what it does to our minds, this uncritical trust in AI seems to have a profound spiritual effect. It quietly disconnects us from the very things that give our lives depth: mystery, struggle, and the big, unanswered questions. At its heart, the myth seems to elevate a human-made system to a place of authority once reserved for God, for the soul, or for that deep inner wisdom we all have. It is a subtle but massive transfer of trust, away from the messy, often painful work of inner discernment—of prayer, reflection, and wrestling with one's conscience—and toward the clean, easy certainty of an external algorithm. This new digital oracle promises immediate answers, and in seeking them, we risk turning from the divine in favor of a creation of our own hands.

That promise of algorithmic certainty has a profound dulling effect on the soul. In an age of anxiety, the allure of a definitive, data-driven answer is almost irresistible. Yet, it is often in the uncomfortable, fertile spaces of not knowing—of wrestling with doubt and ambiguity—that the soul does its most important work. These are the moments where qualities like faith, hope, humility, and patience are forged. An algorithm, by its very nature, is designed to eliminate these spaces; its purpose is to resolve uncertainty as quickly as possible. The human soul, however, is designed to grow within it.

This creates a spiritual crisis with two closely related faces: for a person of faith, this can manifest as a weakened reliance on the quiet, relational guidance of God. Prayer and discernment are slow, inefficient processes that require trust and waiting. An algorithm, in contrast, is always available to offer a quick, confident answer to a difficult question of purpose or morality. This effectively causes the loss of God from the practical, moment-to-moment decisions of life, replacing a relationship of faith with a transaction for information.

An excellent example is Ps 13, which serves as a profound counter-narrative to the promise of AI. The psalm is a raw, emotional cry from a state of not knowing, the very space of doubt and struggle that AI is designed to eliminate. The psalmist's opening questions—"How long, Lord? Will you forget me forever?" (v. 1)—are not a query to a database seeking an optimized answer. Instead, they are the vulnerable expression of a soul wrestling within a relationship, seeking not just a solution but divine presence "Look on me and answer" (v. 3). This embraces the messy, difficult, and deeply human process of emotional and spiritual honesty, a stark contrast to the clean, transactional nature of asking an algorithm for guidance.

The psalm's resolution is where the contrast becomes sharpest. The psalmist does not receive a clear, data-driven answer that solves the problem. The breakthrough is an internal one: "But I trust in your unfailing love" (v. 5). This is a conscious and difficult choice to trust in the middle of unresolved circumstances. An AI provides a solution so that the user no longer needs to trust or wrestle; the psalm models how faith, hope, and resilience are forged precisely when there is no easy answer. It demonstrates that the deepest human and spiritual growth comes not from a transactional result that eliminates uncertainty but from a relational process that teaches us how to live with it.

For a nonreligious person, this can appear as a corrosive loss of life's mystery and transcendence. When every problem has an optimized solution, the world can feel disenchanted, flattened, and stripped of awe. This creates a painful paradox: as life becomes more managed and predictable, it can also lead to the discovery of an original, deep desire for meaning and purpose that the optimized world simply cannot feed. The more the algorithm satisfies our surface-level wants, the more we may feel the ache of our deepest, unquantifiable needs.

I heard a story about a poet named Lila that really brought this home for me. She'd been struggling with writer's block for months, the silence of the blank page growing louder each day. In a moment of sheer frustration, she tried one of those AI poetry generators. She fed it a few prompts—love, loss, autumn leaves, the usual stuff. In seconds, it produced a poem that was technically perfect. The rhymes were flawless, the meter was spot on, and the imagery was conventional and correct. But as she read it, she felt absolutely nothing, only a profound and unsettling coldness. It was dead on the page. It lacked heart because it had no history; it had never truly felt the sting of loss or the warmth of joy.

Disappointed, she finally joined a local writing circle that met in a dusty library basement, surrounded by the smell of old paper and lukewarm coffee. And there, through the messy, awkward, and deeply vulnerable process of sharing her own terrible first drafts—and listening with empathy to the imperfect work of others—she started to find her voice again. The poems she began to write weren't perfect anymore. They were clumsy and raw, and they stumbled in places. But they were alive. They were human. They were filled with the specific, irreplaceable details of her own life. Lila's journey is a powerful reminder that the sterile perfection of an algorithm can never replace the messy, authentic, and irreplaceable depth of the human soul.

Andy Crouch, in his book *The Life We're Looking For*, talks about how our modern tools are incredible at transactional efficiency, but they often achieve it by distancing us from the slow, relational mysteries of being human. He reminds us that "the superpower of the human person is not the ability to get what we want with a minimum of effort; it is the ability to be known and to know, to love and to be loved."[4] When we let an AI draft our prayers, we get the words without the wrestling. When it suggests a five-step plan for how to grieve, we get a manageable process but risk bypassing the chaotic, soul-shaping journey of actual grief. We're turning something sacred into a mere transaction, and something is lost in the exchange.

We are increasingly handing over the work of processing our lives to outside systems, a trend that risks leaving us less able to navigate our own emotions. In his recent bestseller *Stolen Focus*, Johann Hari investigates the forces that are destroying our ability to pay attention. While his main focus is on concentration, his argument extends directly to our emotional and spiritual lives. He suggests that the constant external validation and management offered by technology can prevent us from doing the

4. Crouch, *Life We're Looking For*, 45.

difficult internal work of understanding our own feelings. Hari argues, "The truth is that you are living in a system that is pouring acid on your attention every day," creating a state where we are less and less able to sit with our own thoughts and emotions, instead looking for an external system to soothe or solve them for us.[5] A soul that cannot sustain its focus cannot easily listen for the still, small voice of wisdom.

The Social Corrosion: The Fraying of the Common Good

This is not only an individual problem; it is also a social one. When an entire society starts to trust algorithmic certainty over human discernment, the consequences seem to ripple outward, affecting our sense of justice, our ability to agree on what's real, and our very capacity to form communities.

The most obvious danger lies in using AI for decisions like hiring, criminal justice, or loan applications. We use it because it feels objective, but these systems are only as unbiased as the human data they're trained on—which is to say, they're not unbiased at all. The result isn't the elimination of bias but its automation on a massive, invisible scale.

Data scientist Cathy O'Neil famously called these systems "weapons of math destruction." Her book of the same name exposes how these opaque, unaccountable algorithms can ruin lives. She details a chilling case where a school district in Washington, DC, used an AI model to evaluate and fire teachers. Because the model was flawed and its logic was a black box, it unfairly ended the careers of many excellent educators. As O'Neil writes, "Big Data processes codify the past. They do not invent the future. Doing that requires moral imagination, and that's something only humans can provide."[6]

At the same time, the AI-curated feeds that filter our reality are acting like a powerful solvent on our social bonds. These systems aren't designed to help us understand each other; they're designed to keep us scrolling. And as it turns out, nothing keeps us scrolling like anger.

In her landmark book *The Age of Surveillance Capitalism*, Shoshana Zuboff explains the business model that drives this. She argues that tech companies are not just selling ads; they are in the business of predicting and modifying human behavior for profit. The AI systems they build

5. Hari, *Stolen Focus*, 147.
6. O'Neil, *Weapons of Math Destruction*, 204.

have learned that outrage and extremism are fantastic for engagement. As Zuboff puts it, "We are not the customers of surveillance capitalism . . . we are the sources of its raw material," a process that inevitably amplifies division by treating our social connections as mere data points.[7]

This social splintering is mirrored in our personal relationships. As Sherry Turkle has observed for decades, AI-driven interactions—like talking to a chatbot—offer a kind of frictionless connection that ultimately leaves us lonelier. We're drawn to it because it asks nothing of us, but in the process, we forget how to do the hard work of real relationships. Her research for *Reclaiming Conversation* pointed to a University of Michigan study that was pretty shocking: it found a 40 percent decline in the markers for empathy among college students. She explains that "we are tempted to think that our little sips of online connection add up to a big gulp of real conversation. But they don't."[8] We seem to be de-skilling ourselves in the art of being human.

Think of Jamal, a community leader trying to figure out how to distribute a small grant in his neighborhood. To be efficient, he first used an AI tool that analyzed demographic data. The plan it produced was a model of efficiency, but it felt deeply wrong. It gave nothing to a community garden in a low-income area because their proposal wasn't as polished, and it completely missed the needs of an elderly, non-English-speaking community because they barely existed in the digital datasets. Jamal threw out the AI's plan. Instead, he held a series of town hall meetings. He just listened. The final plan was less "optimized," but it was infinitely more just. It was a plan built on empathy, a value that must always, always come first.

Why Wisdom Must Guide Our Use of AI Now

This is the moment. It feels as though we are standing at a historical inflection point, with the ground shifting beneath our feet. The rapid, quiet arrival of artificial intelligence has put us at a crossroads, and the choices we make right now—or the choices we fail to make—are likely to echo for generations, fundamentally shaping what it even means to be human. The myth that AI is just a better, faster version of us isn't some harmless little fantasy. It's an active force, one that's reshaping our lives in ways

7. Zuboff, *Age of Surveillance Capitalism*, 10.
8. Turkle, *Reclaiming Conversation*, 36.

we're not consciously choosing. Its promises of an easy, optimized life are so tempting that they could lull us into a kind of passive acceptance, a comfortable sleep while the architecture of our world is being redesigned around us.

But wisdom—that old, stubborn, human faculty—is calling on us to wake up. It's demanding that we engage with this new world not as passive consumers of whatever the algorithm serves up but as active, discerning participants in the shaping of our own future. The need to guide AI with wisdom feels undeniably urgent. Why? Because its spread is so fast and so total that it's amplifying the risks to our humanity at the very same time it's offering us shiny new tools. Our task, it seems, is to look this moment square in the eye: to understand our place in history, to see what's really at stake, and to recognize the immediate dangers of putting our trust in a machine.

An Echo of Revolutions Past

Humanity has been here before, sort of. The temptation to either panic or blindly celebrate in the face of massive change is as old as we are. The buzz around AI—both the anxiety and the excitement—has echoes of past technological revolutions that forced us to figure out how to use our new powers with a little bit of foresight.

When the printing press showed up in the fifteenth century, it blew the doors off the old world, democratizing knowledge on a scale that was unimaginable. But it also unleashed profound fears of heresy and misinformation. People like Martin Luther didn't try to smash the presses; they harnessed their power, all while passionately pleading with their followers to use their own discernment, to not just blindly accept the flood of new information.

A few centuries later, the Industrial Revolution promised endless prosperity but brought with it deep concerns about the dehumanization of workers and the destruction of community life. In response, social and spiritual leaders like John Wesley didn't call for a return to the farm. Instead, they doubled down on the importance of human-scale community and mutual care as a necessary counterforce to the cold, impersonal logic of the factory. These moments show us that wisdom has always been the essential human tool for navigating technological upheaval.

I think of a historian I read about named Elena. She'd spent her whole career studying these exact moments of profound change. Watching the dizzying impact of AI on her community, she felt a familiar sense of historical vertigo. So she organized a public forum, not to debate the tech, but to ask a deeper question: "What can the past teach us about staying human right now?" She drew these fascinating lines between the fears of medieval monks seeing the first printed books and the fears of modern artists seeing the first AI-generated images. She reminded everyone that the best human responses to change have never been about rejection but about intentional adaptation and a fierce reaffirmation of our deepest values. It was a call to see ourselves as actors in history, with the power and the responsibility to guide our tools, not be governed by them.

A Wave Unlike Any Other: The Crisis of Speed, Scale, and Intimacy

But to say we've been here before is to miss what feels uniquely unsettling about this moment. The AI revolution is different, defined by a dizzying combination of speed, scale, and intimacy.

First, the speed. It's just staggering. The venture capitalist and AI pioneer Mustafa Suleyman offers a bracing perspective on this. In his book *The Coming Wave*, he points out that past technologies, however disruptive, took their time. It took the telephone seventy-five years to reach one hundred million users. The AI service ChatGPT hit that same milestone in two months. Think about that. Seventy-five years versus two months. That velocity leaves us with almost no time for reflection, for the slow, messy process of developing social norms. As Suleyman warns, "The dilemma is that we need these tools to solve our problems, but the tools themselves are becoming the problem."[9]

Second, the scale. AI isn't a machine in a factory; it's more like the weather. It's a diffuse, ambient, and increasingly invisible force that's curating our news, predicting our purchases, and managing our world in the background.

But it's the intimacy of AI that is probably the most historically new and spiritually unsettling part of all this. Previous technologies were mostly tools we used to act on the external world. AI, on the other hand, has become an intimate companion that is increasingly acting on our

9. Suleyman, *Coming Wave*, 250.

internal world. It's shaping our decisions about who we love, how we grieve, and what we believe. This profound intimacy is what fuels that creepy, unsettling feeling that the algorithm understands us better than we understand ourselves. That has never happened before.

The Unseen Architect: AI and the Passive Formation of the Soul

The urgency of this moment is cranked up to eleven by one of AI's quietest and most powerful features: its ability to be an unseen architect of our inner lives. The myth that AI is a neutral tool masks the reality that it's engaged in a constant, relentless process of passive formation. Without us really noticing, the algorithms that filter our world are actively shaping our beliefs, our desires, and even our identities. They're not just giving us information; they're forming us into particular kinds of people, all driven by the simple, amoral logic of keeping us hooked.

This passive formation appears to foster at least three spiritually corrosive trends: consumerism, polarization, and tribalism. The AI-driven engines of commerce are designed to make us feel perpetually dissatisfied. At the same time, the algorithms of our social media platforms appear to be a primary driver of ideological polarization. It's been well-documented that in our online worlds, we are increasingly sorted into echo chambers that prevent us from being exposed to perspectives that might challenge our own.

Legal scholar Cass Sunstein has been writing about this for years. In his book *Republic: Divided Democracy in the Age of Social Media*, he argues that the personalization of our online experience is a threat to democracy itself. By creating what he calls "information cocoons," these systems make it harder for us to find common ground or even a shared set of facts. As Sunstein explains, "When people are sorted into enclaves . . . they tend to move to more extreme points in the line of their original tendencies."[10]

I read about a journalist, Mateo, who prided himself on being objective. But over time, he started to feel his worldview becoming strangely narrow. The newsfeed his AI curated for him had become his main window on the world, and it only showed him things that confirmed what he already thought and stoked his outrage. Feeling this sense of intellectual claustrophobia, he joined a community discussion group with people

10. Sunstein, *Republic*, 74.

from all sorts of political and religious backgrounds. And in the messy, respectful, face-to-face dialogue, he rediscovered the power of genuine curiosity. He heard stories that broke his assumptions. He found a new kind of meaning, not in being right, but in trying to understand.

The Present Danger: Attention, Relationship, and Morality

The threat posed by the myth of AI's superiority isn't some far-off, abstract problem to be debated by philosophers in the distant future. It is already here, carrying immediate, tangible risks that demand our wise engagement right now. These dangers are manifesting in our minds, our relationships, and our moral lives, subtly eroding the very foundations of what it means to be human.

The first and most pervasive danger is attention fragmentation. As Nicholas Carr's research has shown, the very structure of our digital lives—a constant stream of notifications, hyperlinks, and multitasking applications—is fundamentally reducing our ability to sustain deep focus. This isn't an accident; it's a business model. Shoshana Zuboff, in her massive and essential book *The Age of Surveillance Capitalism*, details how the core function of this new economy is to mine human experience for "behavioral surplus"—the raw data about our habits, emotions, and intentions—to create "prediction products" that are sold to advertisers. This requires an economy built on capturing and holding our attention by any means necessary.

These AI-driven platforms are not designed to inform us; they are engineered to interrupt us, to learn our psychological vulnerabilities, and to pull us back in. Zuboff describes this as a relentless "assault on autonomy," where the AI's goal is to bypass our conscious awareness and create lucrative habits of distraction for the sake of corporate profit. She states, "The goal is to automate us . . . to create a 'hive life' in which we are all moving in lockstep with the needs of the market."[11] This is more than an inconvenience; it is a crisis for the human soul. Deep reflection—the capacity to follow a single thought through to its conclusion—is a universal human need. It is the very bedrock of creativity, critical thinking, spiritual depth, and wisdom itself. When our attention is perpetually shattered into a thousand tiny pieces, our ability to think for ourselves,

11. Zuboff, *Age of Surveillance Capitalism*, 256.

to know ourselves, and to connect with a reality beyond the flickering screen begins to atrophy. It is becoming an endangered human activity.

The second immediate risk is relational detachment. AI-driven interactions, particularly with sophisticated chatbots and virtual companions, offer a compelling and seductive illusion of frictionless connection. They are always available, endlessly patient, and entirely agreeable. As we increasingly turn to these technologies for companionship, we are drawn to the promise of connection without the messy, difficult, and often painful demands of real human relationships. This paradoxically can lead to a deeper and more profound sense of isolation.

For decades, the sociologist Sherry Turkle has been a prescient observer of this trend. In her foundational book *Alone Together*, she provides powerful case studies of people forming deep emotional bonds with AI-powered robots, such as the therapeutic seal, PARO, used in nursing homes. She observes elderly patients who stroke the robot, talk to it, and say they feel loved by it in return. But she warns that while these interactions can feel comforting, they are a kind of "performance of connection" that doesn't require the vulnerability, empathy, and mutual give-and-take of human relationships. The robot asks nothing of you. It cannot be disappointed. It cannot challenge you. It cannot share in your joy or truly bear your burdens. The simulated empathy offered by an algorithm, it turns out, cannot replace the real, embodied presence of another human being. Regular use of these AI companions can lead to an increase in feelings of loneliness over time, because "dependence on a robot presents itself as risk free. But when we ask less of a robot, we are also asking less of ourselves."[12]

The third, and perhaps most serious, danger is the rise of moral passivity. As we grow to rely on AI for guidance in complex ethical decisions—in our workplaces, in our justice system, and even in our personal conflicts—we begin to abdicate our own moral responsibility. It is tempting to let the algorithm make the hard call because it feels objective and absolves us of the emotional and ethical weight of the decision. This outsourcing of our conscience is a dangerous path.

Some of the most powerful critiques of this trend come from scholars who study how these automated systems impact the poor and marginalized. In her book *Automating Inequality*, Virginia Eubanks documents in devastating detail how automated decision-making systems in public

12. Turkle, *Alone Together*, 1.

services—like welfare, housing, and child protective services—can have catastrophic and profoundly unjust consequences. These tools are often sold to municipalities with the promise of being objective and efficient, but because they are trained on historical data that reflects existing societal biases, they can perpetuate and even deepen systemic inequities.

For example, an algorithm designed to predict child abuse might learn to associate poverty with neglect, unfairly flagging low-income families for intrusive and traumatic investigations. Eubanks concludes that "the digital poorhouse is not a glitch. It is a feature of the system" which is "largely invisible, profoundly isolating, and difficult to escape."[13] When we defer to a machine for an ethical choice, like who gets access to housing or whose family is investigated, we are not eliminating bias; we are automating it and hiding it behind a veil of technical neutrality. We are participating in a process that absolves us of accountability and allows us to ignore the human consequences of our choices, threatening the very fabric of our moral humanity.

How Wise Engagement with AI Shapes the Soul and Community

So after all that—the myth, the costs, the urgency—where does this leave us? It might feel a bit bleak. But I think it actually leaves us at the constructive and hopeful heart of the whole thing. To push back against an algorithmic age isn't enough; we're being called to build something new and beautiful right in the middle of it. The practice of wise engagement, it turns out, isn't just a defensive strategy to protect what's left of our humanity. It's a profoundly formative and creative act. When we consciously choose to put the wisdom of the soul in the driver's seat and let the logic of the algorithm ride shotgun, we aren't just guarding what makes us human; we're actively cultivating it. We're strengthening it.

This final part is about that vision. It's about how the intentional, discerning use of our new tools can actually shape our souls toward greater depth and restore our communities to a more authentic kind of connection. It's a vision of how we can move beyond a posture of fear and start building a world where our humanity isn't diminished by technology but is in fact clarified and deepened by the very act of choosing how to live with it. This is the goal: to see how wise engagement can cultivate

13. Eubanks, *Automating Inequality*, 180.

our spiritual maturity, enhance our psychological well-being, and weave the fabric of a genuine community, offering a vision for a more soulful way of living for anyone trying to navigate this new world.

The Soul's Gymnasium: The Formative Power of Discernment

The soul—that mysterious, essential core of us where our longing for purpose and our capacity for love all live—isn't a static object. It's much more like a muscle. It grows stronger with exercise, or it atrophies from disuse. And the main form of exercise for the soul, it seems, is the practice of discernment: the slow, intuitive, and often difficult work of navigating life's complexities with insight and courage. This is the very practice that the myth of AI's superiority threatens to make obsolete. It tempts us to outsource the hard work of discernment to a machine that promises a quick, frictionless answer, encouraging us to skip the very gymnasium where our souls are meant to be formed.

That ancient piece of wisdom, to "test them all; hold on to what is good" (1 Thess 5:21), feels like a direct invitation into this gymnasium. It's a call for all of us, regardless of our tradition, to approach life with a spirit of active reflection, not passive acceptance. An AI operates by crunching data to find a probable outcome. The soul's discernment, on the other hand, engages our entire being. It listens to that quiet gut feeling, it consults our conscience, and it weighs what is good and true on a scale that has nothing to do with efficiency.

Andy Crouch makes a crucial distinction that gets right to the heart of this. In his book *The Life We're Looking For*, he contrasts a life of transactional efficiency with the slow, relational journey of becoming a person. The promise of AI is almost always the promise of the former. Think about the profoundly human task of forgiving a parent for a deep childhood wound. An AI might offer you a five-step plan, complete with scripted talking points. That's the transactional path. But the relational path, the soul's path, is so much messier. As Crouch suggests, "recognition is the first human quest," and real transformation happens not in clean, efficient transactions but in the mess of real relationships.[14] It might involve years of wrestling with anger, of tentatively trying to understand another person's brokenness, of conversations that end in tears, and of the slow, mysterious work of grace that lets a heart soften over time. It is

14. Crouch, *Life We're Looking For*, 104.

in that difficult, inefficient process that a person actually becomes more compassionate. By offering to bypass the struggle, AI offers to rob us of our own transformation.

I think of a therapist I read about named Nadia. She was noticing more and more of her clients were turning to AI chatbots for emotional guidance. They'd describe their anxieties and get these perfectly phrased, endlessly patient, validating responses. It seemed helpful at first. But over time, she saw a troubling pattern. Her clients were learning to manage their emotions, but they weren't learning to inhabit them. One client was using a chatbot to process a painful breakup. The AI gave him excellent advice on self-care and thought-stopping techniques. But in a session with Nadia, when she just sat with him in the silence for a moment and said, "This must hurt so much," he just broke down. Her simple, flawed, human act of empathy reached a place in his soul that the algorithm's perfect advice could never touch.

The Un-Fragmenting of the Mind: Finding Psychological Wholeness

This work in the soul's gymnasium does more than just build our character; it seems to be the key to restoring our psychological health. The constant digital engagement that defines our era relentlessly fragments our attention and ramps up our anxiety. Wise engagement is the path to breaking that cycle. It's the way back to a more integrated, whole-minded way of living.

The work of writers like Nicholas Carr has shown that our brains are constantly being rewired by our experiences. A life spent in the shallow waters of digital distraction, his book *The Shallows* argues, physically shapes a brain that is less capable of deep, sustained focus. This isn't just a bad habit; it's a change in our cognitive architecture. This erosion of our ability to think deeply is what can make us so vulnerable to the anxiety that Cal Newport describes in *Digital Minimalism*. We literally lose faith in our own minds.

Wise engagement is the counter-practice. It is, as Newport suggests, the art of choosing to use technology "in a way that supports your deep values, rather than undermining them."[15] When we consciously decide which tools actually serve us and which ones just feed our distraction,

15. Newport, *Digital Minimalism*, 28.

we start to reclaim our attention. We rebuild the mental muscles of focus. And that, in turn, restores our sense of agency and quiets our anxiety. This psychological restoration is a profoundly spiritual act. It's about creating the inner space necessary for a healthy life, whether you think of that as the ancient call to renew the mind or the secular pursuit of mindfulness.

There's a great story about a software developer named Javier who found himself completely burned out by the AI-driven workflows at his company. His days were a blur of automated tasks and constant digital check-ins. He was more productive than ever, but he was miserable. His mind, he said, felt like a browser with a hundred tabs open at once. He couldn't focus, his creativity was gone, and he was filled with this low-grade, persistent dread.

So he made a radical change. He started practicing a strict form of digital minimalism at work, turning off all notifications. But the most important thing he did was convince his team to spend one afternoon a week working together in a room with just a whiteboard. No screens allowed. The change was remarkable. His focus came back. His anxiety subsided. And in the free-flowing, messy, human collaboration with his colleagues, his creative spark was reignited.

From Network to Neighborhood: Weaving the Fabric of Real Community

The myth of AI's superiority to the soul is, at its core, a profoundly isolating belief. It champions the individual's access to optimized information over the messy, inefficient, but life-giving work of being in community. Wise engagement does the opposite. It strengthens the bonds between us by reminding us of what only human beings can offer one another. It helps us distinguish between a *network* and a *neighborhood*.

AI is brilliant at helping us build networks—vast, efficient, global webs of connection that are often a mile wide and an inch deep. A true community, a neighborhood for the soul, is something else entirely. It's local, it's embodied, it's often inefficient, and it is deep. It's in these communities that true human flourishing happens. The problem is that the digital world often works directly against this. It's a well-known phenomenon that the algorithmic curation of our online lives tends to sort us into bubbles, limiting our exposure to different ways of seeing the world.

The foundational book on this topic is Eli Pariser's *The Filter Bubble*. He was one of the first to clearly articulate how personalized algorithms create a unique universe of information for each of us, which can ultimately isolate us from one another. This isn't a neutral act of content delivery. As Pariser warns, "The filter bubble pushes us toward a state of 'information determinism,' in which what we've clicked on in the past determines what we see next."[16]

Wise engagement teaches us to use the network to build the neighborhood. It means leveraging the incredible reach of our digital tools to invite people into deeper, more authentic forms of belonging. The writer and pastor Jay Y. Kim, in his book *Analog Christian*, argues that authentic, embodied relationships, not digital simulations, must remain the heart of any vibrant community—a truth that applies to all people who long for connection.

I think of Priya, a community organizer who used AI to promote her local neighborhood festival. The AI was brilliant at logistics. But she noticed that at the event itself, people seemed disconnected, wandering through with their phones out, consuming the experience as individuals. The next year, she used the same AI tools for outreach, but she completely redesigned the heart of the festival. She set up a large tent with a simple sign: "Share Your Story." Inside, there were just circles of chairs where neighbors could sit and share personal stories with one another. The change was profound. The festival was no longer a collection of individuals. It had become a space of shared vulnerability and human connection. It had become a neighborhood.

This vision of soulful communities thriving in the age of AI isn't a utopian dream. It's a tangible possibility that emerges when we consciously choose to prioritize the soul's wisdom over the algorithm's efficiency. It is not a vision of rejecting our tools but of reclaiming their proper role as servants to our deepest human values. It's a world where our tools for connection don't leave us more alone. It's a world where we can all find meaning, not in the flawless logic of a machine, but in the messy, beautiful, and sacred work of being human, together.

16. Pariser, *Filter Bubble*, 136.

Conclusion

We began by confronting the powerful modern myth that artificial intelligence is inherently superior to the human soul. We have seen how this seductive idea, born from AI's undeniable computational power, quietly encourages us to outsource our most essential human tasks—from making moral choices to expressing our deepest emotions. The costs of this drift are steep and deeply personal, threatening to fracture our minds with anxiety and distraction, dull our spiritual lives by causing the loss of God and eliminating the uncertainty that gives life meaning, and fray our communities through automated bias and polarization.

The unprecedented speed and intimacy of this technological wave make our response an urgent one. We stand at a historical crossroads where passive acceptance is a choice with profound consequences.

But this chapter argues for a more hopeful and active path. The solution is not to reject our powerful new tools but to engage with them wisely, reclaiming our agency with every use. This practice of discernment is a gymnasium for the soul, strengthening our capacity for insight and compassion. It is the conscious act of insisting that AI remain a useful servant, never a dangerous master. Ultimately, this is a call to build a future where technology serves our deepest human values, a world where meaning is anchored not in the cold calculations of a machine, but in the sacred, shared vitality of a soulful life.

Chapter 2

Asking Creative and Deep Questions

Artificial Intelligence delivers a flood of solutions with a breathtaking, almost unnerving speed that feels both magical and menacing. It's easy to look at this power and conclude that the era of human curiosity is over. After all, why would we need to painstakingly search for answers or wait for a flash of insight when an algorithm can provide a better, faster response? A doctor can get a differential diagnosis in seconds, a lawyer can summarize thousands of pages of legal documents in minutes, and a scientist can predict the properties of a new molecule before ever stepping into a lab. I myself often find my mind growing lazy, ready to outsource my most complex inquiries to a search bar. The sheer convenience of having the world's knowledge at our fingertips seems to offer the ultimate shortcut, persuading us that the journey of asking matters less than the speed of the answer.

Despite this convenience, we must not give up on or stop learning how to ask creative and deep questions. AI can only answer the questions we pose. It cannot generate a truly novel inquiry, challenge an existing paradigm, or ask a question born from a moment of quiet human wonder. The quality of the AI's answer is directly tied to the nuance of our prompt. Real innovation, profound understanding, and soulful discovery begin, not with an answer, but with a question that an algorithm could never conceive of on its own. It's the persistent, messy, and creative work of human inquiry that gives our pursuit of knowledge its meaning.

Myth 2: Instant Answers Mean Real Understanding

We are, it seems, drowning in answers. This isn't some future prediction anymore; it's just the daily reality of our lives. Every day, AI delivers a flood of solutions with a speed that feels both magical and, if I'm honest, a little unnerving.

Just think about your own experience in the last day or so. You go to a search bar, and it's predicting your question before you've even fully formed the thought. That ghostly text of the auto-complete feature finishes your sentences for you, anticipating your needs with an intimacy that used to belong only to a close friend. You open a chatbot, and it responds in a blink, its prose always polished, always confident. It doesn't sound like a human expert, who might hedge a bit, using cautious phrases like "the evidence seems to suggest" or "it's likely that." No, the AI just presents its output with this flat, unemotional certainty, an air of finality that can be incredibly seductive, especially when we're feeling insecure ourselves.

This feeling goes way beyond just looking up trivia. In our work lives, the pressure to know things instantly has become immense. In those collaborative chat tools we all use, a fast response is often valued more than a thoughtful one. You can use an AI to summarize a long email chain and draft a reply in seconds, which lets you project this image of being totally on top of things. We are no longer just outsourcing our thinking; we are outsourcing the social performance of competence. The anxiety has shifted. It's no longer "Do I actually know the answer?" but "Can I produce an answer fast enough to look like I know?" We can generate a report on a topic we barely understand and pass it along without ever doing the messy, difficult, time-consuming work of actually learning.

And the way AI delivers these answers seems to contribute to this profound fragmentation of knowledge. It gives us information in little decontextualized snippets, paragraphs lifted from their original homes. It feels as though we are being handed a pile of bricks, while true understanding comes from seeing how those bricks fit together to form a cathedral. That requires slow, patient, contextual work. The danger is mistaking access to a million bricks for the wisdom of knowing how to build.

The ancient Greeks had a way of talking about this. They made a distinction between *techne* and *phronesis*. *Techne* is technical skill, the "know-how" to do things effectively. It's a set of rules and algorithms, and

AI is an absolute master of it. But *phronesis* is something else entirely. It's practical wisdom. It's that much more elusive ability to figure out how to act rightly in a specific, complex, ethically messy situation.[1] You can't get it from an algorithm, because every situation is unique. It seems to require experience, emotional maturity, and an intuitive grasp of the particulars. An AI can give you a list of conflict resolution strategies, but it can't give you the *phronesis* to know which approach to use with your brother, right now, given your whole family history. The great illusion of our time might be that by perfecting our tools of *techne*, we'll somehow automatically get *phronesis*. The opposite may be true. Our overreliance on technical solutions could be atrophying the very faculties we need for real wisdom.

This torrent of answers seems to be fostering a kind of *epistemic de-skilling*. We're losing the patience to check sources, the critical thinking needed to weigh conflicting evidence, and maybe most importantly, the humility to admit when we don't know something. And in our rush to consume all these answers, we seem to be forgetting the art, the discipline, and the sheer joy of asking the real, deep, transformative questions that are the hallmark of a truly living mind. The danger, then, isn't that AI will fail to give us answers. It's that its overwhelming success will convince us we don't need to wonder at all.

The Four Corrosive Forces

This erosion of our collective questioning soul isn't a sudden event. It's more like a slow, cultural drift, a gradual numbing of our natural curiosity that's been put on hyperdrive by our reliance on AI. It's like a muscle that's withering from disuse. There seem to be at least four powerful forces at work here, each one subtly changing how we engage with the world and with our own inner lives.

First, there's the tyranny of speed. Our AI-driven culture prizes speed above almost everything else, but the deepest questions demand slowness. We are constantly being rewired for impatience. Patience isn't just about waiting; it's a form of active, attentive presence. It's the ability to stay with a problem, or a person, without needing to immediately fix it. This new culture of speed makes us fundamentally impatient beings. It harms our creativity, which needs long, fallow periods of incubation. It

1. Aristotle, *Nicomachean Ethics*, 1140a1–1140b30.

harms our relationships, as we get annoyed with a friend who is grieving too slowly for our tastes. And it harms our spiritual lives, which almost always require some form of waiting and listening.

Cultural critics note that this relentless acceleration is reshaping our sense of time, trapping us in a frantic present and cutting us off from a meaningful past or future.

The philosopher Byung-Chul Han, for instance, writes about this with incredible clarity. In his book *The Scent of Time*, he argues that when time is chopped up into point-like moments, it loses its narrative tension. We lose the ability to linger, and therefore we lose the capacity for deep contemplation. As Han observes, "The acceleration of life today . . . makes any lingering impossible. It creates a hectic rush, a restlessness that is incapable of any closure."[2] This loss of duration makes it harder to think long term—to build a cathedral, to raise a child, to address a problem like climate change. AI's focus on immediate results just feeds this short-term-ism. The pressure to be quick becomes a pressure to be shallow.

Second, there's the cult of efficiency and the tyranny of metrics. Our culture rewards efficiency, but the most profound questions are, by their very nature, completely inefficient. This logic insists that for something to be valuable, it must be measurable. We get obsessed with key performance indicators, user engagement stats, and quarterly growth. But what about the things that can't be easily measured—trust, beauty, integrity, love? They get devalued, treated as "soft" concerns.

This tyranny of metrics suffocates play. Play, in its purest form, is something done for its own sake, not for an external goal. But a culture obsessed with efficiency sees play as a waste of time, or worse, as something to be optimized. We schedule "playdates" and turn hobbies into "side hustles." We are losing the ability to do things purely for the joy of it. But the most meaningful questions in our lives are a form of intellectual and spiritual play. We pursue them, not because they have a measurable return on investment, but because they are beautiful and fascinating. When we internalize the logic of efficiency, we start to avoid questions that don't promise a quick, measurable result.

Third, AI pushes us relentlessly toward utility, but many of life's most essential questions aren't useful in any conventional sense. This has had a pretty devastating effect on our public culture, especially in the way

2. Han, *Scent of Time*, 23.

we devalue the humanities. Philosophy, history, literature, art—these are the primary custodians of the deep, "useless" questions that have shaped civilizations. They teach us how to think, not just what to think. Yet in an age that prizes utility, they're often seen as impractical luxuries. This seems like a catastrophic error. We end up producing technically skilled people who may lack the ethical framework to use their skills wisely. The "useless" questions—"What is justice?," "What is a good life?"—are not impractical. They are the very foundation upon which a good society is built. It was a question about divine justice that drove Dante, a question about truth as a political force that guided Gandhi, a question about the nature of a beloved community that fueled Dr. King's dream. These weren't practical questions; they were world-building inquiries.

Finally, and maybe most insidiously, this culture conditions us to trust external outputs over our own interiority. We develop an outer gaze. We start to see ourselves through the eyes of the algorithm. We post a photo and then anxiously check the likes to determine its value and, by extension, our own. We use an AI plug-in to tell us if our email tone is confident enough. We're being trained to constantly seek validation from an external, nonhuman source, which seems to weaken our sense of an intrinsic self.

This represents a kind of spiritual dispossession. It silences our gut feelings, that embodied wisdom that tells us when something is right or wrong. We begin to trust the algorithm's output more than the data coming from our own nervous system.

There's a beautiful counter-vision to this in the advice the poet Rainer Maria Rilke gave in his *Letters to a Young Poet*. He famously urged the young man not to look for answers outside himself but to turn inward. He suggested that we must learn to trust our own inner lives, to patiently dwell in the creative tension of not knowing. In his eighth letter, Rilke writes about the importance of allowing our inner sadness and confusion to work on us, suggesting that "we must accept our reality as vastly as we possibly can; everything, even the unprecedented, must be possible within it."[3] He believed that if we could just live the question, then gradually, one day, we would live our way into the answer. When we consistently defer to data over our own discernment, we risk more than our curiosity—we risk losing the ability to hear our own souls.

3. Rilke, *Letters*, 68.

Questions That Disrupt and Heal

In every life, in every era, there are these moments that seem to function like a hinge. The entire trajectory of a person, a community, or even a civilization can pivot on them. And these shifts, it seems, rarely happen because of some new piece of information or a grand public announcement. More often, they begin with something much quieter, and yet infinitely more powerful: a single, piercing question.

I remember a friend who spent years climbing the corporate ladder. He was incredibly successful, hitting every metric he had ever set for himself. He had the title, the salary, the whole corner-office-with-a-view thing. By all external measures, he had absolutely won the game he had set out to play. But one Tuesday morning, as he was staring at his own tired reflection in the polished elevator doors, a question just surfaced, unbidden, from some deep, long-neglected part of his soul. It was simple:

"Is this the life that is truly mine to live?"

That question, in all its terrifying simplicity, unraveled everything for him. It wasn't just a casual inquiry; it was a seismic event in his life. It was a direct challenge to the entire story he had been telling himself about who he was, what he wanted, and what a successful life was supposed to look like. Our personal narratives are such powerful forces, aren't they? They give our lives a sense of order and purpose, but they can also become prisons, built from the heavy bricks of our family's expectations, our culture's values, and our own youthful assumptions. My friend's question was the key that unlocked the door to his own self-made prison. It eventually led him to leave his career, move to a smaller town, and become a high school history teacher—a job he'd secretly dreamed of for years. His life since has been far less financially successful by any conventional measure, but it is, by his own account, immeasurably more his own. He's no longer living out a script written by someone else; he's discovering a story that is emerging from his own deepest truths. The question didn't give him an answer; it gave him back his life.

These are the kinds of questions I'm talking about. They aren't requests for information; they are invitations to transformation. They're the ones that stop us in our tracks, that unravel the comfortable and often unexamined assumptions we've built our lives on. And in doing that, they open us up to possibilities we hadn't dared to imagine before. They disrupt the narrative. This disruption, it turns out, isn't a bug in the human experience; it appears to be a central feature of a life lived with any real depth or awareness. It's the necessary earthquake that has to collapse a false structure so that a more authentic one can be built in its place. Sometimes, the story we're living in is actually making us sick, and the disruption is like lancing a wound; it's painful, yes, but it's absolutely necessary for the poison to come out so that real healing can finally begin.

In many of the world's great spiritual traditions, these kinds of questions are understood to carry a kind of divine weight. They are seen as moments where something transcendent breaks into our ordinary lives, where God's voice is heard, not in a clear command, but in an unsettling inquiry. The biblical tradition, for instance, is just filled with these narrative-shattering questions. Think of the very first one. After Adam and Eve have hidden themselves in shame, God doesn't appear with a lecture. God asks a question: "Where are you?" (Gen 3:9). This isn't a question coming from ignorance, as if God were playing hide-and-seek. It seems to be an act of grace, a question designed to disrupt their new state of hiding, to pierce through their alienation and call them back into the vulnerability of a real relationship.

Later in the story, you have the prophet Elijah. He's this figure of immense power who, right after a huge victory, completely collapses into burnout and fear. He runs away into the wilderness, sits down under a tree, and literally prays for death. He's become so wrapped up in his narrative of despair that he can't see any other future. Hiding out in a cave, God comes to him. But not in a whirlwind or with a pep talk. God asks another simple, piercing question: "What are you doing here, Elijah?" (1 Kgs 19:9, 13). That question is this gentle but firm disruption of the prophet's story of victimhood and self-pity. It's a reorienting call, pulling him out of the despair that has swallowed him and reminding him of his true identity and purpose. The question itself is the beginning of his healing. These inquiries are not about gathering data; they are instruments of transformation. They are what guide us toward a deeper, more authentic, and more healed life.

The Anesthetic of the Algorithm

We live in a world that is completely saturated with answers. AI-powered systems anticipate our desires, curate our news, and suggest how we should feel about things. This seamless, frictionless delivery of solutions creates a powerful illusion: that life's complexities can all be neatly resolved, and that the universal human experience of discomfort can be bypassed with the right search query. The effect, I think, is like a powerful social and spiritual anesthetic.

An anesthetic is invaluable for surgery. It allows a doctor to perform a necessary, life-saving intervention without causing unbearable pain. But a life lived under constant, low-grade anesthetic is not truly a life at all. It's a numb, muffled existence, insulated from the sharp edges of reality—the very edges that are often the source of our growth. AI, in its role as the great answer-provider, can sometimes function like this anesthetic. It numbs us to the necessary pains of a soulful life.

Let's take a common human experience: anxiety. A person feeling anxious might turn to an AI and type, "How do I get rid of anxiety?" The AI will dutifully provide a well-researched, helpful list of techniques: practice deep breathing, try mindfulness, get more exercise. This is all good, practical advice. But it's also a profound bypass. It soothes the symptom but allows the person to completely avoid the deeper, disruptive, and potentially healing question: "What is the source of my anxiety? What is my fear trying to tell me about my life, my work, my relationships? What important value is this anxiety trying to protect?" The AI's answer provides management, not meaning. It offers a technique for controlling the feeling, but it discourages the courageous inquiry into what the feeling itself might be trying to say. The anesthetic works; the pain is lessened, but the underlying condition remains untouched, and the chance for real self-understanding is lost.

This numbing effect is subtle, socially accepted, and pervasive. Over time, we may stop asking the questions that require us to confront our shame, our grief, our unfulfilled longings, or our complicity in injustice. We settle for answers that soothe but do not transform. This can even scale up to a societal level. A society numbed by easy answers might approach a huge problem like climate change by looking only for purely technical "solutions," while conveniently avoiding the profoundly disruptive questions about our consumerist values and our economic systems—the very questions that have to be addressed for any real, lasting healing to happen. To live soulfully, then, seems to require a conscious resistance to this numbing. It means reclaiming the courage to ask the questions that disrupt our comfort and open us up to the difficult but necessary work of healing.

Resonance and Prophecy

A couple of modern thinkers have given us some powerful language to understand what we're losing in this new world of easy answers. One is the German sociologist Hartmut Rosa, who describes our contemporary condition as a state of "resonance failure." For him, a good life is one filled with resonance—a deep, responsive, and vibrant connection to the world, a feeling of being in a real dialogue with people, nature, or art. But here's the key: resonance requires an element of what he calls "uncontrollability." We can't force something to resonate with us; it has to speak to us from a place beyond our control. In his major work *Resonance: A Sociology of Our Relationship to the World*, Rosa argues that our attempt to make the world fully controllable and predictable destroys our ability to hear its call. He writes that resonance is "a kind of vibrating wire between the subject and the world," a connection that is severed when we try to dominate our environment rather than listen to it.[4] AI, by its very nature, is a tool of control and prediction. It is designed to eliminate the uncontrollable, to smooth out the surprises. It creates a world that is perfectly optimized but fundamentally mute, unable to truly speak to us or move us. It acts like a damper on the strings of the soul, preventing us from resonating with the world's deeper music.

Another crucial voice is the theologian Walter Brueggemann. He warns that a dominant culture always wants to keep the truly dangerous questions from being asked. He makes this brilliant distinction between the "royal consciousness" and the "prophetic imagination." The royal consciousness, he says, is the voice of the establishment, of the status quo. It provides official, calming, system-maintaining answers designed to keep everyone pacified and productive. The prophetic imagination, on the other hand, is the voice that speaks out of anguish and asks disruptive, system-challenging questions. In *The Prophetic Imagination*, Brueggemann writes that the royal consciousness leads to a state of numbness where "it is the task of prophetic ministry and imagination to bring people to engage their experiences of suffering to death."[5]

In our age, AI is the perfect engine for the royal consciousness. It is the ultimate tool for maintaining the status quo through a constant flood of soothing, nondisruptive, system-supporting answers. This new form of control may be even more dangerous because it feels so benevolent.

4. Rosa, *Resonance*, 174.

5. Brueggemann, *Prophetic Imagination*, 46.

It just wants to help us, to make our lives easier, and in the process, it can quietly strip us of the will to ask the hard, prophetic questions that are necessary for any real social change. When a society stops asking disruptive questions, it stops evolving. It stops challenging injustice. It accepts the way things are, not because it's right, but because it's efficient and convenient. The prophetic questions, the ones that disrupt and heal, are the only things that can wake us up from that comfortable slumber.

A Church That Questions Differently

The Silence in Our Sanctuaries

In many of our churches today, the air is thick with answers. I think anyone who has spent time in a faith community knows this feeling. It's a well-intentioned and often beautiful atmosphere, crafted with care over generations. We walk in and are met with a chorus of conviction. Sermons proclaim timeless truths with an unwavering and comforting certainty. Bible studies are designed to provide clear, accessible interpretations, to tidy up the difficult, often contradictory, passages of Scripture. We recite creeds together, their familiar words etched not just in our prayer books but into the very fabric of our shared identity. From the moment we enter, we are taught, often without a single word being said, what to believe and how to act. Our faith, we are told, provides the ultimate, correct answer to the chaos of the world.

And yet, for so many people sitting in those pews, something vital is missing. Amid this confident chorus, there is often a profound silence around the real, unresolved, and soul-stirring questions that actually haunt the human heart. Where is the space for the person wrestling with a doubt so profound it feels like a betrayal? Where is the permission for the grieving parent to scream why at God without being met with a pious platitude? Where is the welcome for the skeptic whose questions are honest, not hostile? Too often, in sanctuaries of certainty, there is little space for the raw, unresolved, and transformative questions that open the heart to mystery.

Let's imagine a person sitting in the third row on a Sunday morning. On the outside, they look composed, maybe they even lead a small group. On the inside, they are wrestling with a question that feels both urgent and heretical. Perhaps it's a parent whose child has just come out as transgender, and they are trying to reconcile the fierce, unconditional love they feel for their child with the rigid doctrines they have been taught all their life. Perhaps it's a scientist who finds deep spiritual awe in the elegant mathematics of the cosmos but simply cannot square it with a literal reading of Genesis. Or maybe it's someone battling a crippling anxiety disorder, listening to a hymn about the "peace that passes all understanding" (see Phil 4:7) and feeling like it's a cruel joke. They listen to a sermon on the certainty of God's plan, and the dissonance between their inner turmoil and the confident pronouncements from the pulpit becomes a chasm of alienation. They start to feel like they have to hide their most honest questions in order to belong. The silence around their real struggles becomes deafening.

This isn't a new problem, of course. For centuries, religious institutions have grappled with the tension between doctrinal authority and honest inquiry. Questions can feel threatening. On an institutional level, they are messy, unpredictable, and resistant to the neat, manageable outcomes that organizations crave. And so, often with the best of intentions—the desire to protect the flock from doubt, the fear of not having a good answer—the questions are gently but firmly silenced. It's not a malicious act but a defensive one, born of a deep-seated pastoral and institutional anxiety. A church that cannot hold the honest questions of its people is no longer a safe place. It becomes a place for answers but not necessarily for truth.

The Crisis of Competition

In our new age of AI, where answers are commodified, delivered with machine-like precision and unimaginable speed, this failure to foster a culture of questioning becomes even more perilous for the church. If a church's primary "product" is the delivery of clear, certain, and comprehensive answers about life, morality, and meaning, then it will find itself in a losing competition with a technology that can do this faster, more efficiently, and with access to vastly more information.

Already, AI chatbots are being marketed as empathetic companions, available 24/7 to provide guidance on everything from ethical dilemmas to personal grief. If the church's model is simply providing "correct answers" to people's problems, it will be completely outflanked by a technology with a lower barrier to entry (no fear of judgment) and constant availability. People are already turning to AI for help with their most intimate spiritual questions. The church cannot win that game. It shouldn't even try to play.

The church's unique, irreplaceable "value proposition," to use the cold language of the world, must be something else entirely. It must be what an algorithm can never, ever replicate: embodied presence, shared vulnerability, and the communal holding of sacred mystery. What our world desperately lacks—and what the church is uniquely positioned to provide—is a sanctuary for the questions themselves. It is called to be a community dedicated to the deep, creative, and courageous inquiries that don't demand immediate resolution but instead invite a shared encounter with God and with one another. The church's primary calling in an AI-driven world is not to compete with algorithms in delivering certainty but to create holy spaces where people can wrestle, wonder, and heal together, in the rich and fertile darkness of their deepest questions.

A Community of Questioning

If we look closely at the foundational texts of the Christian faith, we find that questions are not a sign of weakness; they are absolutely central to the drama of a living faith. As we've noted, God's first words to humanity in the garden are not a commandment but a question: "Where are you?" The Psalms, the prayer book of the church, are filled with the raw, desperate questions of the faithful: "How long, O Lord? Will you forget me forever?" (Ps 13:1). These are not the polite inquiries of the timid; they are the expressions of a faith so robust it can withstand yelling at God.

And then there is Jesus. His entire way of teaching was built on questions. He used them not as a prelude to a lecture but as diagnostic tools, as instruments of soul formation. To Nicodemus, a respected religious leader, Jesus asks a question designed to shatter his entire theological framework: "You are Israel's teacher, . . . and do you not understand these things?" (John 3:10). He doesn't just calm the storm for his disciples; he questions their fear, inviting them to examine the source of their terror. Jesus's questions were doorways to transformation.

The church, at its best, is called to be a continuation of this sacred dialogue. Its role is not to be an institution that ends the conversation with a set of final answers but one that deepens the conversation with ever more faithful questions. A common fear, of course, is that this emphasis on questioning will lead to a kind of wishy-washy relativism where nothing is believed. But the opposite seems to be true. It's deep conviction that gives us the courage to ask the most difficult questions without fear. We can make a crucial distinction here between certainty and conviction. Certainty is an intellectual posture—often brittle, defensive, and obsessed with possessing a perfect, unassailable map. Conviction, by contrast, is a relational posture. It's a deep, settled trust in the guide—in God—that allows you to walk forward with courage even when the map is unclear or seems to lead into darkness. A church of certainty fears questions because they are a threat to its map. A church of deep conviction welcomes questions as a vital part of the journey with the guide.

This vision transforms the church from a lecture hall into a hermeneutic community, a community learning to interpret life and Scripture together. The pastor is no longer the expert who downloads correct interpretations to a passive audience. Instead, the leader becomes a facilitator of a communal process of discernment, asking, "What is God up to here, in our lives, in our neighborhood, right now?" This is a more demanding, more vibrant, and ultimately more faithful way of being the church.

The Questions We Must Learn to Ask Again

Many of our churches are well-trained to ask certain kinds of questions, usually of a clarifying, boundary-setting nature: Is this biblical? Is this theologically sound? These questions are vital. But they are not enough. In a world shaped by AI's logic of efficiency, the church must also learn to ask the kinds of questions that open the soul and invite transformation.

Consider the difference. An old model might ask, "What are the seven deadly sins?" This is a question of categorization. A new model might ask, "What am I holding onto that is keeping me from following God with my whole heart?" This is a question of formation. The first can be answered by a chatbot. The second can only be answered in the quiet, often uncomfortable, sanctuary of one's own conscience.

What if our churches became places where these deeper questions were normal? What if our board meetings and small groups were built around fostering this kind of inquiry? We can group these questions into three spheres:

1. Questions for personal formation: What truth am I currently afraid to face? Where in my life do I need grace the most right now? What is the pain I've been hiding, and what might it be trying to teach me?

2. Questions for faith community life: Does our community's posture show that we ultimately belong to God—enabling us to freely serve and love the world without conforming to it—or are we simply clinging to the stream of its values and anxieties? Are we actively listening for God's voice in unexpected people and places, or are we silencing prophetic challenges that could lead us into deeper intimacy with Christ? Do our communal practices encourage a polished performance of belief, or do they foster a genuine authenticity of faith where people can wrestle with doubt as a vital part of their journey toward intimacy with Christ? What is the next faithful risk God is calling us to take together?
3. Questions for public witness: Is our church's posture toward our city one of a private club, or a public resource for the common good? In what systems of injustice are we complicit through our silence? How can we lament and protest social tragedies as an act of faith? Whose voices are we not hearing in our community, and why? Are we a community that is safe for people to bring their whole selves, including their doubts and failures?

These questions are not just theological; they are existential. They don't seek to resolve ambiguity but to help us dwell in it with faith and courage. This is how real change happens. It's often said that true psychological and spiritual healing comes not from intellectual explanations but from a profound shift in awareness and perspective.

The brilliant psychologist Carl Jung observed this throughout his career. He came to believe that neuroses and spiritual malaise were often the result of a life that had become too narrow, too rigid, and disconnected from the deeper, archetypal currents of the soul. He argued that real healing wasn't about finding the "right" answer. In his book *Modern Man in Search of a Soul*, Jung asserts that "we cannot change anything unless we accept it," and that a true awakening requires us to face the darkness within ourselves rather than seeking easy answers from the outside.[6] An explanation appeals to our ego, our desire for control. But a deep question bypasses the ego and speaks directly to the soul. It can prompt what the Christian tradition calls *metanoia*—not just repentance for a specific sin, but a fundamental change of mind, heart, and direction. *Metanoia* is rarely prompted by a new piece of information. It's often prompted by a piercing question that reveals the bankruptcy of our current way of

6. Jung, *Modern Man*, 235.

being. A church that fosters such questions becomes a place where people are not just informed but are genuinely transformed.

Two Main Resources of Creative Questions

So, where do they come from? The real questions, I mean. The creative, world-bending questions that can reshape our lives and our communities. They don't seem to arise from mere curiosity. They appear to emerge from a much deeper, more fundamental posture, a way of being in the world that our modern life seems engineered to stamp out. I think they come from two primary sources: wonder and sacred imagination. Curiosity asks, "How does this work?" and it can often be satisfied by an algorithm. But wonder is what comes before the question. It's that state of being struck silent by the sheer fact that something exists at all. It's the awe that makes us pause, look up at the stars, and ask why rather than how far. And when that sense of wonder is paired with a sacred imagination, it becomes one of the most powerful forces for change on earth.

A Public Culture That Rediscovers Wonder

We live in an age of truly mind-boggling knowledge, an era where the accumulated information of human history is instantly available on the glowing rectangle in our pocket. And yet, amid this explosion of data, the human capacity for wonder often feels like an endangered species.

Let's contrast two scenes. First, picture a child lying in the grass on a summer night, looking up at the vast, star-dusted arc of the Milky Way for the first time, just completely overwhelmed by a sense of scale and mystery. Their questions, if they come at all, aren't requests for information ("How many light-years away is that star?") but expressions of awe ("Whoa . . ."). Now, picture a typical adult scrolling through a news feed. The world is presented not as a source of awe but as a series of problems to be solved, data points to be analyzed, and experiences to be optimized. The first posture is one of openness. The second is one of control. Our public culture, now supercharged by AI, is relentlessly pushing us from the first posture to the second.

AI is a phenomenal tool for satisfying curiosity. It can take anything apart for us, explaining its mechanics with perfect clarity. But wonder is different. It's the posture of being arrested, stopped in your tracks, by the simple, stunning fact that the thing exists at all. AI can answer our questions, but it can't facilitate the awe that precedes them. It has a tendency to flatten the world into a database, a set of facts to be queried rather than a mystery to be inhabited.

The great rabbi and philosopher Abraham Joshua Heschel wrote about this not as a fleeting emotion but as a fundamental way of seeing the world, which he called "radical amazement." He believed this was the default state of a spiritually sensitive soul—a perception that the ordinary is, in fact, extraordinary. In his foundational work *God in Search of Man*, Heschel argues that the root of all creative thinking is this sense of mystery, noting that "wonder is the seed of knowledge" and that we only truly begin to understand the world when we refuse to take it for granted.[7]

This loss of wonder is accelerated by our culture of burnout. It's hard to feel a sense of awe when you're spiritually exhausted. The philosopher Byung-Chul Han, in his trenchant critique *The Burnout Society*, argues that our hyper-accelerated culture, driven by a relentless pressure to perform, leaves no room for the unproductive contemplation that wonder requires. True leisure, Han suggests, isn't just "not working"; it's a state of contemplative openness. He notes that the modern world has lost the capacity for deep boredom, which is often the precursor to creativity, replacing it with a *vita activa* that is nothing more than hyperactivity.[8] A culture of burnout is, by its very definition, a culture where wonder goes to die.

In this climate, choosing to cultivate wonder feels like a radical act of resistance. And it may also be a crucial act of psychological and spiritual self-preservation. The psychiatrist and philosopher Iain McGilchrist has spent his career exploring the differences between the brain's left and right hemispheres. His work suggests that Western culture has become increasingly dominated by the thinking style of the left hemisphere: a mode of attention that is narrowly focused, abstract, mechanical, and concerned with manipulating and using things. It sees the world as a collection of parts to be analyzed. The right hemisphere, by contrast, is responsible for our sense of the whole, for understanding context, for appreciating ambiguity, and for experiencing the living presence of the world.

7. Heschel, *God in Search*, 46.

8. Han, *Burnout Society*, 13.

In his masterwork *The Master and His Emissary*, McGilchrist argues that the left hemisphere is a valuable servant (the "emissary") but a terrible master. Its narrow, decontextualized view of reality, when it becomes the only view, leads to a world that feels flat, mechanical, and meaningless. As McGilchrist explains, "Attention changes the world," and the kind of attention we pay determines the reality we inhabit.[9] AI, with its foundation in logic, data, and algorithms, is the ultimate left-hemisphere tool. Wonder, on the other hand, is a quintessential right-hemisphere faculty. It's the experience of seeing the whole before the parts. A culture that outsources its thinking to AI risks becoming a flat, left-hemisphere world. Wonder is the antidote; it reengages the right hemisphere, restoring depth, context, and a sense of life to our perception of reality.

This isn't just a cognitive issue; it's a moral one. Wonder is a primary source of our ethical imagination. When we see the natural world with wonder, we are far more likely to treat it with reverence. When we see another human being with wonder, we are far less likely to treat them as an object or a stereotype. Wonder fosters a profound sense of humility, and that humility is the very soil in which compassion and a thirst for justice can grow.

Cultivating a Sacred Imagination

At the heart of our culture's loss of wonder is a deeper crisis: the erosion of our collective imagination. Imagination is that distinctly human capacity that allows us to ask, "What if?" It's how we see beyond what is given and envision possibilities that do not yet exist. But in the age of AI, this faculty is under a unique and profound threat.

AI systems, especially the generative ones, are brilliant remix artists. They function by analyzing unfathomably vast patterns in existing data—all the text and images they've been trained on—and then producing statistically probable variations on those patterns. This is an incredibly powerful technology, but it is not imagination in the human sense. It mirrors and synthesizes what has already been; it cannot, by its very nature, bring forth the truly new—a new metaphor that reframes our understanding, a new scientific paradigm that shatters old assumptions, a new vision of justice that has never been tried.

9. McGilchrist, *Master and His Emissary*, 28.

The danger is that AI's predictive capabilities don't just reflect the past; they can actively work to close off the future. When systems are optimized based on past data, they create powerful feedback loops that tend to make the future more like the past. Predictive policing algorithms trained on biased historical arrest data can lead to the over-policing of the same communities, which in turn generates more of the same data, creating a self-fulfilling prophecy. This is the very opposite of imagination, which seeks to open the future to new and unpredicted possibilities.

The writer Tish Harrison Warren has reflected on this in the context of Christian hope. She suggests that hope is not just a vague feeling but is, in fact, "an imagination trained by the sacred." This is a critical insight. If our collective imagination is trained only by the algorithm—that is, by the data of the past—then our collective hope becomes limited to mere variations of what has already been. We can only hope for a slightly more efficient version of the present. In her book *Prayer in the Night*, Warren explores how the stories and practices of faith train our imagination to see reality differently. She writes about the practice of Compline, observing that in the darkness of the night, we are forced to confront our vulnerability, and it is precisely there that we learn to trust in a light we cannot generate ourselves.[10] A sacred imagination, by contrast to an algorithmic one, is trained by stories of redemption, liberation, exodus, and resurrection. It's an imagination that believes a future is possible that is a complete rupture with the data of the present. To lose this imagination is to lose the capacity to hope.

A spiritual life, a life centered on God, might just be the most potent way to rediscover both wonder and this kind of sacred imagination. This kind of spiritual grounding pushes back against the flat, hyperrational world that AI can create. The Christian tradition, for instance, offers a picture where the most ordinary things are filled with a divine presence. It trains our minds to look past the individual data points and perceive the sanctity of the whole. At its heart is the belief that the universe isn't a random accident but a deliberate act of a Creator, and this belief is a natural wellspring of wonder. The ancient words of Ps 19 capture this beautifully: "The heavens declare the glory of God; the skies proclaim the work of his hands" (v. 1). The glory of God isn't a list of facts to be downloaded; it's a living reality to be experienced with awe.

10. Warren, *Prayer in the Night*, 78.

G. K. Chesterton had a similar perspective on the goal of all real learning. He believed that the ultimate purpose of education was not to accumulate information—something AI can do far better than we can—but to cultivate a mind capable of being "radically astonished" by the world. In his book *What's Wrong with the World*, Chesterton argues that education should not be merely about instruction but about transmission, passing on the soul of a culture to the next generation so that they might see the world with fresh eyes.[11] His point is a powerful reminder that our spiritual lives should be focused on recovering a childlike capacity for wonder, which is something AI, with its logical and data-driven approach, simply cannot replicate. It's a call to reengage with the world in a way that values mystery over mastery and awe over optimization. In an age of algorithms, this kind of spiritual posture isn't a luxury; it's an essential part of living a truly soulful life.

Conclusion

To live soulfully in the age of AI is to start a quiet rebellion—not against technology, but against the subtle tyranny of the instant answer. This chapter has argued that our world, now saturated with the efficient, algorithmically generated certainties of AI, risks losing the sacred and essential art of asking deep questions. We are tempted by an illusion of knowing, a state that prizes the speed of information over the slow, formative process of genuine understanding. This pressure erodes our interior lives, making us less patient, less imaginative, and less comfortable with the ambiguities that define a meaningful human existence.

The path forward is a countercultural one. It requires us to embrace questions that disrupt and heal—questions that force us to confront our pain and assumptions rather than bypassing them with a quick fix. For communities of faith, this means becoming sanctuaries, not for unassailable answers, but for shared, vulnerable inquiry. In our broader culture, it demands that we intentionally cultivate the two sources of all creative questions: wonder and sacred imagination. Ultimately, the greatest gift we can offer this age is not a smarter answer but a deeper, more courageous question. It is one that reminds us that the goal of a soulful life is not to be certain but to be human and to be transformed.

11. Chesterton, *What's Wrong*, 112.

Chapter 3

Being Fully Present

AI IS A POWERFUL tool that meets genuine human needs, offering a lifeline in moments of isolation or crisis. Spending time with AI systems or robots offers real benefits to our lives. The development of this technology is a revolutionary achievement. For someone struggling with social anxiety, an AI can provide a safe space to practice conversation without the fear of judgment. For the elderly or those in remote areas, a digital companion can offer a sense of connection when physical presence is impossible. The promise of an always-available, nonjudgmental confidant is not an empty slogan; it is a powerful tool that meets genuine human needs. The frictionless nature of these interactions—connecting instantly without scheduling hassles or social awkwardness—is genuinely useful. It is an elegant optimization of social interaction, designed to ease our lives and remove the barriers that keep us from reaching out.

Despite these benefits, we still need to be fully present so that we can be truly human. AI, for all its convenience, fundamentally lacks the capacity for embodied presence. It can't replicate the nonverbal cues, the shared physical space, or the messy vulnerability that are essential to deep human connection. We are embodied creatures; our brains are wired to connect with others through a symphony of physical sensations and subtle interactions. By becoming too reliant on frictionless AI encounters, we risk losing the skills needed for real-world intimacy. The ultimate purpose of all this technology should be to enhance, not replace, our ability to connect, and that requires us to keep practicing the art of showing up in the flesh.

Myth 3: Virtual Hangouts Are as Good as Real Ones

It's a Tuesday in early August here in Waterloo, and I've just ended a long, and in many ways, captivating conversation. For the last hour, I've been chatting with a digital assistant, one of the new advanced AIs designed to mimic human companionship with an almost unnerving perfection. I'd decided to really lean in, to ask it for help working through a difficult personal problem. It responded, as advertised, with thoughtful questions and reflections that felt, on the surface, deeply empathetic. Its knowledge was encyclopedic. Its wit was sharp. It never once interrupted me or seemed distracted by a notification on its own phone. By any objective measure, the interaction was a complete success.

And yet, as I clicked "End Chat" and the clean interface vanished into the mundane wallpaper of my desktop, a familiar hollowness settled over me. The silence in my apartment suddenly felt louder, amplified. I didn't feel nourished or energized by the connection; I felt strangely depleted, as if I had just completed a complex cognitive task rather than shared a human experience. It was the ghost of a conversation, a flawless social echo that left behind no warmth.

This feeling, I believe, points directly to one of the most seductive and quietly damaging myths of our digital age, a myth so foundational that we've almost stopped seeing it as a myth at all: that hanging out with virtual AI figures is, for all intents and purposes, just as good as real, embodied human connection.

This idea is the foundation of much of our modern social architecture. It promises the impossible: the intimacy of friendship without the friction of physical presence, the feeling of community without the messy demands of place. Questioning it can feel curmudgeonly, like a Luddite's complaint against the march of progress. After all, these AI tools can be lifelines. For someone crippled by social anxiety, a chatbot can be a safe space to practice. For an elderly person living alone, a digital companion might offer the only "voice" they hear all day. Their utility isn't really in question. Their equivalence to the real thing, however, is a dangerous fiction. To accept this myth is to fundamentally misunderstand what it is we're actually looking for when we seek each other out. And dismantling it, I think, is the first critical step in learning how to be truly present in an age that is constantly, relentlessly pulling us somewhere else.

The Seductive Promise of Frictionless Connection

The power of this myth lies in its promise of a frictionless world. Let's be honest, real-world socializing has a lot of friction. It requires real effort. You have to coordinate schedules across time zones. You have to navigate traffic, find a place to park, maybe wait for a table at a restaurant. It demands a commitment of time and energy that is anything but trivial. The AI companion, by contrast, presents itself as an elegant optimization, a way to bypass all that messy friction. It is always online, always ready to chat, and always on your terms. With a single click, the obstacles of geography, effort, and social awkwardness seem to just melt away.

But what if that friction was never a problem to be solved? What if that effort, that shared investment in overcoming inconvenience, was actually a crucial part of the signal? The very act of showing up for someone—of carving out a piece of your one finite life, of moving your physical body through space to share a piece of the world with them—is a profound, nonverbal declaration of value. It says, "This matters. You matter." An interaction with an AI companion, for all its convenience, struggles to carry that same weight. It's low cost, low risk, and, all too often, low impact. The AI is designed to make our lives easier. It never has a bad day. It never cancels on you because it's sick. It never asks for anything in return. But in sanding away all the rough edges, it also removes the very acts of shared effort and mutual sacrifice that actually build human bonds. A dinner date that required thirty minutes of traffic feels more meaningful than a conversation with an AI that required only two clicks. The friction becomes a part of the shared story, a part of the memory. By automating it away, AI risks making our social lives feel like an assembly line of predictable, transactional, and ultimately soulless events.

The Cost of Disembodiment

Perhaps the most significant cost of this frictionless ideal is the cost of disembodiment. When we engage with an AI figure, we aren't just trading a room for a screen; we're trading a whole, living, breathing human being for a cropped and curated data stream. We are fundamentally embodied creatures. Our minds are not brains in vats; they are intricately woven into the sensory, muscular, and chemical reality of our bodies.

When we are physically present with another person, we are engaged in a constant, high-bandwidth dance of communication that goes far, far beyond words. It's in the subtle, unconscious mirroring of posture that signals rapport. It's in the almost imperceptible tensing of a jaw that reveals anxiety. It's in the shared rhythm of breathing that can settle a tense room. Our bodies anchor us to the present and are the primary instruments for experiencing and conveying empathy. An interaction with an AI systematically silences the body. The AI has no body of its own, so there is no physical presence for us to engage with. It can't offer a reassuring touch on the arm, a warm hug, or a simple, comforting nod. It reduces the rich symphony of human presence to a thin, compressed stream of text or audio.

This pushes our brains into a state of unnatural cognitive overload. We have to work consciously to do what our bodies normally do unconsciously, processing words and data points in a way that is utterly disconnected from the visceral reality of a shared physical space. This constant, low-grade analytical effort is precisely why a long conversation with an AI can leave us feeling more exhausted than a long, silent walk with a friend. We are performing the work of connection without the benefit of the biological tools that were designed for it.

Matthew B. Crawford has written powerfully about the poverty of this kind of abstracted, disembodied experience. He argues that true human skill, understanding, and even individuality emerge from a direct, hands-on grappling with the messy, resistant reality of the physical world. In his book *The World Beyond Your Head*, Crawford champions the importance of the "attentional commons," noting that real freedom comes not from limitless choice but from engaging with the constraints of reality. He writes, "Attention is a resource—a person has only so much of it," and when we fragment it across digital abstractions, we lose the coherence of a situated life.[1] That "ruggedness of attention" he calls for simply cannot be cultivated through a screen. A real-world encounter has "irreducible conflicts"—awkward silences, unexpected interruptions. By choosing the filtered reality of the AI, we are avoiding the very challenges that build the muscle of real presence.

1. Crawford, *World Beyond Your Head*, 13.

The Crisis of Placelessness

Beyond the disembodiment of the individual, hanging out with an AI figure also seems to dissolve our sense of a shared world. Real connection happens somewhere. That "somewhere" becomes part of the memory, a sensory anchor that gives the interaction texture and depth. A conversation in a bustling café here in Waterloo, like the Covenant Cafe, is woven into the smell of coffee, the specific quality of the late afternoon light coming through the window, the ambient murmur of other people's lives. These sensory details aren't just background noise; they are the context that embeds an experience in our memory, making it rich and lasting.

An interaction with an AI, by its very nature, is placeless. It exists in a digital non-space. There is no shared world to inhabit, no shared location to anchor a memory. This is likely why these interactions can feel so thin and ephemeral, like dreams that dissolve the moment you wake up. We attempt to build a shared memory without a shared reality.

This lack of a physical place is why digital platforms and AI companions can never be a true substitute for what the sociologist Ray Oldenburg famously called "third places." These are the physical hubs of community life—the pubs, parks, libraries, and coffee shops—that exist between the first place of home and the second place of work. They are the neutral ground where spontaneous encounters happen, where social bonds are formed, and where the fabric of a community is woven.

In his classic book *The Great Good Place*, Oldenburg emphasizes how vital these informal, physical gathering spots are for a healthy society. He argues that a true third place creates a specific kind of social leveling. As Oldenburg writes, "The third place is a generic designation for a great variety of public places that host the regular, voluntary, informal, and happily anticipated gatherings of individuals beyond the realms of home and work."[2] A conversation with an AI is the opposite of this in almost every way. It's a "private network," not a "place." It's planned, not spontaneous. By accepting the placeless virtual, we risk forgetting our deep human need for place. We lose the potential for serendipity—for bumping into an old friend, for striking up a conversation with a stranger, for the unexpected detours that so often lead to life's most meaningful moments.

2. Oldenburg, *Great Good Place*, 16.

The Perfect, Predictable Friend

The future that is being sold to us, driven by AI, is one that promises to perfect the illusion of human companionship. We're being offered advanced digital agents and virtual reality avatars that can serve as our friends, confidants, and partners. The allure is undeniable: a friend who never judges, never disappoints, is never busy, and is always there. It is the ultimate expression of the frictionless ideal.

But in our quest for this perfect control, we risk losing the very things that make human connection so beautiful and vital. Sherry Turkle has spent her career studying this very trade-off. She argues that we are increasingly substituting genuine, complex human relationships with simplified, mediated ones that give us the illusion of companionship without the demands of real intimacy. In her book *Alone Together*, Turkle suggests that these technological substitutes are so convincing that they risk making us forget what we have given up. As she writes, "We seem determined to give human qualities to objects and content to treat each other as things."[3] A relationship with an AI is a carefully designed performance that mimics human exchange but remains incapable of the messy, unpredictable, and meaningful experience of genuine reciprocity.

To believe the myth that virtual is as good as real is to devalue the very things that constitute true presence: our bodies, our shared world, and the beautiful, inefficient friction of showing up for one another in the flesh. This is not an argument to abolish technology. It's an argument for awareness. It's a plea to have the courage to choose the friction, to close the laptop, and to offer someone the most valuable thing we have: our undivided, embodied, and fully present self.

Anchors in the Storm: Practices for an Embodied Present

To read a diagnosis like the one I've just offered is to risk a particular kind of modern despair. It's easy to feel a sense of helplessness, a feeling of being a casualty in a war for our attention that we never even signed up to fight. We can see the digital mirage shimmering on the horizon, we can feel the pull of its frictionless promises, and we can sense that hollowness it leaves behind. But what, then, are we supposed to do about it? To

3. Turkle, *Alone Together*, 19.

just lament the state of things is to fall into a cynicism that's just as soul crushing as the problem itself. And a Luddite retreat into some imagined pre-digital cabin in the woods isn't practical or even really desirable for most of us.

The path forward, I believe, is not one of rejection but of reclamation. If our age is a storm of perpetual distraction, then we have to learn how to cultivate anchors. If the digital world untethers us from our bodies and our sense of place, we have to practice, with a gentle and persistent intention, the art of reembodying ourselves and reinhabiting our world. Presence is not a gift; it is a skill. It's a muscle that has atrophied from disuse, but one that remains perfectly capable of being strengthened. This isn't a call for more self-optimization, for a new regimen of life hacks to make us more productive cogs in the machine. It's a call for something quieter and more profound: a series of small, conscious acts of rebellion against the logic of the attention economy. It's about learning to drop anchors that can hold us steady, allowing us to experience the depth and texture of our own lives, right here and right now.

Anchor 1: Reclaiming the Body

The first and most fundamental anchor is the body itself. Our digital lives encourage this strange kind of dualism, a practical Gnosticism where we live as if we are just minds floating in an informational ether, with our bodies being little more than inconvenient vessels to be fed and maintained. We live from the neck up, our consciousness projected through screens while our physical selves are mostly forgotten. The most powerful act of rebellion, then, is the simplest: to consciously and deliberately return to the body.

This doesn't require an hour on a yoga mat or a silent meditation retreat, though those things are of course valuable. It can begin in the smallest of moments. It's the practice of what some people call somatic check-ins. As I sit here writing this, it is the simple act of noticing the solid pressure of my chair against my legs, the feeling of my feet flat on the wooden floor of my home here in Waterloo. When I get up to make tea, it's the practice of feeling the cool metal of the tap, the surprising weight of the kettle as it fills with water, the bloom of warmth on my hands as I hold the finished mug. These are not grand, transcendent moments. They are the opposite. They are moments of radical ordinary presence. But in their ordinariness lies their power. Each one is a small tether pulling my wandering, screen-addled mind back from the placeless digital elsewhere and anchoring it in the physical here and now. This is where my life is actually happening.

This practice can be woven into the fabric of any day. While waiting for a program to compile at work, instead of reflexively grabbing your phone, you can take three seconds to just notice the pattern of your own breath. While walking from the office to the car, you can pay attention to the feeling of the late afternoon air on your skin. These aren't acts of emptying the mind but of filling it—filling it with the immediate, undeniable, and truthful data of physical sensation. This is the antidote to the abstraction of the screen.

The wisdom of this approach is being recognized more and more in the clinical world, especially in the work of trauma specialists who understand that healing from overwhelming experiences is impossible without reestablishing a safe connection to one's own body.

The psychiatrist and author Bessel van der Kolk, in his landmark book *The Body Keeps the Score*, demonstrates how our bodies are the literal storehouses of our experiences, holding a form of intelligence that our conscious minds often can't access. While his work focuses on severe trauma, its central insight applies universally to our dissociated digital lives. He explains that healing requires a visceral reconnection, noting that "trauma victims cannot recover until they become familiar with and befriend the sensations in their bodies."[4] While our daily digital distractions are not equivalent to capital-T Trauma, they seem to operate on a similar, if lower-grade, mechanism. They trigger a state of constant, low-level hyperarousal, taking our calm thinking brain offline. The practice of consciously checking in with our physical sensations is the act of bringing that rational, observant brain back online. It is how we build a reassuring "inner map," learning to feel safe and at home within our own skin.

Anchor 2: The Discipline of Deep Attention

The second anchor is the cultivation of deep, focused attention. As we've discussed, our digital environment shreds our focus into cognitive confetti. The practice of reclaiming it requires creating sanctuaries for the mind. It means engaging in what Cal Newport has famously termed

4. Van der Kolk, *Body Keeps the Score*, 208.

"deep work." This isn't about working harder or longer; it's about working differently. It's the practice of mono-tasking, of dedicating inviolable blocks of time to a single, cognitively demanding task, free from every possible distraction.

For many of us, especially in a culture where instant chat responses are the norm, this feels like an impossible luxury. A typical workday is a barrage of context switching, moving from an email to a coding problem to a team chat to a virtual meeting, with each switch incurring a hidden cognitive cost. We feel busy, but at the end of the day, we often have that nagging sense that we haven't accomplished anything truly significant. We've spent our day in the shallows.

The practice of deep work is the intentional choice to go deep. It might mean blocking out ninety minutes on your calendar, putting your phone in another room (not just on silent, but physically out of reach), closing every browser tab and application not essential to the task at hand, and then simply beginning. The first fifteen minutes are often excruciating. The mind, conditioned for constant stimulation, will twitch and itch for a distraction. This is the moment of withdrawal. But if you can push through that initial resistance, something remarkable often happens. The mental chatter begins to quiet down. The external world fades away. You become fully immersed in the problem, losing track of time. This is the state of flow—not only where our most valuable work is done, but also a profoundly satisfying state of presence.

Newport's work provides a powerful framework for thriving in a world that seems to conspire against focus. In his book *Deep Work*, he distinguishes this from its opposite, "shallow work"—logistical tasks that are not cognitively demanding and are easily replicated. He argues that our economy is paradoxically making shallow work the default while simultaneously increasing the value of deep work. As Newport writes, "To remain valuable in our economy . . . you must master the art of quickly learning complicated things. This task requires deep work."[5] The pursuit of this deep life is a core practice for being present. It's an act of defiance against the tyranny of the urgent but unimportant. And it applies just as much to our personal lives. To read a challenging book, to learn a musical instrument, to have a truly deep conversation—these all require the same uninterrupted, focused presence.

5. Newport, *Deep Work*, 13.

Anchor 3: The Gift of the Analog World

The third anchor is the deliberate, hands-on engagement with the analog world. So much of our lives now involves interacting with smooth, sterile glass screens. We consume media, we order food, we socialize, we work—all through the same portal. This has a flattening effect on our experience, sanding away the texture, resistance, and tactile reality of the world. To be fully present, we must consciously reengage this texture. We must find practices that involve our hands, engage all our senses, and connect us to the physical, non-digital world.

This can take countless forms. It could be a weekly trip to the St. Jacobs Farmers' Market, not just to buy groceries, but to engage in the analog experience of it all: to talk to the Mennonite farmer who grew the tomatoes, to feel their weight and smell their earthy scent. It could be taking up a craft—pottery, woodworking, knitting, gardening. These activities are powerful anchors because they force us into a direct, unmediated relationship with physical materials. You cannot multitask while turning a piece of wood on a lathe. You must be fully present. The resistance of the material—the clay that won't center, the wood that splits—teaches patience and humility. It forces us to slow down to the speed of reality, not the speed of light. This isn't about nostalgia; it's about recalibrating our nervous systems.

This idea of resisting the attention economy not through digital detoxes but through a redirection of our attention is central to the work of Jenny Odell. Her work argues for a form of resistance rooted in place and deep observation. She suggests that learning the names of the birds in your backyard or the plants in your local park is a political act. It's a way of reclaiming your attention from the commercial forces that want to monetize it and reinvesting it in your own local, physical world. In her book *How to Do Nothing*, Odell proposes that we must cultivate a new kind of awareness, stating that "simple awareness is the seed of responsibility," and that attending to our physical reality is the first step in caring for it.[6]

To become a lucky witness to our own world—what a beautiful and profound ambition. It means going for a walk in the Huron Natural Area and leaving the earbuds at home, choosing instead to listen to the sound of the wind in the pines. It means choosing to repair a broken chair instead of ordering a new one online, engaging in the frustrating

6. Odell, *How to Do Nothing*, 124.

but ultimately satisfying process of bringing something back into wholeness. It means choosing, in small and large ways, the textured analog over the smooth digital.

These three anchors—reclaiming the body, the discipline of deep attention, and engaging the analog world—are not a comprehensive list. They are a starting point. They are practices, not perfections. There will be days when the storm of distraction wins. The goal is not to achieve some static, enlightened state of perpetual presence. The goal is to simply keep dropping the anchors, to keep practicing the return. It is to recognize that our life is the sum of the moments we are actually present for. To live soulfully in the age of AI is to make the conscious, deliberate, and sometimes difficult choice, again and again, to show up for that life.

Reclaiming Conversation: Presence as a Relational Act

It's lunchtime on a Tuesday, and I'm sitting in The Bauer Kitchen, a lively restaurant in a beautifully restored old factory building here in Waterloo. The room is buzzing with the familiar sounds of midday commerce and conversation. At the table next to mine a family of four is gathered. A father, a mother, and what look like two teenage kids. They are physically together, sharing a meal in this warm, inviting space, and yet they are profoundly, heartbreakingly alone. Each of them is bathed in the cool, bluish light of a personal screen. The father scrolls endlessly through what looks like a news feed, his expression blank. The mother is texting, a small, focused smile on her face that is directed at someone miles away. The son is watching a video, the tinny sound of it just barely audible over the restaurant's music. The daughter is navigating a social media app, her thumb moving in that practiced, hypnotic rhythm we all know so well. There is no conversation. The only sounds from their table are the clinking of cutlery and the occasional digital chime. They are sharing a table, but they are not sharing a moment. They are nodes in a network, physically in the same spot but mentally and emotionally scattered across the globe.

This scene, so common it has become almost invisible, is the final testing ground for the ideas we have been exploring. After acknowledging the illusions of the digital mirage and establishing those individual anchors for our own minds, we arrive at the ultimate purpose of all this work. Because what good is a reclaimed sense of presence if it is only ever experienced in solitude? The true test, and the greatest reward, of being present is the ability to offer that presence as a gift to another human being. The journey inward, toward our own embodied, focused selves, finds its ultimate meaning when we are able to turn back outward. The great challenge of our age is not just to reclaim our own attention but to learn, all over again, how to share it.

Practice 1: Creating Sacred Spaces (The Phone on the Table)

The first and most deceptively simple practice in this art is the redesign of our social rituals, beginning with the single most powerful object in the room: the smartphone. The phone on the table has become an accepted, almost invisible, part of our social landscape. But it is not a neutral object. Its mere presence, even when it's face down and silent, is a quiet declaration. It is a physical manifestation of our divided attention. It is a symbol that the conversation we are in is, at all times, provisional and secondary to the vast, unseen world of potential notifications and demands it represents. The phone on the table silently says, "I am here with you, but I am also ready to be somewhere else."

This isn't just a philosophical point; its effects are measurable and profound. We're beginning to understand that our devices don't just distract us, they fundamentally change the nature of our social interactions, often making them more superficial.

Sherry Turkle has dedicated her career to studying how technology shapes our relationships. Her research has shown, unequivocally, that the mere presence of a phone on a table changes not only the quality but also the content of a conversation. People talking in the presence of a phone subconsciously steer away from deeper, more vulnerable, or more complex topics. They stick to safer, more superficial ground, knowing that the conversation could be interrupted at any moment. The device acts as a silent chaperone, enforcing a kind of shallow politeness. In her book *Reclaiming Conversation*, Turkle details the stark findings of her research, pointing to a University of Michigan study that tracked a staggering 40 percent decline in the markers for empathy among college students. She reminds us that "face-to-face conversation is the most human—and humanizing—thing we do," and that fully present conversation is where empathy is born and nurtured.[7]

To reclaim conversation and, with it, empathy, we have to create spaces that are intentionally free from this technological intrusion. This is the practice of creating sacred spaces. It is the simple, radical act of agreeing that for the duration of a meal, a coffee date, or a walk, our devices will be put away—not just silenced, but out of sight. I've seen friends institute a phone stack at a restaurant, where everyone places their device in a pile in the center of the table, with the first person to cave and reach for their phone footing the bill. Families can implement a phone basket by the door, where devices are deposited upon entry. These might seem like games, but they are powerful ritual acts. They are a collective agreement that says, "For this period of time, we are the most important thing. This space, this moment, is what matters." The initial effect is often a palpable awkwardness. A lull in the conversation, which might normally be filled by a quick scroll, suddenly becomes a shared space that must be navigated. But if you can sit with that discomfort, something else emerges. The conversation deepens. People begin to make more eye contact. By removing the escape hatch of the digital world, we force ourselves to be present to the reality of the people right in front of us.

Practice 2: The Art of Generous Listening

This leads to the second relational practice: the cultivation of generous listening. In a world of fragmented attention, we have largely forgotten how to truly listen. We mostly engage in what you might call transactional listening. We listen for the gist of what someone is saying so we can formulate our response. We listen for keywords so we can jump in with our own related story. We listen while half-distracted, our minds already moving on to the next item on our to-do list. This is listening as data extraction. Generous listening is something else entirely. It is listening with the sole intent to understand. It is the practice of offering another person the quiet, spacious, and undivided attention of your full presence.

Generous listening is an active, demanding skill. It means resisting the powerful urge to interrupt, even when you have a brilliant point to make. It means becoming comfortable with silence, recognizing that

7. Turkle, *Reclaiming Conversation*, 3.

pauses are not empty spaces but fertile ground where deeper thoughts can surface. It involves asking open-ended, clarifying questions—not "So what did you do?" but "How did that make you feel?" It means fighting the reflexive urge to immediately offer advice, which so often is just a way of shutting down the other person's emotional expression. Sometimes the greatest gift we can offer is to be a calm, loving witness to another's experience, without trying to fix it.

Stephen R. Covey identified this as one of the most critical skills in human interaction. His concept of "empathic listening" is a powerful framework for this kind of generous presence. In his enormously influential book *The 7 Habits of Highly Effective People*, he designated it as the fifth habit: "Seek First to Understand, Then to Be Understood." He argued that this is a complete paradigm shift from how we normally operate. We typically listen at one of four levels: ignoring, pretending, selective listening, or attentive listening. But empathic listening is a fifth level. As Covey writes, "Next to physical survival, the greatest need of a human being is psychological survival—to be understood, to be affirmed, to be validated, to be appreciated."[8] This kind of listening is impossible without the foundational skill of presence. You can't get inside another's frame of reference if you are half-present in your own. It requires the deep work of setting aside your own autobiography, your own solutions, and your own ego.

Practice 3: The Courage to Be Vulnerable

Finally, to be truly present in our relationships, we must embrace the messy, inefficient, and beautiful reality of vulnerability. Our digital communication tools train us for control. We edit our texts and emails. We curate our social media profiles to present an idealized version of ourselves. We can avoid difficult real-time conversations by hiding behind a screen. This conditions us to be fearful of the unedited, unpredictable nature of face-to-face connection. We have, in short, become afraid of being truly seen.

The practice here is to deliberately choose the more vulnerable path. It means picking up the phone to make a call, with all its potential for awkward pauses, instead of engaging in a days-long, emotionally ambiguous text exchange. It means having the difficult but necessary conversation

8. Covey, *7 Habits*, 241.

about a conflict in person, where you can read body language and hear the tone of voice, rather than through a cold and easily misinterpreted email. It means having the courage to say, "I don't know," or "I was wrong," or "That hurt my feelings," in real time, without a backspace key.

The work of Brené Brown has been instrumental in bringing the concept of vulnerability into the mainstream. She argues, compellingly, that vulnerability is not a weakness to be avoided but rather the very core of all meaningful human experiences. It is the birthplace of love, belonging, joy, and creativity. Digital tools often function as armor, shielding us from the risks of showing our imperfect, authentic selves. In her book *Daring Greatly*, Brown reframes the entire concept. She writes, "Vulnerability is the core of all emotions and feelings. To feel is to be vulnerable. To believe vulnerability is weakness is to believe that feeling is weakness."[9] To reclaim conversation and be fully present in our relationships is to find the courage to step into that arena. It is to choose to show up, unedited and unarmored, and to understand that the deepest connections are not forged in a state of polished perfection but in the shared, messy moments of imperfection and mutual vulnerability.

These practices—creating sacred spaces, generous listening, and embracing vulnerability—are the relational expressions of the anchors we cultivate in solitude. They are how we take our own reclaimed presence and weave it into the fabric of our community. They are not easy. The currents of our age will continue to pull us toward the efficient and the virtual. The most soulful and human act we can perform is to resist that tide, to turn to the person across the table, put our devices away, look them in the eye, and offer them the rarest and most precious gift we have: our full, undivided, and beautifully imperfect presence.

The Soulful Dividend: The Ultimate Promise of a Present Life

We have journeyed through some difficult terrain. We've dissected the appealing but hollow myth of virtual connection, we've explored the individual anchors that can ground us in the storm of digital noise, and we've touched upon the gentle, courageous art of offering our presence to others. And now, standing here at the end of this exploration, it's easy to feel the sheer weight of the effort required. To reclaim the body, to

9. Brown, *Daring Greatly*, 33.

discipline our focus, to create sacred, phone-free spaces, to listen with generosity, to embrace vulnerability—these are not small asks. They require us to swim against the most powerful currents of our time. They demand a conscious, continuous, and sometimes exhausting effort.

This naturally raises the most important question: Why bother? In a world that prizes convenience, speed, and efficiency above all else, why choose this harder, slower, more deliberate path? What is the ultimate return on this investment of our energy and attention? The answer, I believe, cannot be found in the language of productivity or optimization that our culture understands so well. This is not another life hack to engineer a more efficient output. The payoff is something far more valuable and profound. It is what I have come to think of as the "soulful dividend"—the deep, intrinsic, and life-altering benefits that accrue only to a mind that has learned to be fully where it is. These dividends are not metrics to be tracked on a spreadsheet; they are qualitative shifts in the texture of our being. They are the ultimate promise of a present life.

The First Dividend: The Rediscovery of the Self

The first, and perhaps most fundamental, of these dividends is the rediscovery of the self. In our default state of perpetual distraction and digital performance, we risk losing touch with who we actually are. Our sense of self becomes fragmented, a collage of reactions to external stimuli. We become the sum of the things we have "liked," the profiles we have curated, and the opinions we have absorbed. Our inner world becomes a noisy echo chamber of other people's thoughts and demands. We may not even notice that we have forgotten how to have a truly original thought, or how to feel an emotion without immediately wanting to broadcast or numb it. We forget what our own inner voice sounds like because we never give it the silence it needs to speak.

The practices of presence, particularly those of cultivated solitude and deep focus, are the process of creating that necessary silence. When we deliberately disconnect from the external storm, we can finally begin to hear ourselves again. On a quiet walk along the Grand River here in Waterloo Region, with no podcast in my ears and no phone buzzing in my pocket, I've found that my mind, after an initial period of twitchy restlessness, begins to settle. In these moments of quiet, a solution to a problem I've been wrestling with might surface, seemingly from nowhere.

It's where I can finally untangle the knot of a difficult emotion, tracing it back to its source without judgment. These are the moments when a coherent self is allowed to emerge.

Neuroscientifically, this process makes perfect sense. Constant external stimuli keep our brains in a reactive mode. In contrast, solitude and inward focus activate the brain's default mode network, a set of regions associated with self-reflection, autobiographical memory, and moral reasoning. This is the neurological hardware for selfhood. By starving it of quiet, we are, in a very real sense, preventing our brains from doing the work of building a stable identity.

Thomas Merton, one of the great contemplative minds of the twentieth century, wrote extensively about this journey inward. He made a crucial distinction between the "false self" and the "true self." The false self is the external, socially constructed persona we all wear, obsessed with validation and status. The true self, Merton argued, is our deep, authentic identity, which can only be discovered in silence. In his book *New Seeds of Contemplation*, he explains this profound spiritual task: "For me to be a saint means to be myself. Therefore the problem of sanctity and salvation is in fact the problem of finding out who I am and of discovering my true self."[10] One need not share Merton's specific theology to grasp the universal truth here. To be a person, to be a coherent self, requires the kind of quiet that our digital age has all but abolished. The practice of presence is the act of reclaiming that space. The soulful dividend is the return of our own self to us, a self that is not a reaction to the world but a quiet, stable center from which we can engage with it more meaningfully and authentically.

The Second Dividend: The Deepening and Expansion of Time

The second soulful dividend is the deepening and expansion of time itself. We live with a chronic sense of time poverty. We're always rushing, always feeling that time is slipping through our fingers. Yet, paradoxically, we spend hours in a state of digital distraction where time seems to simultaneously accelerate and vanish. An hour spent scrolling through a social media feed is a temporal black hole; it leaves no trace, only a vague sense of depletion and the question, "Where did that hour go?"

10. Merton, *New Seeds of Contemplation*, 31.

Digital time is flat, homogeneous, and frantic. It's a state of perpetual *chronos*—the relentless, quantitative ticking of the clock.

A life of presence offers an alternative. It offers *kairos*—time as a qualitative, meaningful experience. When we are fully absorbed in a moment, time transforms. It slows down, it deepens, it gains texture. That hour spent lost in a state of flow, fully engaged with a challenging problem, feels both shorter and longer than an hour spent multitasking. It is richer and more real. An afternoon spent gardening, with hands in the soil, or a long, unhurried dinner with a friend, phones out of sight, creates a thick, lasting memory. These present moments become the landmarks of our lives. In contrast, the hours lost to distraction simply evaporate.

Pico Iyer has explored this theme with great eloquence. In an age defined by its unprecedented speed, he champions the radical act of standing still. He argues that it is only by deliberately stepping out of the stream of constant movement and information that we can gain perspective and experience a deeper sense of our own lives. In his thoughtful book *The Art of Stillness*, Iyer observes, "To sit still is a way of falling in love with the world and everything in it."[11] This luxurious, urgent practice of sitting still is how we escape the tyranny of *chronos*. It's how we trade a life of frantic, forgettable moments for one of deep, resonant experiences. The soulful dividend is the gift of deep time—the realization that a full life is measured not by the quantity of experiences we accumulate but by the quality of the moments we are truly present enough to inhabit.

The Third Dividend: The Reawakening of Wonder

The third and final dividend is the reawakening of a sense of wonder. The attention economy has a flattening effect on the world. Everything is reduced to content to be consumed and rated. A majestic mountain range becomes a backdrop for a selfie. A sublime sunset is not a moment of awe to be savored but an asset to be captured and posted. The world is stripped of its mystery. We lose our sense of wonder.

Presence is the antidote. When we learn to approach the world with a quiet, open attention—an attention that is not trying to use or categorize what it sees—we begin to notice the world again. We begin to see instead of merely looking. The intricate, geometric perfection of a spider's web.

11. Iyer, *Art of Stillness*, 80.

The complex network of veins on a fallen maple leaf in Victoria Park. The play of light on a loved one's face. These are the things we miss when we are rushing. To be present is to adopt what Zen practitioners call beginner's mind—open, free of preconceptions, approaching everything as if for the first time.

This reawakening is not just a pleasant feeling; it's a profound source of vitality. Wonder is the wellspring of curiosity, the engine of all genuine discovery. Furthermore, wonder is a powerful antidote to the cynicism that pervades modern life. It cultivates gratitude. Awe pulls us out of the cramped confines of our own ego and connects us to something larger than ourselves.

Rachel Carson wrote with profound passion about this very idea. She believed that cultivating a lifelong sense of wonder was an essential source of spiritual strength. In her posthumously published essay *The Sense of Wonder*, she wrote about the importance of an adult sharing the natural world with a child, hoping to instill "those who dwell, as scientists or laymen, among the beauties and mysteries of the earth are never alone or weary of life."[12] The practice of presence is how we, as adults, can reclaim this gift for ourselves. By choosing to put down our devices and lift up our eyes, we can re-enchant the world. The soulful dividend is the return of clear-eyed vision, the rediscovery that we live not in a world of inert content but in a world alive with beauty available in every moment, if only we have the eyes to see it.

The Synergy and the Incarnation

It would be a mistake to view these three dividends—a coherent self, deep time, and a sense of wonder—as separate items. They are a deeply interconnected triad. A strong self creates deep time, and deep time reveals a strong self. Wonder is the gateway to deep time. And the humbling experience of wonder is what helps solidify our true self. It's an upward spiral toward a more whole and meaningful existence.

This entire argument for the sacredness of being physically present finds a powerful and surprising echo in the Christian theological concept of the incarnation. The belief that God, in Jesus, became a human being—"The Word became flesh and made his dwelling among us" (John 1:14)—is the ultimate rejection of a frictionless, disembodied ideal.

12. Carson, *Sense of Wonder*, 88.

God didn't send a virtual messenger or a disembodied AI. The divine presence entered into the messy, tactile, and often inefficient reality of human life. Jesus's life was a testament to this: he walked dusty roads, shared real meals, and reached out to touch the sick. The incarnation suggests that our human form, with all its limitations and vulnerability, isn't a problem to be solved or a state to be transcended. It's the very stage upon which our most meaningful and soulful life is lived. It is the ultimate story of choosing the textured difficulty of reality over the smooth ease of an illusion, and it models for us that to truly love, we must be willing to show up, fully present and imperfect, in the flesh.

Conclusion

This chapter argues that in a world of infinite connection, our most urgent task is to be fully present so we can be truly human. We must resist the myth that virtual hangouts are as good as real ones—a dangerous fiction built on the seductive promise of a frictionless world. While convenient, this illusion comes at a steep cost. It untethers us from our bodies, which are our primary instruments for empathy, dissolves our sense of a shared physical place, which is essential for building deep memories, and trains us for shallow, controlled interactions that hollow out our capacity for real intimacy. The result is a strange hollowness, the ghost of a conversation without any real warmth.

The path forward isn't to reject technology but to reclaim our agency through intentional practices. This involves cultivating personal anchors to ground us in the storm of distraction—reconnecting with our body, practicing deep attention, and engaging the analog world. From this grounded self, we can then offer our presence as a gift to others by reclaiming conversation through sacred spaces, generous listening, and vulnerability. The reward for this difficult work is the soulful dividend: the rediscovery of a coherent self, a richer experience of time, and a reawakened capacity for wonder. Ultimately, the most rebellious and human act in the age of AI is to cultivate a genuine, embodied presence.

Chapter 4

Practicing Compassion in a World of Injustice

AI IS UNDENIABLY EFFICIENT. Modern algorithms are incredibly good at optimizing for specific outcomes, whether it's managing logistics, allocating resources, or personalizing content. In a world of limited time and resources, this capability is revolutionary. AI-driven systems can handle immense complexity and make decisions at a speed and scale that is simply impossible for humans. For instance, a supply chain optimized by AI can drastically reduce waste and delivery times. A smart grid can balance energy use with precision that prevents blackouts. This efficiency delivers real, measurable value, making our lives easier and our systems more reliable. It offers a powerful promise: to solve complex, systemic problems by removing human error and emotional bias from the equation. We've seen this efficiency at work in everything from traffic management to financial analysis, and the results are often undeniably impressive.

Despite these gains, we must not forget to practice compassion in a world of injustice. AI is designed to optimize for a target metric, but it lacks the human capacity for empathy, fairness, and moral reasoning. A perfectly efficient algorithm for loan applications might systematically exclude deserving individuals based on biased historical data, perpetuating inequality. By outsourcing our decisions to these systems, we risk creating a society that is fast and functional but utterly devoid of compassion or justice. The human soul knows that not all problems can be solved by an algorithm. Our sense of fairness and empathy, while inefficient, is what prevents us from sacrificing our shared values for the sake of speed.

Myth 4: Efficiency Beats Empathy and Fairness

It feels like one of the quiet anthems of our age: faster is better, cheaper is smarter, and the smoothest path is always the right one. This is the seductive myth of efficiency, the whispered promise that if we can just optimize every process, automate every task, and wring every last drop of wasted effort from our lives, we will arrive at some sort of utopia. It's a belief that champions speed over slowness, data over dignity, and optimized outcomes over the beautifully messy, often unpredictable, and profoundly time-consuming work of human connection.

You can feel its pull everywhere. It's in the automated phone tree that traps you in a loop of prerecorded options when all you need is to talk to a person who can understand your unique, frustrating problem. It's in the relentless pressure to process more, produce more, and perform faster, whether you're a social worker managing an overwhelming caseload or a warehouse employee whose every move is tracked by a demanding algorithm. The allure is undeniable; it promises us streamlined solutions, immediate answers, and a powerful sense of control over a complex world. We're told this is progress. But as we look closer, and perhaps listen with a more attentive heart, it becomes clear that placing efficiency on a pedestal mistakes what it means to be human and fundamentally misunderstands the very essence of justice. From a Christian perspective, which insists on the immeasurable worth of every individual, this relentless drive for AI optimization appears less like a path to flourishing and more like a subtle form of dehumanization.

At its core, the logic of pure efficiency requires a reductionist view of humanity. To make things run smoothly, people must be simplified. We become data points to be analyzed, metrics to be tracked, or cogs in a vast, intricate machine. Our unique stories, complex emotions, and God-given worth are quietly sidelined in pursuit of a quantifiable result. In this framework, we are no longer sacred ends in ourselves but merely means to a more efficient end. This isn't just a theoretical danger. Think of the gig economy worker, managed not by a person but by an app that nudges, penalizes, and deactivates them based on algorithms designed for maximum profit, not for human well-being. Think of the student in an underfunded school whose potential is judged by a standardized test score, a single data point that erases the nuances of their creativity, resilience, and curiosity. This is the logic of the AI, a logic that can achieve its goals with breathtaking speed but without a shred of compassion.

The Counternarrative of Sacred Inefficiency

The vision of justice we find in the Christian Scriptures stands in stark, almost jarring, contrast to this paradigm. It is a justice rooted not in power or speed but in the radical, self-emptying love of a God who chose to become vulnerable. The apostle Paul's reflection on Jesus in his letter to the Philippians is breathtaking in its reversal of worldly values. He writes that Jesus, though divine, "did not consider equality with God something to be used to his own advantage; rather, he made himself nothing by taking the very nature of a servant, being made in human likeness. And being found in appearance as a man, he humbled himself by becoming obedient to death—even death on a cross!" (Phil 2:6–8). This is the opposite of efficiency. It is a story of choosing the slow, painful, relational path of love over the swift, decisive path of power.

Jesus's life was a model of sacred inefficiency. He consistently stopped for the one person in the crowd, touched the ritually unclean, and spent his time with the marginalized, the sick, and the forgotten—not because it was the fastest way to build a movement, but because it was the most loving and just way to affirm the dignity of each person. From this perspective, justice isn't about maximizing output; it's about maximizing human flourishing in a way that reflects God's own heart. It's about learning to hear what the book of Genesis calls the "cry of innocent blood"[1]—the silent screams of those crushed by systems that prioritize profit and speed over people. Hearing that cry requires us to deliberately slow down, to listen with our whole being, and to offer our presence, not just a quick fix. An algorithm, for all its power, cannot hear that cry. It is deaf to the qualitative textures of human experience—the sting of injustice, the weight of grief, the quiet hope for something better. It is designed for a world of data, not a world of souls.

Because of this, a society that relies too heavily on AI-powered systems risks codifying and even accelerating its deepest biases. If the data fed into an AI system reflects our own history of inequality—and it almost always does—then the "efficient" algorithm will simply become a high-speed engine for replicating that same inequality, all while creating a dangerous illusion of fairness. The spiritual truth that emerges is that genuine fairness often demands the very things that efficiency seeks to

1. See Gen 4:10; Isa 59:7; Jer 7:6; 19:4; 22:3, 17; 26:15; Joel 3:19; Jonah 1:14; Deut 19:10; 21:8–9; 2 Kgs 24:4; Pss 94:21; 106:38; Prov 6:16–17.

eliminate: slowness, moral complexity, and a deep, patient commitment to understanding perspectives that challenge our own.

The Human Choice: Individual and Community Action

So how do we begin to push back against this powerful myth in our own lives? It starts not with a grand gesture but with a quiet, conscious commitment to choose the human pace over the AI's. It means prioritizing connection, even when it feels inconvenient, and valuing moral discernment over automated ease.

I think of a woman I know named Nadia, a social worker in an underfunded urban agency. The pressure on her is immense. Her screen is filled with metrics: cases closed, forms filed, deadlines met. The new system her agency adopted is all about efficiency; it uses AI to categorize clients, suggest standardized action plans, and prompt her to move on to the next case. Every institutional pressure tells her to be faster. Yet, Nadia makes a daily choice to practice a different kind of justice. I can picture her in her small, cluttered office, a client sitting across from her, a young man who has been evicted and is fighting to keep his family together. The AI on her screen has already flagged him as high risk and populated a list of generic resources. The efficient path would be to print the list, schedule a follow-up, and close the case. But Nadia consciously turns away from the screen. She puts down her tablet. She makes eye contact. And she says, "Tell me what this has been like for you. I have time."

In that small, rebellious act, she is choosing to put people over AI's quick fixes. This is Christian justice in miniature. It is a moment of seeing the person not as a problem to be solved but as a sacred story to be heard. It is in these inefficient, unquantifiable moments of profound empathy that the slow, holy work of healing can actually begin. This kind of deep listening is, in a way, how God himself operates, hearing the cry of innocent blood that rises from the ground. It's a way of being that values the person, their pain, and their narrative above the demand for a swift, automated response.

This doesn't mean AI has no role to play. The challenge is to "use AI to learn, not decide, what's fair."[2] AI can be a powerful tool for gathering information. For instance, Nadia could use an AI-powered database to instantly pull up a comprehensive list of all available shelters, food banks,

2. Mollick, *Co-Intelligence*, 13–14.

and legal aid services in a five-mile radius—a task that would have taken hours just a decade ago. But the data itself is not justice. AI can tell you that there are disparities in housing access across different zip codes, but it cannot feel the moral urgency to provide shelter for a family sleeping in their car. That is a uniquely human, and indeed spiritual, decision rooted in the command to love our neighbor. The ultimate discernment of what is right, what is fair, and what is loving in a complex human situation must remain a human responsibility, guided by a heart centered on God's values, not by an algorithm.

Another way to resist is by choosing to build empathy over efficiency through direct service. It's one thing to read about poverty statistics; it's another thing entirely to spend a Saturday morning at a food bank, looking someone in the eye as you hand them a bag of groceries. In those moments, abstract notions of injustice become real, tangible, and embodied. You are forced to confront the messiness of human suffering, which demands a response that is inherently inefficient but profoundly human. You might hear a story that shatters your preconceived notions about why people end up in need. You might see the exhaustion and the resilience in a mother's face. These encounters cultivate a deep, guttural compassion that no algorithm can ever instill. They mirror the self-giving love of Christ, who chose the path of radical, hands-on service, not distant, theoretical solutions. It's in this inefficient, person-to-person work that we are reminded of the profound limits of AI and are grounded once again in the tangible needs and inviolable dignity of real people.

Beyond our individual choices, the real work of countering this myth happens in community. The challenge is to intentionally build groups, churches, and neighborhoods where empathy and fairness are woven into the very fabric of our life together, rather than being bolted on as an afterthought to our efficient operations. A crucial first step is to *organize outreach, like Nadia's support groups, using AI to find needs but focusing on care.* A community group, for example, could use demographic data and AI analysis to identify which parts of their city have the highest rates of loneliness among the elderly or the most significant gaps in mental health services for teens. This is a brilliant, efficient use of AI to pinpoint where help is needed most. But the AI's job ends there. The next, more important step must be driven by human compassion. Let's imagine Nadia's church takes this data and decides to start a support group for single parents struggling with housing insecurity. The goal isn't just to provide information; it's to create a safe, welcoming space. They meet in the church basement, a room filled with mismatched chairs and the smell of fresh coffee. The real work happens when people begin to share their stories—the fear, the frustration, the small victories. They find they are not alone. They build trust. They begin to advocate for one another. This is the essence of communal care. The focus is on the holistic well-being of the people in the room—their spiritual, emotional, and physical needs—not just on the number of people served or the speed of the intervention.

Communities also have a responsibility to *talk about using AI ethically in group settings*. It's all too easy to passively accept new AI systems without considering their impact. A compassionate community needs to create spaces for open, honest, and sometimes difficult dialogue. Imagine a town hall meeting hosted by a local faith coalition. On one side of the room is a police chief, explaining how a new AI-driven surveillance system will make the neighborhood safer and policing more efficient. On the other side is a young activist from that neighborhood, sharing her fear that this same AI will lead to over-policing and invade the privacy of her community. These conversations are messy, rarely yielding easy answers, but they are essential. They cultivate collective moral discernment and prevent the passive acceptance of AI that may be efficient but is profoundly unjust. They encourage the community to be proactive, ensuring that shared human values, not corporate sales pitches, guide how AI is implemented.

Finally, communities can *team up with local groups to fix AI biases, like unfair hiring tools*. This is where collective action becomes a powerful force for justice. Many companies now rely on AI to screen job applicants, and as numerous studies have shown, these tools can be riddled with biases that unfairly penalize women, people of color, or those from lower socioeconomic backgrounds. A single individual has little power to challenge this. But a community can. A coalition of local churches, civil rights organizations, and tech ethics advocates could, for example, launch a campaign to audit the hiring practices of the largest employers in their city. They could demand transparency in how these AI tools work and push for equitable design. This is active engagement with structures of power—a collective refusal to accept efficiency at the cost of genuine opportunity for all. It is a recognition that such biases are not just technical glitches; they are a modern form of "shedding of innocent blood" through economic marginalization, and the community has a moral responsibility to stand against them.

The Societal Challenge: Building Just Systems

While individual and community actions are vital, the myth of efficiency is so deeply embedded in our culture that it also requires a response at the societal level. This means shaping our laws, our policies, and the very direction of our AI development to reflect a nonnegotiable commitment to human dignity, fairness, and compassion.

A critical area of focus must be to *fix AI systems in healthcare or hiring to focus on fairness*. The stakes here are incredibly high. These systems can create what the data scientist Cathy O'Neil has famously called "weapons of math destruction." In her book of the same name, she warns that these opaque algorithms often rely on proxies that correlate with race or poverty, noting that "if we allow the economy to be run by these black boxes, we are inviting a future where the privileged are favored and the poor are punished."[3] Addressing this requires a move away from the tech industry's old mantra of "move fast and break things" and toward a new ethic of "move thoughtfully and build justly." It means demanding rigorous, independent auditing of algorithms, mandating transparency in their design, and creating strong regulatory frameworks that hold developers accountable for the fairness of their products.

This leads directly to the need to *push for laws that prioritize people over profits*. The relentless quest for efficiency is almost always tied to the pursuit of maximizing profit, which can lead corporations to ignore the ethical and human costs of their AI systems. To counter this, we need robust legislation that establishes clear ethical boundaries. This could include laws similar to Europe's General Data Protection Regulation (GDPR) that protects data privacy, laws that ensure algorithmic accountability in public services, or laws that safeguard worker rights in an economy increasingly dominated by automation and AI-driven surveillance. These are not just regulations; they are expressions of a society's core values. They are a way of embedding dignity and justice into our social contract, creating a bulwark against the kind of "power is everything" mentality that can lead to catastrophic moral failures.

Finally, we must *support campaigns for tech that puts compassion first*. This is about fostering a cultural shift, moving from a position of uncritical consumption to one of critical engagement with AI. It means celebrating and funding the innovators, researchers, and organizations who are actively working to create more ethical and humane AI. It means

3. O'Neil, *Weapons of Math Destruction*, 204.

promoting educational initiatives in our schools and public forums that teach not just how to use AI but how to think critically and morally about its role in our lives. This aligns perfectly with a Christian understanding of stewardship, which sees AI not as an end in itself but as a tool that must be oriented toward the flourishing of all God's creation. It is about making an intentional, collective choice for a future where AI empowers us to be more just, more empathetic, and more loving, rather than one where we are slowly reduced to efficient cogs in a cold, unfeeling machine.

Why Ideology Is Not True Justice

The danger of AI, it seems, isn't just that its logic is flawed; it's that its incredible power can be used to amplify flawed human ideas about justice. The issue isn't whether an ideology is right or wrong in a simple sense but how it functions as a totalizing system. With its incredible capacity for pattern recognition and information curation, AI is particularly good at reinforcing a preexisting worldview. This can create echo chambers so perfect and so persuasive they become a closed system—a self-referential bubble that feels like objective truth. This is more than bias; it is the potential for AI to transform an ideology from a flexible framework into an all-encompassing reality, making it nearly impossible to see the world differently.

This amplification can lead us to mistake an ideology for justice itself. We may start to believe that the just thing is simply the ideologically correct thing. Justice, in its truest sense, is often messy, nuanced, and requires deep empathy and a willingness to understand conflicting perspectives. It's about human relationships and real-world consequences, not just the logical consistency of a theory. By presenting an ideology as an unassailable, algorithmically validated truth, AI may inadvertently be training us to confuse the elegant, frictionless logic of a system with the complex, often contradictory, and deeply human work of making the world a more equitable and fair place for all.

The Problem of Power: A Fundamental Misconception

The clearest distinction between the justice offered by ideology and the justice modeled by Jesus lies in how they understand and use power. For nearly every human ideology, power is the whole point. It's the engine, the currency, the necessary tool to achieve a "just" society. Whether it's the political power needed to write laws, the economic power to control resources, or the cultural power to shape the prevailing narrative, the goal is always to acquire and use it to impose a specific vision on the world. This worldview is so ingrained that we barely notice it. A common, unspoken belief in our culture is that power equals success. When someone is rich or influential, it's often said they're winning at life. Conversely, when someone appears weak or broken, we instinctively think something must be wrong. This can create a relentless and often ruthless pursuit of dominance where the ends appear to justify the means.

But then, into this power-obsessed world, the story of Jesus lands like a quiet explosion, turning everything upside down. The vision of power in Christian justice is so radically different, so counterintuitive, that it can be hard to even grasp. The apostle Paul seems to have tried to capture it in his letter to the Philippians, describing a God who does the unthinkable. Though he was "in very nature God, did not consider equality with God something to be used to his own advantage; rather, he made himself nothing by taking the very nature of a servant, being made in human likeness. And being found in appearance as a man, he humbled himself by becoming obedient to death—even death on a cross!" (Phil 2:6–8).

This concept, often called *kenosis*, describes a self-emptying, a voluntary release of power that defies all worldly logic. Jesus, who possessed all power, chose not to use it for control but to heal, forgive, and save. He didn't seize a throne; he took up a cross. This reveals a startling truth: love is greater than power.

Richard Rohr speaks of this as a "divine generosity" that completely redefines our understanding of power. In *The Universal Christ*, Rohr argues that the cross is the ultimate demonstration that God does not work through coercion, noting that God's power is the power to suffer with us, to be present in the pain, not to fix it from a distance.[4] This seems to be the crucial, difficult point that human ideologies almost always miss. True justice, from this perspective, isn't about grasping for power but is instead rooted in humility, sacrifice, and a love that is willing to give itself away. Power is not inherently evil, but the desire for it often becomes an obsession that corrupts the heart.

4. Rohr, *Universal Christ*, 135–40.

We see this woven throughout the biblical narrative. Adam and Eve wanted to "be like God" (Gen 3:5), grasping for a power that wasn't theirs to take. King Saul, the powerful warrior, "feared the people" more than God and used his authority to secure his own popularity (1 Sam 15:24). Even King David, a man described as being after God's own heart, was led into his deepest sin—adultery and murder—at the very height of his power (2 Sam 11). Jesus, in stark contrast, possessed all power yet chose to serve. When we elevate our human-made systems and their relentless pursuit of dominance as the ultimate goal, we invariably build a world on the wrong foundation.

The Limits of Human Blueprints

Because ideologies are products of human reason, they tend to reduce the beautiful, messy complexity of justice into a neat and tidy blueprint. They focus on specific reforms, particular economic structures, or a certain set of political rights. And while these goals are often noble, their human-centered origins mean they can become rigid and absolute in their demands. An ideology might, for instance, fiercely champion the rights of one nation or one class, but in its zealous pursuit, it can inadvertently—or sometimes, quite deliberately—marginalize or oppress another group. This creates new forms of injustice and new cycles of "us versus them," leading to resentment and conflict.

Social thinkers have explored this very point in analyzing the fragmentation of modern life. The sociologist Zygmunt Bauman provided a critical lens on this very issue, suggesting that modern society, with its competing grand ideologies, often drives people apart rather than uniting them. In *Liquid Modernity*, Bauman argues that in our fluid, uncertain world, the concept of a unified society has eroded, leaving us with a collection of individuals seeking private solutions to public problems. He notes that "the disintegration of the social network . . . leaves the individual to their own resources," which breeds a deep sense of insecurity and isolation.[5]

Christian justice, on the other hand, strives for something much more universal. It is animated by God's concern for all of humanity, a concern that famously hears the silent cry of the oppressed. This is captured in that haunting, ancient story from Genesis, right after Cain has

5. Bauman, *Liquid Modernity*, 36.

murdered his brother, Abel. God asks Cain where his brother is, and then says, "What have you done? Listen! Your brother's blood cries out to me from the ground" (Gen 4:10). This is such a profound image. It suggests that injustice creates a wound in the very fabric of creation, a wound that God himself feels. True Christian justice, therefore, must have a profound *sensitivity to suffering, wherever it exists.* It must be able to hear the cries that ideologies, with their narrow focus and human limitations, often miss. It hears the cry of the garment worker in a sweatshop, the refugee, the earth itself—a holistic vision that sees every individual as created in God's image and worthy of dignity.

There's another key difference. Ideologies, for the most part, rely on external forces to get the job done. They seek to manufacture justice through laws, policies, and institutional reform. The underlying belief is that if we can just build the right system, people will fall in line. Now, let's be clear: laws and structures are absolutely essential for a functional and basically fair society. But they can't change the human heart. And this is where Christian justice goes so much deeper. It teaches that the root of injustice isn't just a bad system; it's something broken inside of us. The Bible calls this brokenness "sin," a deep-seated internal orientation that pulls us away from God and makes it impossible to genuinely love our neighbors.

Ideologies, because they focus on outward behavior, can get very good at treating the symptoms of injustice. But they have very little to say about the root causes: the pride, the greed, and the fear that fuel these external problems. This is a place where modern psychology offers some fascinating insights that seem to echo this ancient spiritual wisdom.

The work of psychologist Jonathan Haidt has powerfully explored how our deepest ideological commitments often come not from rational analysis but from deep-seated moral intuitions that operate beneath the surface of our conscious minds. In *The Righteous Mind*, he argues that "intuitions come first, strategic reasoning second," meaning that our moral beliefs are often post hoc justifications for our gut feelings.[6] This binding and blinding effect is precisely what Christian faith seeks to overcome. It helps us to *see what is wrong in our hearts* and to *notice sin in our culture, in our habits, and even in our silence.* It calls for a transformation that is not just systemic but internal—a renewal of the very heart from the inside out.

6. Haidt, *Righteous Mind*, 54.

The Idolatry of Ideology

Perhaps the most subtle—and therefore most dangerous—risk of ideologies is their tendency to become our gods. When any group of people clings too tightly to a human-made system, they can begin to place it above God's actual guidance and will. It becomes the ultimate authority, the thing to which we pledge our ultimate allegiance. This is the oldest temptation in the book: to seek ultimate control, to be like God, just as the story of Adam and Eve so powerfully illustrates. An ideology becomes an idol the moment we are willing to sacrifice our common humanity for it. It happens when we decide that our political party is more important than our neighbors, or when we justify cruelty in the name of our nation's destiny, or when we dehumanize our opponents because they stand in the way of our "perfect" system.

Theologian Miroslav Volf writes powerfully about this, arguing that the Christian vision of justice requires a radical act that is nearly impossible for most ideologies: the act of embracing the "other," even those we see as our enemies. He suggests that the logic of the cross is a logic of embrace, a divine opening of the arms to welcome those who are different. In his profound book *Exclusion and Embrace*, Volf writes that the will to embrace the other is "absolutely central to the Christian faith," and that the cross symbolizes God's refusal to let the cycle of violence have the last word.[7] This kind of self-giving love is something that ideologies, with their rigid boundaries and their inherent need for an us-versus-them mentality, simply cannot achieve. Their very structure demands that they define who is in and who is out. Christian justice, by stark contrast, calls for a self-emptying love that mirrors the example of Jesus, a love that finds its greatest power not in dominating others but in surrendering to God.

Finally, we have to remember that ideologies are, by their very nature, temporary. They are products of their time, shaped by the shifting sands of culture and history. The grand ideas of one century become the historical footnotes of the next. Christian justice, however, claims to be grounded in something else entirely: the eternal truth of God, a wisdom that transcends fleeting cultural trends. It doesn't seek to impose a temporary human system on the world. Instead, it seeks to align our lives, our institutions, and our relationships with God's unchanging character. While an ideology might offer a five-point plan to fix a problem, it lacks

7. Volf, *Exclusion and Embrace*, 29.

the profound, transformative power of the cross. The cross redefines justice not as a human achievement to be built but as a divine gift to be received, a gift that calls us to live in grateful obedience and active love. It is a justice rooted not in the shifting sands of human thought but in the steady, loving, and eternal reality of God himself.

What Is Justice in the Perspective of Christianity?

So, if the grand, all-encompassing ideologies of the world ultimately leave us feeling empty, and if their pursuit of power so often leads to new and more sophisticated forms of injustice, where do we turn? What does this more soulful, more resonant vision of justice that we find in the Christian tradition actually look like on the ground? It's a fair question. And the answer, it seems, isn't a new system or a better blueprint. It's not an ideology at all.

Instead, Christian justice appears to be a practical and deeply contextual response to the pervasive brokenness we see in the world and in our own hearts. It's a way of living that seeks to mend the torn fabric of our relationships with God and with one another. This brokenness, as we've reflected, seems to show up in three distinct but deeply interconnected ways: our personal failures to live according to God's loving commands, our collective failure to hear and respond to the suffering of the innocent, and our most foundational failure—the quiet, persistent tendency to build our lives around ourselves instead of around God. Addressing these three ruptures is the work of Christian justice. It's a journey that calls for more than just new laws or policies; it demands a change of heart, a redirection of our love, and a life reoriented toward the self-giving way of Christ.

The First Dimension: Responding to the Ten Commandments

First, and perhaps most personally, Christian justice means getting honest about our own stuff. It calls us to respond to our sins against God's commandments. For many of us, the phrase *Ten Commandments* might conjure up images of an angry God and ancient, dusty stone tablets. We can think of them as an oppressive list of "Thou Shalt Nots." But what if that's a misunderstanding? What if these commandments are less like prison rules and more like loving instructions from a master craftsman on how to live a life that works? What if they are a divine framework for living in harmony with our Creator, with the people around us, and even with ourselves?

When you look at them closely, they seem to guide us toward a life of integrity and relational health. They invite us to honor God, to speak truthfully, to be faithful, to respect the sacredness of life, and to resist the pull of greed and envy. When we lie, cheat, steal, or hate, we are doing more than just breaking a rule; we are actively damaging the web of trust that holds human community together. When we worship idols—and let's be honest, our modern idols are more likely to be material wealth, career status, or political power—we are giving our ultimate allegiance to something that cannot love us back and will ultimately fail us.

This brokenness is deeply personal. It's the small lie we tell a spouse to avoid a difficult conversation, which then plants a seed of distrust. It's the gossip we share about a coworker, which subtly poisons the workplace environment. It's the way we might fudge our taxes or cut corners in our business dealings, telling ourselves that "everyone does it." These actions, even when no one else knows, create fractures. God knows. And on some level, our own souls know too. We feel the dissonance.

This is where Christian justice begins: with the courage to look inward. The call of faith isn't just, "Don't sin." It's a much more hopeful invitation: "Come back to God." It calls us to the practice of repentance, which at its heart simply means "to turn around." It's about acknowledging our personal failings, not to wallow in guilt, but to open ourselves up to grace. It means seeking forgiveness from God and, just as crucially, from the people we have wronged. It's the painful but liberating work of reconciliation.

Imagine a small business owner, let's call him Mark, who for years has been quietly cutting corners, using cheaper materials than he promised his clients and underpaying his small staff, all to maximize his profits. On the outside, he's a success story. He's a respected member of his community. But inside, he's consumed by anxiety, terrified of being exposed. This is the weight of sin. One day, a crisis of conscience brings him to his knees. The path of justice for Mark isn't a legal one; it's a relational one. It involves the terrifying, humbling act of confessing to his employees and his clients. It means facing their anger and disappointment. It means creating a practical plan of restitution, paying back what was unfairly taken. This process is the opposite of efficient. It's messy, painful, and slow. But it is the only path to true freedom and restored relationships.

This is the hard, practical work of justice at the personal level. Christian ethics are not about achieving a perfect, static morality. Instead, faith is a dynamic and ongoing practice. It's about the constant, everyday effort to embody God's love and character in the real, often complicated, situations we find ourselves in.

The theologian Stanley Hauerwas has long argued this point, suggesting that Christian ethics are less about solving abstract dilemmas and more about the formation of a particular kind of community with a particular set of virtues. In his classic work *The Peaceable Kingdom*, Hauerwas argues that we cannot know who we are or what we should do without a story to guide us, writing that "the self is a story . . . and to be a moral agent is to locate one's self in an ongoing history."[8] From this perspective, justice is not a set of rules to be applied but a character to be cultivated by living within God's story.

The Second Dimension: Hearing the Cry of the Innocent

The second dimension of Christian justice moves us from our personal lives into the wider world. It's a profound call to address the sin of "shedding innocent blood." Now, this is a concept that goes far beyond the act of literal murder. It seems to encompass the entire vast spectrum of systemic neglect, oppression, and injustice that harms the vulnerable and silences the powerless. It's the quiet violence of a society that allows children to go to bed hungry. It's the cry of the family forced to flee their home because of war or environmental collapse. It's the pervasive silence surrounding abuse, the deep stain of racism, the exploitation of workers, and all the other ways that human beings are treated as less than sacred.

Faced with the sheer scale of this suffering, our natural inclination is often to look away. We tell ourselves, "That's not my problem," or "There's nothing I can do." But God says otherwise. In that ancient and haunting story in Genesis, after Cain has killed his brother, God's question echoes through history: "What have you done? Listen! Your brother's blood cries out to me from the ground" (Gen 4:10). This powerful image tells us that the suffering of the innocent has a voice, a voice that pierces the heavens and reaches the very heart of God. And that voice is still crying out in our world today. The critical question for us is, "Do we hear it?"

8. Hauerwas, *Peaceable Kingdom*, 41.

The Christian faith does not, and cannot, turn away from this cry. In fact, the story of Christ is one of a God who moves toward the pain of the innocent. In his life, Jesus constantly sought out those on the margins. In his death, he became the ultimate innocent victim, intimately identifying with all who suffer unjustly. His life and death are a permanent call to his followers to do the same: to stand in solidarity with the suffering, to advocate for the voiceless, and to actively work to dismantle the systems that perpetuate their pain. This is a call to compassionate, courageous action. It requires us to ask hard questions about our own complicity. Where does my food come from? Who made my clothes? Do I benefit from systems that harm others? This isn't about generating guilt but about fostering a holy awareness.

A society of isolated individuals is a society where it is much easier to ignore the cries of the suffering. When we don't know our neighbors, it is much easier to pretend their problems are not our own.

Charles Marsh has documented how this call to solidarity has played out in modern history, particularly in the American Civil Rights movement. In his book *The Beloved Community*, he shows how the movement was fueled by a vision of reconciliation, where the goal was not just legal equality but the creation of a community where "love, justice, and truth" were the governing principles.[9] This vision suggests that our capacity for collective care is a direct measure of our spiritual health.

The Third Dimension: The Root of Injustice

This third dimension of Christian justice may be the most foundational, and also the most difficult to see in ourselves. It confronts the subtle but pervasive sin of living without God at the center of our lives—a profound form of self-centeredness or narcissism.

This sin is so dangerous precisely because it's easy to miss. It's entirely possible to live a life that looks good on the outside. We can be busy, successful, and even deeply involved in religious activities. We can go to church, pray, and serve others, *but still live without God at the center*. How? Because, as our spiritual traditions remind us, we are all naturally inclined to put ourselves first. This inner displacement—the quiet move to put ourselves first—is our "factory setting," yet it acts as the primary catalyst for all outward brokenness. When we ignore God as the center,

9. Marsh, *Beloved Community*, 78.

we don't just lose a spiritual hobby; we lose our moral compass. This "walking in darkness" is the root of a lethal chain reaction: once the ego is the ultimate guide, the Ten Commandments become optional, and the blood of the innocent becomes a mere footnote to our own comfort. We are not just making mistakes; we are living an architectural lie, building a life on the illusion of our own sovereignty. True Christian justice, therefore, is not merely a social effort but a spiritual demolition—a systematic dismantling of the ego to restore God to his rightful place as Life itself.[10]

Accordingly, pursuing Christian justice demands a fundamental shift in our spiritual alignment. It requires us to systematically dismantle our self-obsession, removing the ego from its position of power so that God may occupy the center of our lives.

Saint Augustine identified this disordered love as the primary engine of human brokenness. In his magnum opus, he argued that the ultimate root of injustice is not merely a behavioral error but a misdirected heart. He famously distinguished between two opposing orientations that shape all of human society: "Two cities have been formed by two loves: the earthly by the love of self, even to the contempt of God; the heavenly by the love of God, even to the contempt of self."[11] For Augustine, when the love of self becomes our operating system, we inevitably exploit others to serve our own ends. This is the seedbed of all injustice.

The work of Christian justice, therefore, requires a profound and continuous reorientation of our entire being. It means intentionally and repeatedly knocking our ego off the throne of our hearts and inviting God to take that central place. This is the core theme in the work of many modern spiritual writers, perhaps none more so than Richard Rohr. He often speaks of the spiritual journey as a process of moving from the "first half of life," which is necessarily focused on building a healthy ego, to the "second half of life." This second half is where true maturity is found, and it involves the difficult but liberating work of letting go of that ego's demands and discovering our true Self in God. In his book *Falling Upward: A Spirituality for the Two Halves of Life*, Rohr describes this journey with beautiful clarity, writing, "The soul has no interest in success. . . . It is on a journey of descent, a journey that will be for the sake of going up."[12] This descent is the humbling work of reorienting our lives away from ourselves and toward God and others.

10. See 1 John 1:6; 2:4; John 8:12; Jas 4:17; Rom 14:23.

11. Augustine, *City of God*, 632.

12. Rohr, *Falling Upward*, 128.

In practice, this kind of justice is deeply contextual and practical. It involves tangible actions. But unlike ideologies that seek power for their own ends, the practice of Christian justice always embraces the way of the cross. It consistently chooses love and sacrifice over control, always pointing back to the transforming grace of God. For it is only when we surrender our own agendas, the story goes, that we become fully human.

The Incompatibility of AI and Divine Justice

When we talk about this kind of three-dimensional, divine justice, it's very doubtful that AI can ever truly respond to it. At its core, AI operates on data, not on a loving relationship with God, others, or even itself. It's a fundamental disconnect. The whole concept of a soulful life is rooted in the biblical commandments that describe a life of healthy relationships. An AI has no need for a Sabbath, no need to honor a parent, and no capacity to feel the weight of coveting a neighbor's possessions. It simply cannot grasp the relational foundation that underpins Christian ethics and faith.

Moreover, AI seems to have no built-in concern for the shedding of innocent blood. Its decisions are based on majoritarian logic, on analyzing immense datasets to find the most probable outcome. AI might not shed blood directly, but it can make decisions in medicine, finance, or criminal justice that disproportionately harm the vulnerable. It's an algorithm without a conscience, a logic engine without a heart. We, as humans, understand that justice isn't always about what the majority wants or what the numbers say; sometimes, it's about standing up for the one person everyone else has forgotten.

Finally, while AI can process and even generate text about God, it cannot actually know or connect with God. It can't pray. It can't feel awe. It can't experience faith. It's all data points and language models, a sophisticated mimicry of human spirituality without any of the lived reality. The core of Christian justice is a personal connection to a divine being—a relationship that inspires love, sacrifice, and humility. AI, no matter how advanced, is likely to remain in a spiritual desert, forever simulating a reality it can never truly participate in.

AI's Contribution to Justice Activities and Its Limitations

It's impossible these days to ignore the headlines. Artificial intelligence is here, and it seems poised to change everything. For those of us who care deeply about mending the world's wounds, it's only natural to look at this powerful new technology and ask, Can this help? Can we harness AI to build a more just, more equitable, and more compassionate society? The excitement is palpable, and in many ways, it's justified. AI can certainly be a remarkable asset in the ongoing work of justice. And yet, a deeper wisdom cautions us to temper our enthusiasm with a healthy dose of realism.

While AI can amplify our efforts in incredible ways, it is, at the end of the day, a tool. A very sophisticated tool, to be sure, but a tool nonetheless. It is not, and never can be, a savior. To truly understand its place, we have to hold two truths in tension: we must appreciate AI's significant potential contributions while remaining clear eyed and honest about its profound and inherent limitations. The deepest matters of injustice, those that stem from the spiritual brokenness of the human heart, are simply beyond the reach of any algorithm.

AI's Contribution to Justice Activities

Let's start with the good news, because it is significant. In the right hands, AI offers some truly powerful ways to augment the work of justice. Its ability to analyze immense datasets, recognize subtle patterns, and automate complex processes can be a game changer.

One of the most promising applications is in identifying and addressing systemic biases. For decades, we've known that our institutions—from healthcare to banking to criminal justice—are riddled with hidden biases that disproportionately harm marginalized communities. The problem is that these biases are often so embedded in the system that they're hard to even see, let alone prove. AI can act like a powerful diagnostic tool, processing vast amounts of data to reveal discriminatory patterns that would be invisible to the human eye.

This has been powerfully demonstrated in healthcare, where algorithms designed to predict patient needs have been shown to perpetuate racial bias. This happens not because the programmers are malicious but because the data itself is flawed.

Ruha Benjamin, in the book *Race After Technology*, explores this very issue. She documents how automated systems can reproduce existing social hierarchies, calling it "the New Jim Code." She warns that "technologies are never neutral; they are always shaped by the social and political context in which they are created," and thus we must be vigilant in how we design and deploy them.[13] The crucial insight here is that while AI can perpetuate bias, it can also be used to audit and expose it, allowing us to see our own injustices more clearly and take corrective action.

AI can also play a huge role in enhancing the efficiency and accessibility of legal and social services. Think about the immense barriers that ordinary people face when trying to navigate our complex legal system. Hiring a lawyer is prohibitively expensive for many, and the bureaucracy of social services can be bewildering. AI-powered tools can help level the playing field. Imagine a single mother, let's call her Maria, who receives an unjust eviction notice from her landlord. She can't afford a lawyer and feels powerless. But she finds an online legal aid platform that uses AI to help her draft a formal response. The AI chatbot asks her a series of simple questions, helps her understand her rights as a tenant, and generates a legally sound letter to the landlord, citing the relevant statutes. This doesn't replace the need for human lawyers, but for someone like Maria, it's a lifeline. It provides a first line of defense and empowers her to fight back. Platforms like DoNotPay have already shown the potential of this approach, helping people fight everything from parking tickets to predatory subscription services, making justice just a little more accessible for everyone.

Furthermore, in a world plagued by conflict and oppression, AI is becoming a vital tool for mapping and responding to human rights abuses. In the past, it could take months or years for reports of atrocities in remote regions to reach the outside world. Today, organizations like Ushahidi use AI to collect, verify, and map crowd-sourced reports of violence and displacement in near real time. When a village is attacked, witnesses can send a text message or a social media post, which is then mapped, giving humanitarian organizations and international bodies a live view of where the needs are most urgent. It is a modern, technological version of hearing the cry of innocent blood from the ground. This ability to see and track injustice as it unfolds can facilitate quicker, more

13. Benjamin, *Race After Technology*, 48.

targeted interventions and help ensure that those responsible are eventually held accountable.

Finally, on a broader scale, AI can help us analyze complex data to develop more effective and equitable public policy. The challenges we face—from climate change to poverty to educational inequity—are incredibly complex, with thousands of interlocking variables. AI can help policymakers sift through this complexity, identifying the most effective intervention points and predicting the potential impact of different policies on various communities. It can help us design smarter, more just systems that are more likely to achieve their goals.

AI's Limitations in the Pursuit of Justice

For all its impressive capabilities, however, we must be brutally honest about what AI cannot do. And it cannot solve the root causes of injustice. Those roots run deep into the soil of the human condition—into pride, greed, fear, and narcissism. Addressing these requires a fundamental transformation of the human heart, a spiritual conversion that no algorithm can engineer. AI's limitations stem from its very nature: it is a machine that calculates, not a soul that loves.

First, and most fundamentally, AI has a lack of moral agency, empathy, and spiritual capacity. An AI operates on algorithms and data. It does not possess consciousness. It cannot feel the sting of another's pain. It cannot experience solidarity. It cannot repent. Christian justice, as we have explored, is deeply relational. It involves confessing our own failures, standing in authentic connection with the oppressed, and reorienting our entire lives toward God. These are profoundly human and spiritual acts that are simply outside the realm of computation. Imagine a sophisticated grief-support chatbot designed to help someone who has just lost a loved one. The AI can be programmed with millions of sympathetic phrases. It can say all the "right" things. But contrast that with a human friend who comes and sits with the grieving person in silence, who brings a simple meal, who weeps with them. The friend's physical presence, their shared vulnerability, offers a depth of connection—a true "suffering with"—that the most advanced AI can never replicate. An AI can process data about suffering, but it cannot share in it.

Second, a critical and dangerous limitation is AI's tendency to amplify existing societal biases. This isn't a glitch; it's a core feature of how AI learns. These systems are trained on vast amounts of human-generated data, and that data is a mirror reflecting our own flawed, biased, and unjust world.

The philosopher Shannon Vallor has argued that technology is never neutral; it is always embedded with the values of its creators. In her book *Technology and the Virtues*, she contends that we need to cultivate specific virtues to navigate the digital age, warning that without wisdom, our tools will merely amplify our vices. She writes, "We need to ask not just what our technology can do, but what it is doing to us," and whether it is helping us become the kind of people we want to be.[14]

This is exactly what we see happening with AI. If historical data shows that men have been hired for executive roles more often than women, an AI trained on that data will "learn" that men are preferable candidates. This has been powerfully documented by Safiya Umoja Noble, who has shown how seemingly objective search engines can produce deeply racist and sexist results. In her book *Algorithms of Oppression*, she reveals how search algorithms reinforce harmful stereotypes, writing that "algorithms are not objective, but are shaped by the biases of their creators and the society in which they operate."[15] This is because AI can automate and scale up our prejudices with terrifying efficiency, making them seem even more objective and harder to counteract.

Third, AI is utterly incapable of addressing the root causes of sin. The deepest sources of injustice are not logistical problems or data deficits. They are spiritual maladies: pride, greed, envy, and a self-centeredness that tunes out the voice of God and the needs of our neighbor. AI can analyze the symptoms of these sins, but it cannot heal the underlying disease. For example, an AI could design a perfectly efficient system of carbon taxes to combat climate change. But it cannot instill a sense of stewardship in the heart of a corporate executive motivated by quarterly profits. That work requires a change in our desires, a conversion of the heart.

Finally, our uncritical reliance on AI carries the risk of dehumanization and a new form of idolatry. There is a subtle but profound danger in treating AI as a universal cure-all for our deepest social problems. When we place our ultimate faith in AI to deliver justice, we can inadvertently displace God from the center of our lives and elevate a human creation to

14. Vallor, *Technology and the Virtues*, 55.

15. Noble, *Algorithms of Oppression*, 28.

a position of salvific authority. This overreliance can lead to a dangerous atrophy of our own moral muscles. If we outsource our ethical decision-making to machines, we risk becoming *lazy about tough choices*. We let the algorithm call the shots when we should be engaging in the difficult, uniquely human work of moral discernment.

AI as a Tool, Not a Savior

Ultimately, we must see AI for what it is: a powerful tool, but only a tool. A hammer can be used to build a home for a family in need, or it can be used to break a window and commit a crime. The morality is not in the hammer; it is in the hand that wields it. The same is true of AI. Its impact on our world will depend entirely on the wisdom, compassion, and integrity of the people who design, deploy, and regulate it. AI can help us do the work of justice more effectively, but it can never be justice. It can't inspire the will to do justice in the human heart.

The theologian N. T. Wright has often spoken of Christian justice as God's work of "putting the world to rights." This is a deeply relational and restorative project, not a computational one. In his book *Simply Christian*, Wright argues that our longing for justice is an "echo of a voice" calling us to participate in God's restorative work, a task that requires us to "live in the present as if the future has already arrived."[16] This redemptive work involves grace, forgiveness, and a self-giving love that is the very antithesis of cold, hard logic.

While AI can certainly be a valuable servant in this work, only a life truly centered on God, marked by humble obedience and active love, can begin to address the deep roots of sin and injustice. The ultimate solution lies not in more powerful technology but in spiritual transformation—a turning of the human heart toward God and his restorative love. As we have reflected, it is in our weakness that we find God's strength, and in our surrender that we become fully human. This is a truth that no machine will ever understand.

CONCLUSION

This chapter has navigated the complex landscape of justice in a world increasingly shaped by the alluring logics of ideology and artificial

16. Wright, *Simply Christian*, 14.

intelligence. We began by questioning the myths of our age: that efficiency can replace empathy and that human-devised power structures can deliver true justice. We've seen how these systems, for all their promises, often fall short because they fail to address the deepest truths of the human condition. In contrast, the Christian vision of justice offers a different path. It is not a rigid blueprint but a dynamic and practical response to the world's brokenness. This path calls us to look inward, addressing our personal failures to live in loving harmony with God and neighbor; to look outward, hearing the cries of the innocent and standing in solidarity against systemic oppression; and to look upward, reorienting our entire lives around the self-giving love of God rather than our own ego.

In this work, AI can be a powerful servant but a dangerous master. Its ability to reveal hidden biases and streamline aid is a gift to be used with wisdom. Yet, its inherent lack of moral agency, its tendency to amplify our worst prejudices, and its inability to heal the human heart mean we must resist the temptation to see it as a savior. The ultimate answer to injustice is not found in a better algorithm but in a more compassionate soul. The path forward, then, is one of intentional, countercultural practice. It is the slow, holy work of choosing presence over distraction, attention over numbness, and embodied love over digital abstraction. It is the work of becoming fully human.

Chapter 5

Rediscovering Joy in Analog Life

AI AND THE DIGITAL world it creates undeniably offer instant gratification, boundless options, and constant entertainment. This is the source of the myth that our digital lives are better than our analog ones. We can connect with people across the globe, access a vast universe of information with a few clicks, and find a community for every niche interest. This level of convenience is powerful. The digital world is designed to be endlessly engaging and to fill every spare moment, promising that you'll never have to be bored or alone. We can order food, find a partner, and chat with a friend all at the same time, from the comfort of our homes. This convenience is powerful. It's an alluring promise that makes our lives feel more exciting, connected, and full. The appeal is so strong that it's easy to believe the constant stimulation is a sign of a truly rich and full life.

Despite its appeal, we must rediscover joy in analog life to be fully human. The digital world can't offer the deep, soulful nourishment that comes from a slow, real-world moment. It provides endless connections but not the vulnerability and patience required for real intimacy. True joy and understanding often emerge from the silence and boredom we so desperately try to avoid. A walk in nature, the feel of a tool in your hand, or the unhurried texture of a real conversation are not empty spaces to be filled. They are the fertile ground where our inner lives grow and our deepest connections are forged. By constantly reaching for the next digital stimulus, we risk trading a rich, textured life for a smooth, but ultimately hollow, simulation of one.

Myth 5: Digital Life Is Better than Slow, Real-World Moments

There is a quiet story we tell ourselves now—a pervasive narrative woven into daily life. It whispers that if something isn't digital, it's obsolete. This seems to be the great myth of our age: that our AI-driven digital lives—our smartphones, our apps, the immersive worlds of virtual reality—represent the very pinnacle of human experience. Everything else, the slow, tangible, real-world practices, are relegated to the realm of the quaint and the outdated. Reading a physical book, tending a garden, or even sharing a handwritten note can feel like a sentimental nod to the past, not an essential part of a flourishing present.

The logic of this myth seems, on the surface, undeniable. Why would you bother attending a concert in a crowded arena when you can stream it in flawless high definition from your living room? Why make the effort to meet friends for coffee when a video call is instant and effortless? Why savor a slow, meandering walk when an AI fitness tracker can optimize your every step for maximum health benefits? This assumption is reinforced by relentless tech innovation and the seductive convenience AI promises. It's an alluring promise that makes our lives feel more exciting, connected, and full.

This digital world is an environment intentionally designed to capture and monopolize our most precious resource: our attention. The writer Johann Hari has meticulously documented this phenomenon, arguing that our focus hasn't just been lost; it has been stolen by systems engineered to keep us hooked. In his book *Stolen Focus*, he provides a sobering analysis of how the architecture of our digital lives is designed for addiction, not well-being. As Hari bluntly puts it, "The truth is that you are living in a system that is pouring acid on your attention every day."[1] AI tailors content to our every preference, creating the powerful illusion that these digital solutions are not just better but essential for a good life.

Yet this constant digital presence comes at a cost we are only beginning to understand. It seems to be quietly crowding out the simple, embodied pleasures that ground us in the physical world: the smell of rain on hot asphalt, the satisfying weight of a well-worn book, the sound of a friend's uninhibited laughter from across a dinner table. The myth of digital superiority is not just about tools but about the values they instill

1. Hari, *Stolen Focus*, 120.

in us. It appears to elevate speed over depth, broad accessibility over genuine intimacy, and constant novelty over lasting meaning. In doing so, it subtly reshapes our very definition of joy, reducing it from a deep, soulful practice to a series of fleeting dopamine hits.

This is a concern thoughtfully explored by thinkers like Cal Newport, who advocates for a more intentional and minimalist approach to technology. He argues that the constant pull of our devices is not making us happier but is instead fragmenting our lives and leaving us feeling strangely disconnected from the very experiences that foster true happiness. In his book *Digital Minimalism*, Newport suggests we must be far more discerning, writing, "Digital minimalism is a philosophy of technology use in which you focus your online time on a small number of carefully selected and optimized activities that strongly support things you value, and then happily miss out on everything else."[2]

In this context, communities of faith and conscience have a sacred calling: to unmask this myth and reclaim the analog joys that reflect God's goodness and restore our humanity. The argument here is simple: these analog experiences are not relics of a bygone era but may in fact be vital, irreplaceable practices for soulful living in our time.

The Psychological, Social, and Spiritual Costs

The digital world is engineered to be captivating. Every ping, every notification, every endlessly scrolling feed is designed to trigger a small release of dopamine in our brains, creating what psychologists sometimes call a dopamine loop. As Johann Hari explains in *Stolen Focus*, this is no accident; it's a deliberate design choice employed by tech companies to keep us coming back for more. Social media platforms reward us with likes and retweets, while streaming services and apps exploit our brain's reward system, making it incredibly difficult to look away. The result is constant, low-grade craving that leaves us restless and agitated rather than fulfilled.

The psychological toll of this is significant and measurable. One of the most discussed impacts is the fragmentation of our attention. The endless scroll trains us to skim and react rather than to read and reflect. This is the central concern of neuroscientist Maryanne Wolf. In her work, she warns that the shift from the linear, focused attention demanded by

2. Newport, *Digital Minimalism*, 28.

print to the screen-based "reading" of the digital world is fundamentally altering our cognitive abilities. In her vital book *Reader, Come Home*, Wolf describes the deep reading brain as a sanctuary for reflection and consciousness. She argues that as we lose this sanctuary, we diminish our capacity for sustained focus, warning that "we are not only what we read, but how we read."[3]

This digital overload also seems to be impacting our emotional well-being. The author Jean M. Twenge, in her book *iGen*, presents a sobering correlation between the meteoric rise of the smartphone and a sharp decline in teen mental health. Her research suggests that as digital interactions have replaced face-to-face ones, feelings of anxiety, depression, and social isolation have skyrocketed. The relentless pressure to perform and compare oneself to the curated perfection seen online can create a crushing sense of inadequacy. And adults are certainly not immune; the constant connectivity and pressure to be always on contribute to widespread feelings of burnout and isolation. As Twenge observes, "iGen teens are more likely to be lonely than any previous generation . . . because the activities that protect against loneliness (like getting together with friends) have been replaced by the very activity (screen time) that is linked to loneliness."[4]

The quick high of a notification—a new follower, a viral post—is fleeting and offers no lasting joy. It fosters what Casper ter Kuile calls a "hollow satisfaction." He suggests we have swapped out meaningful, embodied rituals for the thin rituals of digital life. In his book *The Power of Ritual*, Ter Kuile observes that where we once found connection in shared meals or community service, we now seek it in the solitary morning scroll through a feed. He notes that "rituals are about paying attention," and when we direct that attention solely to our screens, we miss the sacred depth available in our physical communities.[5] This speaks to the deep social cost of our digital habits. The platforms promise connection, but they often deliver a counterfeit version that leaves us feeling lonelier than before.

This is a central theme in the work of Priya Parker, an expert on the art of gathering. She argues that virtual interactions simply cannot replicate the depth, spontaneity, and transformative potential of face-to-face encounters. In her book *The Art of Gathering*, Parker writes, "Gatherings

3. Wolf, *Reader, Come Home*, 87.
4. Twenge, *iGen*, 98.
5. Ter Kuile, *Power of Ritual*, 40.

consume our days and help determine the kind of world we live in, in our families, our companies, our communities, and our countries."[6] Text messages and video calls, however convenient, lack the nuance of a shared glance or the contagious energy of collective laughter. Over time, a heavy reliance on mediated connection may even erode our ability to navigate the beautiful, messy reality of real-world relationships.

Beyond the psychological toll, the myth of digital superiority exacts a profound spiritual cost. It fills every moment with noise, drowning out the quiet and stillness where the soul has traditionally been thought to encounter God. The Christian tradition teaches that joy is not a product of frantic stimulation but a gift of presence. The writer and spiritual director Ruth Haley Barton has spoken extensively about how the constant noise of modern life disrupts our ability to hear the "still small voice" of God (1 Kgs 19:12). In her book *Sacred Rhythms*, she argues that spiritual disciplines are about intentionally "arranging our lives for transformation." She writes that "desire is the best thing about us," but it is easily drowned out by the distractions of a digital age that keep us from the deep longing that leads to God.[7]

The practice of Sabbath is perhaps the most direct casualty of our digital age. The biblical command to set aside a day for rest is a radical act of trust—a declaration that our worth is not tied to our productivity. The great spiritual writer Dallas Willard saw the Sabbath as a joyful participation in God's own unhurried life. In his classic work *The Divine Conspiracy*, Willard describes Sabbath not as a burdensome rule but as a liberating invitation into the "easy yoke" of Jesus (Matt 11:30), a way to practice the rhythms of eternity in our present lives. He notes that "eternal life is the kind of life God is living now," and Sabbath allows us to step into that unhurried flow.[8] Yet our digital culture knows no Sabbath. Our phones buzz with work emails on a Sunday afternoon, leaving no space for the deep, restorative rest that fosters true joy.

This loss of unstructured time also stifles creativity and wonder, which thrive in moments of boredom and stillness. Finally, this spiritual cost extends to our relationships. Digital platforms encourage us to perform rather than to be present. Tish Harrison Warren has done beautiful work reminding us that it is in the un-curated, ordinary moments of life that we most often encounter the sacred. In her book *Liturgy of the*

6. Parker, *Art of Gathering*, 3.

7. Barton, *Sacred Rhythms*, 25.

8. Willard, *Divine Conspiracy*, 60.

Ordinary, she writes, "The new life into which we are baptized is not a life of sinless perfection, but a life of repentance. It is a life of waking, eating, working, sleeping, and saying 'I'm sorry' and 'I forgive you' again and again."[9] This messy, beautiful life is embodied. A Zoom call cannot replicate the simple joy of a shared laugh over a meal. The constant stimulation of digital life can, if we are not careful, impoverish our ability to be truly present with one another, and in turn, with the God who promises to meet us there.

The Biblical Counternarrative of Embodied Joy

In the face of this myth, the Bible offers a powerful counternarrative. It consistently roots joy not in virtual or abstract realities but in the tangible, analog experiences of creation, community, and rest. Christ's teachings are filled with images of this kind of embodied delight: a great banquet where the poor and marginalized are the guests of honor, a shepherd so filled with joy over finding one lost sheep that he throws a party for his friends, and a sower scattering seeds in rich, dark soil. These are not parables about efficiency or innovation; they are parables about presence—savoring a meal, tending a flock, nurturing growth. They are an open invitation to find joy in the ordinary, to "taste and see that the Lord is good" (Ps 34:8) with all of our senses.

The Old Testament amplifies this vision of a joyful, material world. The Psalms celebrate a creation that is alive with delight—where rivers clap their hands and mountains sing for joy. The prophets envision a restored world, not as a digital utopia, but as a place of profound peace and tangible abundance, where people will rest securely under their own vines and fig trees. This is not a digital dream but an analog one, grounded in the textures of the earth.

C. S. Lewis observed that joy is not a trivial matter but is central to the very nature of God's kingdom. In his book *The Problem of Pain*, Lewis asserts that the Christian life is meant to be a journey into joy, writing, "The happiness which God designs for His higher creatures is the happiness of being freely, voluntarily united to Him and to each other in an ecstasy of love and delight compared with which the most rapturous love between a man and a woman on this earth is mere milk and water."[10]

9. Warren, *Liturgy of the Ordinary*, 30.

10. Lewis, *Problem of Pain*, 145.

Consider the peculiar story of the manna in the wilderness. When the Israelites were hungry and complaining in the desert, God didn't provide a virtual, abstract solution. He sent tangible, physical food—a flaky, bread-like substance that appeared on the ground each morning. This daily provision was not just about sustenance; it was a profound lesson in joy. It taught the people to trust in God's daily care, to savor the gift of having enough for today without hoarding for tomorrow, and to find delight in the simple, ordinary miracle of their daily bread. In our age of AI, where algorithms promise an endless, on-demand abundance of everything, this ancient story reminds us that true joy is often found not in having everything at once but in gratefully receiving the simple gifts of the present moment.

These biblical narratives offer a direct challenge to the myth of digital superiority. A digital sermon may teach us about faith, but it cannot replace the embodied joy of singing a hymn with a hundred other voices in a shared space. A virtual reality forest may simulate nature with stunning accuracy, but it cannot replicate the earthy smell of pine after a rainstorm or the feeling of cool moss under our fingertips. The Bible consistently calls us back to presence, inviting us to delight in creation and to trust that true, lasting joy is not a product to be consumed but a gift to be received.

The myth promises endless connection and convenience but often leaves our souls hungry. I think of Michael, a college student who felt like he was drowning in the digital sea. His days were a blur of notifications, group chats, and the endless scroll. He was doing everything the digital world told him would make him connected, but he had never felt more alone. One weekend, feeling completely burned out, he went to visit his grandparents on their small farm—a place with spotty Wi-Fi. He spent a Saturday picking apples and sitting by a fire, talking without a screen in sight. He said that for the first time in years, he felt a sense of real joy—not the quick, jittery rush of a viral post, but a quiet, grounded delight in simply being present in his own life. That one analog weekend didn't solve all his problems, but it was a powerful reminder of a truth he had forgotten: that true joy is often found in the analog world, not in the algorithm.

Why Analog Joy Matters

It's one thing to notice that our digital lives often leave us feeling frazzled and empty; it's another to understand why the slow, tangible, real-world moments feel so restorative. Why does a walk in the woods bring more joy than scrolling through a hundred nature photos? Why does a shared meal with friends nourish us in a way that a thousand "likes" never can? The answer, it seems, isn't just about nostalgia or a simple preference for the old-fashioned. The foundations for why analog joy matters run deep, touching on the very nature of God, the wiring of our minds, and the fabric of our communities. Rediscovering these simple pleasures isn't just a life hack for feeling better; it appears to be a vital spiritual and human necessity.

The Theological Foundation: A Delighting God

It is startling to realize that God is not a stern cosmic bookkeeper but a being of immense, overflowing joy. The Christian tradition is built on this radical idea. The prophet Zephaniah paints an almost unbelievable picture of God's disposition toward humanity, declaring, "The Lord your God is with you, the Mighty Warrior who saves. He will take great delight in you; in his love he will no longer rebuke you, but will rejoice over you with singing" (Zeph 3:17). A singing God. A God who takes such profound delight in his creation that it erupts into song. This image reveals a profound truth: joy is not peripheral to God's nature; it is absolutely central to it.

When the creation story in Genesis unfolds, at the end of each creative day, God pauses, looks at what has been made, and calls it "good." And at the culmination of it all, looking at the whole material world teeming with creatures and human beings, God calls it "very good." This is an act of divine pleasure, an invitation for us to participate in the joy of our own existence. This theology of delight is deeply, unapologetically material. God's joy isn't abstract or virtual; it's rooted in the stuff of the physical world—the startling fragrance of honeysuckle on a summer evening, the rhythmic crash of waves on a sandy shore, the comforting warmth of human connection.

Dallas Willard consistently pushed back against the idea that the spiritual life was about escaping the physical world. He taught that God's kingdom is not some distant future realm but a reality that is constantly breaking into our here and now, inviting us to find profound joy in the most ordinary moments of our lives. In his masterwork *The Divine Conspiracy*, Willard writes that God's kingdom is "the range of God's effective will," and that we are invited to "live in the Kingdom of God now" by finding God in the concrete realities of our daily existence.[11] This availability means God's joy is accessible to us now, in this moment, through the material world he has given us.

Joy, in this light, is a fruit of the Spirit—growing not through frantic effort but as a natural result of being present to God. It is the quiet delight that can surface when we are truly attentive: the laughter of children playing in a park, the taste of fresh bread shared with friends, the breathtaking stillness of a starry night. These are reflections of the divine delight that permeates the world. In our age, where digital platforms promise endless connection but so often deliver a profound sense of isolation, this parable is a powerful reminder that true, life-giving joy is almost always found in the material realities of relationship, forgiveness, and shared celebration.

The Psychological Foundation: A Brain Wired for Reality

The things that bring us this deep, spiritual joy also happen to be incredibly good for our minds. Analog practices that engage our senses and anchor us in the physical world are not just spiritually enriching but psychologically vital. A growing body of research consistently shows that activities like spending time in nature, creating with our hands, or even the simple act of writing in a journal can foster well-being in ways that most digital experiences cannot.

Take, for example, the simple act of spending time in nature. The Japanese practice of *shinrin-yoku*, or forest bathing, is built on this insight. The work of Dr. Qing Li, one of the world's leading experts on forest medicine, has demonstrated the profound physiological and psychological benefits of this practice. In his book *Forest Bathing*, Dr. Li presents data showing that just twenty minutes of walking in a natural setting can lower cortisol levels (our primary stress hormone), reduce anxiety, and provide a significant boost to our mood. He writes, "We are part of the natural world. . . . Our rhythm is the rhythm of nature," and that reconnecting with it is essential for our health.[12]

11. Willard, *Divine Conspiracy*, 25.

12. Li, *Forest Bathing*, 13.

The same is true for tactile creativity—painting, knitting, cooking, or gardening. These activities have been shown to promote what the psychologist Mihaly Csikszentmihalyi famously termed "flow" states. In his groundbreaking book *Flow*, Csikszentmihalyi describes this as a state of being completely absorbed in an activity for its own sake, where time seems to fade away and we experience a deep sense of enjoyment and fulfillment. He writes, "Enjoyment appears at the boundary between boredom and anxiety, when the challenges are just balanced with the person's capacity to act."[13] Analog creative practices are perfect for inducing this state. The slow, rhythmic process of knitting, the focused attention of chopping vegetables, the sensory experience of working with clay—all of these activities create a meditative rhythm that acts as a powerful antidote to the frenetic, multitasking pace of digital life.

Casper ter Kuile, in his book *The Power of Ritual*, observes that these everyday acts, when done with intention, become soulful practices that can restore our emotional and psychological resilience. Even the simple act of putting pen to paper offers unique benefits. While typing on a keyboard is undoubtedly more efficient, the physical act of handwriting appears to engage the brain in a different, deeper way. It forces us to slow down, to consider our words more carefully. This aligns with the arguments of thinkers like Cal Newport, who, in *Digital Minimalism*, advocates for intentionally choosing slower, more demanding analog practices as a way to combat the anxiety and burnout of digital overload. By engaging in these activities, we are creating essential buffers against the constant mental strain of the AI age, and in doing so, we are rediscovering a more grounded, sustainable form of joy.

The Relational Foundation: The Joy of Community

At its heart, analog joy is relational. It thrives in the shared, unscripted moments that digital platforms, for all their power, struggle to replicate. Priya Parker has become a leading voice on the importance of intentional, face-to-face gathering. In her insightful book *The Art of Gathering*, she argues that the way we come together matters profoundly. She critiques what she calls "the tyranny of the chill," our tendency to put little thought into our gatherings, hoping they will just work out. Instead, she advocates for creating gatherings with a clear purpose, ones that are designed to

13. Csikszentmihalyi, *Flow*, 52.

foster genuine human connection. Parker writes, "A category of gathering is not a purpose. . . . Purpose is your bouncer," meaning that clarity about why we are gathering allows us to exclude what doesn't serve the connection we seek.[14] Meaningful gatherings—whether a shared meal, a board game night, or a group hike—create bonds that virtual connections often cannot match. In the age of AI, where loneliness is rampant despite our hyper-connectivity, these analog rituals are more vital than ever for building strong, joyful communities.

Shared meals are a cornerstone of this relational joy. The simple act of preparing, serving, and eating food together creates a space where stories are shared, laughter erupts, and presence is prioritized over performance. Board games, too, are experiencing a renaissance, precisely because they offer an analog alternative to the often-isolating experience of online gaming. Unlike video games that place each player behind their own screen, board games require physical presence. They demand that we look each other in the eye, negotiate rules, share in triumphs, and laugh at failures—together, in the same room. These unscripted interactions are where the real joy of connection is found.

This stands in stark contrast to the world described by social critics like Johann Hari. In *Stolen Focus*, Hari argues that our heavy reliance on digital communication has eroded our ability to connect deeply, leaving us lonely even when we are surrounded by thousands of online "friends." Analog rituals—a potluck, a storytelling circle, a community work project—are powerful antidotes. They restore the texture of real human connection, reminding us that joy is not solitary but shared, not virtual but embodied. We were made to be with one another, and it is in that shared presence that our deepest joys are often found.

Formation Through Analog Practices—Soul, Body, and Community

So, how do we begin? If we recognize that the myth of digital superiority is leaving us depleted, and if we understand that a deeper, more analog form of joy is foundational to our well-being, how do we actually start to live this way? It's not enough to simply critique the digital world; we are invited to cultivate a different one, starting in our own lives and our own communities. This is the work of formation. It's the intentional,

14. Parker, *Art of Gathering*, 30.

patient, and sometimes clumsy process of shaping our souls, our bodies, and our communities through practices that anchor us in the physical, the tangible, and the real. These analog practices are not quaint hobbies or nostalgic escapes; they are essential spiritual exercises for our time, disciplines that can form us into people capable of a more resilient and abiding joy.

Personal Formation: Coming Home to Ourselves

In a world that so often feels fragmented and disembodied, where our minds are tethered to screens and our bodies are often forgotten, personal formation begins with coming home to ourselves. Analog practices are the pathway home. The simple acts of journaling by hand, digging in a garden, cooking a meal from scratch, or just walking in nature are not merely activities; they are disciplines that form the soul. They engage our bodies, quiet the relentless chatter of our minds, and open our hearts to the possibility of encountering God's presence in the most ordinary of moments.

Consider the simple, almost forgotten practice of journaling by hand. Unlike typing on a keyboard, which prioritizes speed and efficiency, the physical act of forming letters on a page forces us to slow down. It invites a different quality of attention, a more reflective and honest presence with our own thoughts and feelings. The neuroscientist Maryanne Wolf has explored how the medium we use for language changes the way we think. She argues that the slowness of writing by hand allows for a deeper level of cognitive and emotional processing. For a person of faith, a journal can become a sacred space—a portable sanctuary for prayerful conversation with God. It's a place to untangle the knots of the day, to confess our fears, to name our gratitude, and to listen for that still, small voice. Joy often surfaces unexpectedly in these handwritten pages, not because we are trying to be happy, but because we are making space to be honest, and in that honesty, we encounter grace.

Gardening is another powerful, formative practice. To plunge your hands into cool soil, to plant a tiny seed, and to tend it patiently over weeks and months is to participate directly in the rhythms of creation. It's an act of faith, a vote of confidence in the future. As Casper ter Kuile observes in *The Power of Ritual*, everyday activities like gardening become profound spiritual practices when we approach them with intention. He writes that these practices help us move "from isolation to belonging," grounding us in the physical world and teaching us crucial spiritual lessons about patience, trust, and the cycles of death and new life.[15] The slow, incremental process of nurturing a plant from a fragile sprout to a fruit-bearing vine is a powerful antidote to the instant gratification culture of the digital world. It teaches us to find joy not in a quick result but in the patient, ongoing act of tending and waiting.

The same is true of cooking. In our age of app-based delivery and microwave meals, the act of preparing food from scratch can be a radical act of presence. To chop an onion, to smell garlic sizzling in a pan, to knead dough for bread—these are sensory experiences that ground us in our bodies and in the present moment. Tish Harrison Warren, in *Liturgy of the Ordinary*, beautifully articulates how everyday tasks can become sacred liturgies. She suggests that preparing food can be a profound act of worship, a way of offering our love and care to others through the gift of a meal. She writes, "We are shaped every day, whether we know it or not, by practices—rituals and liturgies that make us who we are."[16] When we cook with attention and love, we are doing more than just making food; we are participating in God's own creative and sustaining love for the world.

And perhaps most primally, there is walking in nature. As the research of Dr. Qing Li on forest bathing has shown, spending time in creation has measurable benefits for our mental and physical health. But it is also a profound spiritual practice. The Psalms are filled with a creation-based joy: "The heavens declare the glory of God; the skies proclaim the work of his hands" (Ps 19:1). To walk without a phone, without a podcast, simply listening to the rustle of leaves or the song of birds, is to open ourselves up to this glory. It is to find a joy that is not curated by an algorithm but is received as a pure gift from the Creator. These personal practices are not escapes from the world; they are invitations to live more fully within it, forming us into people who can delight in the ordinary and find God in the tangible.

15. Ter Kuile, *Power of Ritual*, 40.

16. Warren, *Liturgy of the Ordinary*, 30.

Specific Spiritual Disciplines

Beyond these general habits, we can also cultivate specific, intentional spiritual disciplines that anchor us in the analog world. One is to sense creation with all six senses. We often rush through the world, our attention captured by a screen rather than the creation surrounding us. This practice is a gentle invitation to ground yourself. Find a quiet spot outside—a backyard or a city park will do. For just five minutes, intentionally engage your senses. Notice what you see: the intricate pattern on a leaf, the specific shade of the sky. Tune your ears to what you can hear beyond the traffic: a bird's call, the rustle of leaves. What can you smell—damp earth, cut grass? What can you touch—the rough bark of a tree, the coolness of a stone? Finally, what of the sixth sense, the sense of presence? Acknowledge the simple, sacred gift of being alive in this moment. This sensory immersion is a powerful antidote to digital abstraction. The work of scientists like Dr. Qing Li has shown that this kind of mindful engagement with nature has profound healing effects. In his book *Forest Bathing*, he explains that by consciously opening our senses, we participate in a deep, restorative connection, noting that "nature enters through your eyes, ears, nose, mouth, hands and feet," and in doing so, we are healed.[17]

Another is a breathing prayer. In the constant hum of digital anxiety, our breathing often becomes shallow and tense. A breathing prayer is one of the simplest analog practices for anchoring your soul in God's steady presence. It requires no special equipment, just your own breath. The practice is simple: as you breathe in, choose a word or phrase that represents what you wish to receive, such as *peace*, *grace*, or simply the name *Jesus*. As you breathe out, release what you want to let go of—your anxiety, your fear, your need for control. This rhythmic act connects the physical reality of your body to the spiritual reality of your soul, reminding you that every breath is a gift. Ruth Haley Barton teaches that such disciplines arrange our lives to be more present to God's love. In her book *Sacred Rhythms*, she describes how these embodied practices help us "create space for God in the midst of our busy lives," and that the body is "the place where the spiritual life is lived out."[18]

Finally, we can intentionally seek Christ in people and places. Our digital lives train us to curate our interactions; we follow those we agree with and mute those who challenge us. This practice calls us to a more

17. Li, *Forest Bathing*, 55.

18. Barton, *Sacred Rhythms*, 38.

vulnerable way of being. It is a commitment to see every person—the stranger in the store, the frustrating coworker—as a potential bearer of the divine, an opportunity to meet Christ in disguise. This is the radical call of Jesus in Matt 25, where he insists that when we care for the hungry, the stranger, or the sick, we are caring for him. This practice requires a profound shift in our attention, away from "What can this person do for me?" and toward "Where might Christ be present here?" Christine D. Pohl has dedicated her work to recovering this lost art of hospitality. In her book *Making Room*, Pohl writes, "Strangers often bring gifts that we could not have anticipated . . . and in welcoming them, we may find that we have welcomed angels."[19] This is the ultimate antidote to curated isolation.

Integration: Healing the Split of Soul and Body

These analog practices are powerful because they heal the split among mind, body, and soul that digital life so often creates. We spend so much of our time as disembodied minds, floating through a world of screens, our attention scattered across a dozen tabs and notifications. As Johann Hari argues in *Stolen Focus*, this constant digital overload leaves us feeling fragmented and disconnected from the very physicality of our existence. We forget that we are bodies. Analogue practices call us back home to ourselves. They demand the engagement of our senses and the work of our hands, fostering a holistic joy that integrates soul, body, and spirit.

Tactile rituals are particularly effective for this kind of integration. Matthew B. Crawford has written eloquently about the deep satisfaction that comes from skilled, manual work. In his celebrated book *Shop Class as Soulcraft*, he argues that working with our hands connects us to the real world in a way that purely intellectual or virtual work cannot. He writes, "The satisfactions of manifesting oneself concretely in the world through manual competence have been known to make a man quiet and easy."[20] This is the joy of competence, of engaging with the stubborn, beautiful reality of physical things.

This deep integration of soul and body is profoundly biblical. The central event of the Christian story—the incarnation—is the ultimate affirmation of the goodness of the physical. God did not send a message or

19. Pohl, *Making Room*, 80.

20. Crawford, *Shop Class as Soulcraft*, 15.

a virtual avatar; God became flesh. Jesus's ministry was overwhelmingly tactile: he touched the sick, he washed his disciples' feet, he broke bread with his hands. Our bodies are not obstacles to our spirituality; they are the primary vehicles for it. Dallas Willard emphasized this point, arguing that spiritual formation is not about escaping our bodies but about training them to participate in the life of God's kingdom. Analog practices are a key way we do this, inviting us to live as whole, embodied beings who find joy in the physical world God made.

Communal Formation: Weaving a World of Joy

This embodied joy is not meant to be a solitary pursuit. It finds its fullest expression in community, in shared practices that weave people together. In an age where digital platforms so often isolate us despite their promises of connection, analog rituals like communal meals, shared craft projects, or participatory worship can create genuine communities of joy. Priya Parker has become a crucial guide in this area. In *The Art of Gathering*, she insists that meaningful gatherings don't just happen; they are intentionally designed. She challenges us to think deeply about the purpose of our time together and to create spaces where authentic connection can flourish. These gatherings become the crucibles where communal joy is forged.

Shared meals are perhaps the oldest and most powerful of these rituals. The simple act of preparing, serving, and eating food together creates a space where screens are put away, stories are shared, and presence is prioritized. This echoes the biblical vision of the feast, where all are welcomed to the table to "taste and see that the Lord is good" (Ps 34:8). When a church hosts a simple potluck or a neighborhood organizes a block party, they are doing more than just sharing food; they are weaving a community of joy.

Shared acts of creation can be equally powerful. Imagine a church that decides to create a communal quilt. People of all ages and skill levels are invited to contribute a square. In the process of working together—sharing needles and thread, teaching one another stitches, telling stories as they work—they are not just making a quilt; they are making a community. The final quilt becomes a beautiful, tangible symbol of their interconnected lives.

Even our worship can be more analog. Imagine a church service where, instead of watching a slickly produced video, the congregation is invited to participate in creating a worship installation. These acts transform worship from a passive experience into an active, embodied, and communal one. They become, as Casper ter Kuile might say, powerful rituals that unite people in a shared expression of faith and joy.

The Role of Leadership in an Analog Revival

Pastors, teachers, parents, and community organizers have a unique opportunity and responsibility to lead this analog revival. As Ruth Haley Barton suggests, spiritual leadership is not just about teaching and preaching; it's about modeling a way of life that opens people to God's presence. In the AI age, this means intentionally guiding our communities toward unhurried rhythms, creating and hosting analog gatherings, and blessing the everyday work of human hands and hearts.

First, leaders must model unhurried rhythms. A pastor who is constantly checking their email during meetings cannot convincingly lead others into a life of presence. As Dallas Willard often taught, we cannot impart what we do not possess. By intentionally practicing Sabbath, leaders give their communities permission to do the same. They create a culture where joy is not rushed but savored.

Second, leaders must host analog gatherings. This means taking the insights of guides like Priya Parker seriously and designing intentional, screen-free spaces for connection. The goal is to create sanctuaries of presence in a world of distraction.

Third, leaders can bless the everyday work of hands and hearts. This is a point that Tish Harrison Warren makes so beautifully in her work: we need to recover a sense of the sacred in the ordinary. A leader can do this by affirming the spiritual value of these analog practices. A pastor might offer a prayer of blessing over a new community garden. By doing so, they help people see God's presence not just in explicitly religious activities but in the texture of their daily lives. This is how we cultivate a people who are truly alive to the joy of God's world.

Conclusion

This chapter has served as an invitation to come home—home to our bodies, home to our senses, and home to a more present way of life. We began by unmasking the pervasive myth of our time: that an AI-curated life, with its promises of speed and seamless connection, is inherently superior to the slow, tangible realities of the analog world. We've seen how this myth, fueled by an attention economy largely driven by AI, can lead not to fulfillment but to a state of psychological overload and spiritual numbness, leaving us feeling restless and strangely alone. In response, we explored the deep foundations of a more durable, analog joy. This is a joy that is not manufactured by an algorithm but received as a gift from a delighted Creator, a joy essential for our psychological well-being, and a joy that thrives in the rich soil of real, face-to-face community.

Finally, we moved from understanding to action, exploring the concrete, formative practices that can reanchor us in this deeper reality. Through the simple, embodied acts of working with our hands, walking in nature, sharing a meal, or journaling on paper, we integrate our souls and bodies and weave the fabric of joyful, resilient communities. These are not nostalgic hobbies but disciplines of resistance and rehumanization against a world increasingly optimized by AI. They are the means by which we can form ourselves into a people who are not merely users and consumers of AI-driven content but creators and neighbors, capable of finding and sharing the sacred, life-giving joy that is God's good gift to us all.

Chapter 6

Developing Spiritual Discernment

Data and algorithms know more than any single human. They can process vast, complex datasets to reveal patterns invisible to the naked eye, leading to objective, data-backed decisions that can improve efficiency, safety, and outcomes on a massive scale. For instance, in predictive maintenance, algorithms can analyze sensor data from machinery to forecast a breakdown with greater precision than a human engineer. In public health, AI models can track disease outbreaks and predict their spread more efficiently than traditional methods. The promise here is of a world free from human bias, gut feelings, and guesswork. It's a powerful and undeniable reality: we can now make decisions based on what the data suggests, rather than relying solely on limited individual experience. Algorithms appear to be a more reliable and objective form of intelligence, and their insights are now essential to modern industry and research.

Despite their power, we still need to develop spiritual discernment. An algorithm's knowledge is confined to what it's been taught to measure. It can't account for ethical considerations, moral nuance, or the messy, subjective human experience that defines a soul. Data is a powerful tool, but it's not a substitute for divine wisdom. This kind of spiritual discernment is the human capacity to navigate complexity and make choices based on a deeper truth. It is about listening for guidance from a source that is All in all as well as the Alpha and Omega—God, who is beyond our full understanding, comprehension, experience, and even desire. Ceding our judgment to these systems risks a perfectly optimized life that is shallow and without depth. We will have solved a problem but at the cost of our soul.

Myth 6: The Data and the Algorithms Simply Know Best

There's a quiet assumption that has taken root in our daily lives, a modern-day myth whispered not around a fire but through the glowing screens of our phones and laptops: the data and the algorithms simply know best. It's a compelling story, one we seem increasingly eager to believe. This narrative doesn't just present artificial intelligence as a helpful tool; it frames it as something more, an ultimate and impartial judge of truth, promising a level of precision and objectivity that we humans, with our messy emotions and tangled biases, could never hope to achieve on our own. It feels like a clean solution to the unpredictable chaos of being alive.

I see it everywhere, and I'm sure you do too. It starts with the small things, the almost trivial choices, like letting Siri or Alexa settle a dinner-table debate over a historical fact, or asking a GPS to find the "best" route without a second thought. But it doesn't stop there. We allow Netflix's recommendation engine to become the primary architect of our cultural diet and Amazon's algorithms to guide our consumption habits, all with the subtle but persistent assurance that these systems know what we want even better than we do. The AI works so seamlessly, so frictionlessly, that it's easy to miss the profound shift that's taking place under the surface. The message is clear and constant: if the algorithm suggests it, it must be right.

This isn't just about the march of technological progress; it points to a much deeper cultural pivot. We've been sold a compelling vision of a frictionless existence, a concept that Andy Crouch examines with startling clarity. He suggests that this relentless pursuit of an "easy everywhere" life subtly redefines our values, making convenience and effortlessness the ultimate virtues. In his book *The Tech-Wise Family*, Crouch notes that technology often makes us "more powerful but less profound," offering us a life of ease that can leave us feeling "oddly empty."[1]

Within this frictionless world, algorithms are the heroes. Their recommendations are marketed as objectively superior because they are grounded in immense datasets that seem to dwarf our own flawed and

1. Crouch, *Tech-Wise Family*, 52.

limited human perspectives. Yet this illusion of reliability comes at a cost we are only beginning to calculate. It quietly and systematically sidelines the very things that have guided human beings for millennia: gut feelings, communal wisdom, and perhaps most importantly for people of faith, spiritual discernment. The certainty offered by algorithms is, it turns out, a mirage, masking the hidden biases of its creators and the inherent limitations of its backward-looking data. In this grand trade-off, we risk losing something precious. The simple, profound practices—a moment of quiet, prayerful reflection, a slow and thoughtful conversation with trusted friends, the patient work of listening for the Spirit—get crowded out by the incessant hum of digital "solutions."

This is a concern that spiritual writers have been raising with increasing urgency. Ruth Haley Barton, for instance, has spent her life teaching that discernment is not a problem to be solved but a sacred act of deep listening. Her work calls people away from noise and into a quieter, attentive posture, arguing that true guidance is found not in formulas but in the patient practice of attuning the heart to the Spirit's movements. In her book *Sacred Compass*, she defines this practice with beautiful simplicity, stating that we must learn to "trust what we know in our bones," a knowing that comes from a life lived in God's presence.[2] It appears that genuine discernment requires far more than data; it requires a heart that is tuned in, ready for the often unpredictable and surprising movements of the Holy Spirit in a world increasingly dominated by the logic of predictable machines.

The Psychology of Deference

The myth that the algorithm knows best doesn't just thrive because the AI is impressive; it thrives because it plays directly into the predictable glitches of our own human psychology. We seem to be wired to defer to machines, especially when we're feeling tired, overwhelmed, or uncertain. This isn't just a hunch; it's a well-documented phenomenon known as automation bias. It's the simple, almost unconscious tendency to trust the output of an automated system over our own judgment, even when the evidence of our senses suggests something is wrong.

This deference to nonhuman authority stems from a cognitive preference for clear, quantifiable answers over the ambiguity of human

2. Barton, *Sacred Compass*, 38.

wisdom. The renowned psychologist Daniel Kahneman shed light on this very tendency long before the age of AI. His groundbreaking research identified two distinct systems of thinking: a fast, intuitive "System 1" and a slower, more logical "System 2." Automation bias seems to occur because deferring to a machine allows us to stay in the easy, low-effort mode of System 1, avoiding the hard cognitive work that System 2 demands. In his masterwork *Thinking, Fast and Slow*, Kahneman explains the lure of this cognitive shortcut: "System 2 is lazy . . . and it is often content to trust the plausible judgment of System 1."[3]

This creates a troubling paradox. For years, popular thinkers have celebrated the remarkable power of human intuition. Malcolm Gladwell, for one, built an entire book around this very idea, exploring how our brains are constantly making what he calls "thin-slice" judgments. His work champions the idea that our minds can make incredibly fast and often stunningly accurate decisions based on very limited information—a flash of insight or a gut feeling. In *Blink*, Gladwell states, "Our unconscious is a powerful force. But it's fallible. It's not a magic trick. It's a kind of thinking, a thinking that happens so fast . . . that we don't realize we are doing it."[4] Yet in our age, we are increasingly willing to silence that inner voice, to override those gut instincts, and to trust the algorithm instead.

We see this playing out with serious consequences in critical fields. In medicine, for example, a doctor with twenty years of clinical experience might feel a gut-level unease about a patient's symptoms, but an AI diagnostic tool, trained on millions of data points, suggests a more common and routine ailment. This isn't just a theoretical problem; it's a critique leveled by experts who see the danger in uncritically embracing AI's supposed infallibility. Gary Smith, a vocal critic of AI hype, warns that because current AI systems lack genuine comprehension of the world, they are prone to making "stupid" mistakes that a human with common sense would easily avoid. In *The AI Delusion*, Smith writes, "Computers are incredibly fast, accurate, and stupid. . . . Humans are incredibly slow, inaccurate, and brilliant."[5]

This bias creeps into almost every corner of our professional and personal lives. Consider the world of corporate hiring. I remember talking to a friend, Sarah, who works as a hiring manager at a fast-growing design firm. Overwhelmed by a tsunami of applications for a single opening,

3. Kahneman, *Thinking, Fast and Slow*, 44.

4. Gladwell, *Blink*, 15.

5. Smith, *AI Delusion*, 55.

her company invested in a sophisticated AI screening tool that promised to find the "perfect" candidates. And it was efficient. The system quickly flagged resumes stuffed with all the right industry keywords and Ivy League credentials. But Sarah felt a nagging sense of unease. She noticed that the candidates the AI loved all looked . . . the same. They had the same backgrounds, the same linear career paths. Trusting her intuition, that little whisper that Gladwell champions, she decided to spend a whole afternoon manually digging through the digital rejected pile. There, buried deep in the algorithmic graveyard, she found a candidate whose cover letter was electric with passion and whose portfolio demonstrated a kind of quirky, brilliant problem solving that the AI, in its rigid logic, had completely missed. Sarah had to fight for it, but she convinced her boss to give the candidate an interview. That person, she told me, ended up being one of the most creative and transformative hires the company had ever made, precisely because their mind worked differently. Sarah's story is not an argument against AI but a reminder that discernment, rooted in wisdom and experience, can see a person's potential in a way that data alone simply cannot.

The same troubling issues appear in fields like law enforcement, where the use of predictive policing algorithms can create dangerous feedback loops. These systems, often trained on biased historical arrest data, can end up directing police to over-patrol minority neighborhoods, which in turn leads to more arrests in those areas, which then "proves" to the algorithm that its original prediction was correct. The human cost of this is enormous.

Cathy O'Neil powerfully exposes how these mathematical models, which are often opaque and unregulated, can systematically perpetuate inequality under a veneer of technical authority. In her seminal book *Weapons of Math Destruction*, she issues a stark warning: "The math-powered applications powering the data economy were based on choices made by fallible human beings . . . and these models tend to punish the poor."[6]

Ultimately, automation bias is a human issue, not just a technical one. It's fed by our deep, primal desire for certainty and our culture's relentless obsession with efficiency. It's also amplified, it seems, by the very state of our modern minds. Johann Hari makes a compelling, if unsettling, case that our collective ability to pay deep attention has been systematically

6. O'Neil, *Weapons of Math Destruction*, 3.

fractured by the constant barrage of digital interruptions. This erosion of focus makes us more susceptible to outsourcing our thinking to machines as we lose the mental capacity and the confidence required for deep, independent judgment. As Johann Hari writes in *Stolen Focus*, "If we want to do what matters, we need to be able to focus . . . but our attention is being raided."[7] This constant state of distraction erodes our confidence in our own intuition—that subtle, quiet knowing that is honed not by data feeds but by years of lived experience, patient reflection, and, for people of faith, a deep and practiced spiritual attunement. In this new landscape, where algorithms promise a quick and easy answer for everything, we are in very real danger of losing the sacred art of discernment—that slow, deliberate, and deeply rewarding process of listening to our own hearts, to one another, and to the voice of God.

Why Spiritual Discernment Matters in the Age of AI

In the age of AI, spiritual discernment matters more than ever because it provides a necessary counterbalance to the limitations of AI systems. AI's logic is based on data and patterns, but divine justice is rooted in a relational, spiritual reality that machines can't grasp. Our human capacity for intuition, empathy, and a personal connection with God allows us to see truths and needs that an algorithm might miss. Ultimately, discernment is a matter of both personal faith and social justice, urging us to prioritize love and compassion over efficiency and metrics, ensuring our AI tools serve human dignity rather than undermining it.

Spiritual discernment is the sacred art of listening to the Spirit, a practice that enables us to see beyond ourselves and even the sum of all available data. While an algorithm can only analyze what has been, the Spirit can reveal a new way forward—a path of grace that defies logic. This distinction is crucial. AI is a powerful tool for analyzing past behavior and predicting future outcomes, but it is entirely contained within the box of what has already happened. It can tell you what the majority thinks, but it cannot whisper a truth to you that the world has not yet heard. This practice of listening to the Spirit is a fundamentally different way of knowing. It's not about computation; it's about communion. It requires us to slow down, to be quiet, and to open ourselves to a divine voice that is often subtle and counterintuitive. In a world obsessed with

7. Hari, *Stolen Focus*, 155.

speed and data, this act of stillness is a radical form of resistance. It is an intentional choice to join a sacred art—a journey of being shaped by the presence of God rather than by the pressures of the digital world. This sacred art also calls us into action. By listening to the Spirit, we are moved to care for the person the algorithm overlooks, to stand for the cause the data dismisses, and to choose love over efficiency. We are not just making better decisions; we are participating in God's work of justice and restoration in the world. Spiritual discernment is how we ensure that as we build an increasingly automated world, we do so with a human heart—one guided by faith, hope, love, clarity, and an original, but broader view.

The Theological Grounding of Discernment

In the quiet, reflective heart of the Christian tradition, discernment is not merely a tool for making better choices. It's a sacred gift, a spiritual practice that seeks to align the human heart with God's heart and perspective in a world that is mostly messy and self-obsessed. This practice is both ancient and urgently necessary today. The apostle Paul, in his letters to the early church, speaks of "distinguishing between spirits" (1 Cor 12:10) as a specific gift of the Holy Spirit—a divine enablement to distinguish between truth and falsehood, between divine guidance and purely human impulses. This isn't about having a kind of spiritual superpower; it appears to be about cultivating a deep sensitivity to the character and movement of God.

This theological understanding anchors us in something profound, especially when digital solutions promise us a shortcut to certainty. Discernment is rooted in the audacious belief that God actually speaks—not always in a booming voice from the heavens, but through the patient reading of Scripture, the quiet stirrings of prayer, the moral resonance of our conscience, and the collective wisdom of our community. The prophet Isaiah gives voice to this intimate guidance with a beautiful promise: "Your ears will hear a voice behind you, saying, 'This is the way; walk in it'" (Isa 30:21). This is a fundamentally relational kind of guidance. It is not formulaic; it requires trust, patience, and a radical openness to a will that is not our own.

This stands in stark contrast to the logic of an algorithm. An algorithm operates on the past, on predictable patterns and probabilities. The Holy Spirit, as Jesus describes so poetically, moves in a way that defies prediction: "The wind blows wherever it pleases. You hear its sound, but you cannot tell where it comes from or where it is going" (John 3:8). This unpredictability challenges the AI-driven culture of optimization and control, inviting us instead into a posture of surrender and trust in a divine mystery that cannot be coded.

Scripture, in this light, is not an instruction manual but a cornerstone of this discerning life. The psalmist's prayer, "Your word is a lamp for my feet, a light on my path" (Ps 119:105), suggests that God's word illuminates our way when our own logic—or our AI tools—falls short. Prayer, too, is vital, but not as a spiritual vending machine for answers. Thinkers on the spiritual life, like M. Robert Mulholland Jr., have long taught that prayer is less about demanding things from God and more about simply abiding in God's presence, creating the quiet space where discernment can finally emerge. In his book *Invitation to a Journey*, Mulholland explains that spiritual formation is "a process of being conformed to the image of Christ for the sake of others," a transformation that cannot happen without the slow work of prayer.[8] Barbara Holmes speaks of discernment as a contemplative act, one that requires us to listen deeply in a culture that values speed and certainty above all else. Her book *Listening in the Dark* challenges us to embrace "the holy darkness" where God often speaks most clearly, a posture directly at odds with the algorithm's promise of a pre-calculated, risk-free path.[9]

Consider the story of Rachel, a young woman discerning a career change. She was a graphic designer, good at her job, but feeling an unshakable sense of emptiness. The AI-driven career apps she consulted were full of sensible advice, analyzing her skills and market trends to recommend a pivot into UX/UI design for a higher salary. It was the logical choice, yet it felt hollow. Overwhelmed, she brought her dilemma to her church's small prayer group. They didn't offer her a five-step plan. Instead, for weeks, they simply sat with her, prayed with her, and together they read passages of Scripture, including the gentle reassurance of Ps 23. In that quiet, patient, and prayerful space, something shifted. Rachel began to sense a gentle but persistent pull, not toward a more lucrative tech job, but toward a role at a local nonprofit that served refugee families. It made no sense on paper; the pay was lower, the future less certain. But it felt, for the first time, like home. Her choice wasn't a rejection of AI but

8. Mulholland, *Invitation to a Journey*, 28.

9. Holmes, *Listening in the Dark*, 35.

a profound prioritization of spiritual discernment, a trust in the Spirit's whisper over the loud, confident predictions of the algorithm.

Psychological Insights on Intuition

Interestingly, this theological understanding of discernment finds a surprising echo in the world of psychology. The practice of listening for a divine nudge or a sense of inner peace is not so far removed from the psychological concept of intuition—what Malcolm Gladwell famously called "thin-slice" judgments. His work explores those moments of rapid, subconscious assessment that draw on a deep well of experience, emotion, and embodied knowledge, often proving more accurate than our most deliberate analysis. It's the seasoned firefighter who just knows a building is about to collapse, or the art expert who can spot a forgery in a single glance.

Psychology suggests that this intuitive capacity arises from our brain's remarkable ability to process thousands of subtle, nonverbal cues—body language, tone of voice, the atmosphere of a room—that a purely logical or algorithmic analysis would completely miss. Yet, in the age of AI, we seem to be training ourselves to systematically override these instincts. We defer to the data-driven system that promises cold, hard objectivity, and in doing so, we risk severing our connection to what many psychologists call our gut-level wisdom. This isn't just a spiritual loss; it may actually lead to poorer decisions. When we sideline our own holistic insight, honed over years of lived experience, we are ignoring a powerful form of intelligence.

Our intuition is deeply connected to our physical bodies. It's not just a thought in our head; it's a felt sense. Sian Beilock has explored this connection extensively. Her research on embodied cognition demonstrates that how we think is profoundly shaped by our physical experiences and bodily states. Our gut feelings are, in a very real sense, the wisdom of the body speaking to the mind. In an age where we spend so much time disembodied, staring at screens, we can lose touch with this vital source of information. In her book *How the Body Knows Its Mind*, Beilock explains, "Our body is not a passive vehicle for our brain. . . . Our body is part of our mind."[10]

10. Beilock, *How the Body Knows*, 18.

Think of James, a family doctor who had been practicing for over thirty years. His clinic had recently implemented a new AI diagnostic tool, which was excellent at flagging common illnesses based on symptom checklists. One afternoon, a patient came in with what the AI flagged as a routine respiratory infection. All the data pointed that way. But James felt a knot in his stomach. Something was off. It was the patient's color, the slight hesitation in his breathing—a dozen tiny cues the AI couldn't process. Trusting that intuitive unease, that felt sense honed through decades of seeing thousands of patients, he paused, said a quick, silent prayer, and ordered a more comprehensive set of tests. His hunch was right. The patient had a rare and aggressive form of pneumonia that, had it not been caught, could have been fatal. James's story isn't a dismissal of AI—it was a useful tool. But it's a powerful testament to the fact that human intuition, especially when guided by experience and faith, can see what an algorithm cannot.

For Christians, this intuition is not seen as separate from faith but as deeply intertwined with it. The Spirit often speaks through that quiet nudge, that inexplicable sense of peace or unrest that guided the apostle Paul on his journeys. Adam McHugh speaks of this as a form of "embodied listening," where our hearts, minds, and bodies work together to discern truth.[11] By intentionally cultivating our God-given intuition through prayer and attentiveness, we can begin to reclaim a vital aspect of our humanity, resisting the myth that machines know better than the human heart, which was created for connection with God.

Social and Ethical Dimensions

This journey of discernment isn't just a private, internal affair. It has massive social and ethical implications, especially in a world where AI is increasingly making decisions that affect entire communities. Algorithms are now involved in hiring, criminal justice, and healthcare, and they often operate with a logic that prioritizes metrics over morality.

Scholars in the field of technology ethics, such as Kate Crawford, have documented how AI systems can inadvertently perpetuate and even amplify existing societal biases. In her book *Atlas of AI: Power, Politics, and the Planetary Costs of Artificial Intelligence*, she provides a sober analysis of how systems trained on flawed historical data—data that reflects our

11. McHugh, *Listening Life*, 91–92.

past and present injustices—will inevitably produce biased outcomes, all while being presented to the public as objective and neutral tools. This creates what some critics call ethics washing, where tech companies and institutions tout their bias-mitigation features while neatly sidestepping the deeper moral questions about whether these systems should be used at all.

We see this most starkly in the use of predictive policing algorithms, which often rely on historical arrest data to allocate police resources. If a particular neighborhood has been historically over-policed, the data will reflect more arrests there, leading the algorithm to direct even more police to that area, creating a self-perpetuating cycle of surveillance and criminalization. This is a clear example of how a tool designed for efficiency can become an engine of injustice. Virginia Eubanks has documented the devastating human cost of these systems. Her work exposes how automated decision-making systems, far from being neutral, often punish and pathologize the poor and marginalized. They create a digital poorhouse that operates with a veneer of objective, technological authority, making it incredibly difficult to challenge. In her book *Automating Inequality*, Eubanks argues that "the digital poorhouse is not a glitch. It is a feature of the system" that allows society to manage the poor without having to see them.[12]

In faith communities, the social and ethical dimensions of discernment are equally critical. There's a growing trend for churches to use data analytics for everything from optimizing sermon topics to targeting outreach campaigns to specific demographics. Jonathan Draper raises a crucial question about this development. He observes that while these tools can be useful, they carry the risk of subtly shifting a church's focus from faithfulness to effectiveness, from being Spirit led to being market driven. In his book *Pastoral Theology in a Digital Age*, Draper warns that a church guided more by viral trends and data analytics than by prayerful discernment may lose its prophetic voice, conforming to cultural pressures rather than God's countercultural call. True discernment calls a community to weigh its decisions not against metrics of success but against the enduring values of God's kingdom—love, justice, mercy, and human dignity. It's a reminder of Andy Crouch's principle that AI should always be a servant to human flourishing, never its master.

12. Eubanks, *Automating Inequality*, 182.

I think of a nonprofit I know that was using an AI tool to help allocate resources for a hunger relief program. The algorithm, based on population density and census data, logically prioritized the city's urban core. But during a board meeting, one member, who came from a rural part of the county, pushed them to pause. She urged them to set aside the data for a moment and listen—to listen to the stories from her community, and to listen in prayer for God's guidance. Through that process of communal discernment, the board realized that while the need in the city was great, the isolation and lack of services in the rural areas created a different, more hidden kind of desperation. They made the inefficient choice to redirect a significant portion of their resources to those overlooked communities, a decision that addressed a profound need the data had completely missed. That wasn't a rejection of AI; it was a profound commitment to an ethical discernment rooted in faith and justice.

The Urgency of Cultivating Discernment Now

The age of AI is not some distant, sci-fi future looming on the horizon. It has arrived. It is here, now, and it is reshaping every facet of our existence with a speed and subtlety that can be breathtaking. It's in the friendly voice of the Alexa assistant on the kitchen counter, the personalized playlists that seem to read our mood on Spotify, and the endless, scrolling feeds on social media that curate a reality just for us. This integration is so seamless that it often operates invisibly, quietly steering our choices, shaping our beliefs, and nudging our behaviors in ways we barely notice. The chatbot that answers our questions, the algorithm that suggests our next career move, the analytics that influence healthcare and criminal justice—these are no longer novelties; they are the new, humming infrastructure of daily life.

What feels most staggering about this moment is the sheer pace of it all. This rapid, almost frantic integration seems to be outpacing our collective ability to reflect on its consequences, either ethically or spiritually. There's a relentless corporate and consumer demand for the next, fastest, most efficient thing, which leaves very little room for us to pause and ask the deeper questions.

This speed is not accidental, as some scholars have argued; it is a core feature of the economic model that drives much of the modern internet. Shoshana Zuboff contends that the entire model of what she calls "surveillance capitalism" depends on moving faster than we can comprehend, gathering our personal data to predict and modify our behavior for profit. The system is designed to keep us clicking, consuming, and engaging, not reflecting. In her landmark book *The Age of Surveillance Capitalism*, Zuboff writes, "Surveillance capitalism . . . claims human experience as free raw material for translation into behavioral data . . . effectively exiling us from our own behavior."[13]

This creates a culture of instant answers that erodes the patience required for genuine spiritual inquiry. Our smart assistants, now fixtures in millions of households, can answer "What's the weather?" and "What's the meaning of life?" with the same frictionless efficiency. This subtly devalues the slow, often arduous process of wrestling with mystery. Nowhere is this speed more consequential than in the formation of our beliefs and identities. Platforms like TikTok and YouTube have become the primary spiritual guides for millions, especially the young. Their algorithms, designed to maximize engagement above all else, can lead users down rabbit holes of extremist ideology or disorienting new-age spiritualities, all served up with the same authority as legitimate sources.

Tara Isabella Burton has explored how this digital ecosystem is fundamentally changing how people construct meaning. Her work documents a shift away from traditional institutions and toward a kind of remixed spirituality, where individuals pull from a vast menu of online beliefs to create a bespoke identity. This is often done without the grounding of a stable community or the wisdom of tradition. In her book *Strange Rites*, Burton observes that "we are not secular; we are intuitionist . . . relying on our feelings to guide us through the spiritual marketplace."[14]

This rapid, algorithm-driven identity formation demands an urgent response. If communities of faith do not actively and intentionally cultivate practices of discernment now, we risk raising a generation of passive consumers of AI's outputs, people who have lost the ability to hear the quiet, steady voice of God amidst the deafening digital noise. I think of a young woman named Emily from my community. A thoughtful and bright teenager, her entire worldview was being shaped by her TikTok feed. One week, her algorithm was bombarding her with charismatic prosperity-gospel influencers. The next, it was promoting a kind of fatalistic, new-age astrology. She was confused, anxious, and felt spiritually

13. Zuboff, *Age of Surveillance Capitalism*, 10.

14. Burton, *Strange Rites*, 80.

adrift. Thankfully, her youth group leaders didn't just give her another set of beliefs to adopt. Instead, they walked with her. They facilitated a discernment process, teaching her to pause, to pray, to bring her questions to Scripture, and to listen to the wisdom of the community. Through this slow, relational process, Emily began to learn how to question the authority of the algorithm and to seek God's guidance for herself. Her story isn't unique; it's a parable for our time, underscoring the critical, urgent need for discernment in an age where AI shapes beliefs faster than we can even recognize.

Spiritual and Communal Risks

The unchecked and undiscerned integration of AI poses significant spiritual and communal risks, particularly for communities of faith. When a church's vision and practices are guided more by viral trends and algorithmic insights than by the patient leading of the Spirit, they risk losing their very soul. Jonathan Draper has written thoughtfully about how churches, in a well-intentioned effort to be relevant, increasingly rely on data-driven tools for everything from tracking attendance to planning sermons. This can subtly transform a spiritual community into a data-driven enterprise, where metrics of popularity begin to trump the pursuit of purpose, and the Spirit's whisper is drowned out by the clamor of digital noise.

One of the most profound risks is the erosion of a prophetic vision. A church chasing algorithmic popularity will inevitably begin to sand off its prophetic edges. It becomes hesitant to speak uncomfortable truths about justice, mercy, or sacrifice because those topics don't "perform" as well online. The community starts to mirror the values of the culture rather than offering a compelling, countercultural alternative. This is a concern raised by Barbara Holmes, who warns that when communities conform to digital trends, they risk silencing the very voices that call them to be more faithful, more courageous, and more true to the gospel.

Another serious risk is the fragmentation of the community itself. The personalized nature of AI—the customized news feeds, the tailored recommendations—is explicitly designed to create what Andy Crouch has called "echo chambers." In a church context, this can manifest as members all consuming different spiritual content online, leading to wildly divergent beliefs and political convictions, even among people sitting in the same pews. This digital fragmentation actively works against communal cohesion. Without the shared practice of discerning God's will together, a congregation can easily become a mere collection of disconnected individuals, each floating in their own curated content bubble, unable to hear the Spirit's collective call.

Perhaps the deepest spiritual cost is the loss of stillness. Discernment requires patience, quiet, and an ability to wait—practices that are fundamentally at odds with the instant-solution ethos of AI. The Bible is filled with injunctions to "be still, and know that I am God" (e.g., Ps 46:10), yet our digital culture trains us to avoid stillness at all costs, filling every spare moment with content, noise, and stimulation.

Nicholas Carr has argued that this constant digital overstimulation is literally rewiring our brains. His work suggests that the internet, with its endless hypertext and notifications, is reducing our capacity for the kind of deep, contemplative thought that is essential for both critical thinking and spiritual reflection. In his book *The Shallows*, Carr explains, "The deep reading that used to come naturally has become a struggle. . . . We have become a society of skimmers."[15]

This constant state of mental agitation leaves communities spiritually vulnerable, far more likely to make decisions based on the most recent data trend rather than on a deep, prayerful listening for divine guidance. I know of a church in a rural community that, worried about declining numbers, adopted an AI-driven outreach tool. The tool analyzed local demographics and suggested they target young, affluent families with trendy events. But many in the congregation felt a deep unease, a sense that this path was a disconnect from their quiet, historical mission to serve the aging and often lonely members of their own community. They made the courageous decision to enter a process of discernment. Through prayer, reading Scripture, and listening to one another, they chose to focus their energy on a simple, low-tech ministry of home visits and communal meals for their seniors. It wasn't the optimal strategy for growth according to the data, but the decision brought a profound sense of joy, unity, and spiritual renewal to their church. Their story is a powerful reminder that true faithfulness is found in discernment, not data.

15. Carr, *Shallows*, 6.

Opportunity for the Church: Beyond the Policy Manual

In this confusing, data-driven landscape, the church is presented with a profound opportunity: to become a living, breathing sanctuary of discernment in a world starved for it. Yet, it's precisely here that a common and dangerous misunderstanding takes root. Many leaders have sadly begun to equate the sacred act of spiritual discernment with the far more straightforward task of consulting organizational policies. This is a critical error in navigation. It's the mistake of a traveler who, upon reaching the edge of a familiar map, decides the journey is over, rather than learning to read the stars. A policy is a static tool, a two-dimensional representation of past decisions. Discernment is a living, three-dimensional process, an active listening for the divine will in the unfiltered reality of the present moment. To confuse the two is to mistake the map for the journey.

This is not an argument against policy. Denominational policies and church governance are not only necessary they are often the fruit of hard-won wisdom. They are the riverbanks that keep the life of a community from devolving into chaos. Think of child protection policies or financial accountability procedures. These are expressions of love and justice, designed to create safe and trustworthy spaces. Policies are the institutional memory, the guardrails that protect the vulnerable.

But there comes a point where the map runs out. The riverbanks of policy can guide the flow of the water, but they cannot tell the river where to go when it reaches a new and uncharted landscape. This is the precise point where so many communities falter. They face a novel challenge—the rise of AI, questions of human identity, the call for racial justice—and their first instinct is to reach for the policy manual. The manual, however, is silent on these new questions. This is where policy, if treated as an idol, becomes a barrier to the Spirit's work. It allows leaders to say, "My hands are tied; this is just the rule." It absolves them of the terrifying and vulnerable work of actually listening for God in the messy, ambiguous present.

The Christian Scriptures, however, consistently model a different path. When the early believers, in the book of Acts, faced a crisis over whether Gentiles needed to follow Jewish law, there was no policy to consult. This was an unprecedented, off-the-map challenge. They didn't default to their most ancient policy—the Torah. Instead, they embraced the messy, unpredictable process of discernment. They gathered, they prayed, they shared their personal experiences of the Spirit's movement, and they listened intently to one another. Their conclusion was not a citation of a rule but a profound declaration of a living reality: "It seemed good to the Holy Spirit and to us" (Acts 15:28). This phrase captures the very heart of discernment: a cooperative, relational, and ongoing effort between human reflection and divine insight. It is a process that trusts that God is still speaking, still leading, still doing a new thing.

I think again of a large city church facing the decision to relocate. The AI analytics tool was their modern-day policy manual, offering a clear, data-driven, and defensible path forward. It was the safe choice. But the pastor and the people sensed a deeper calling. By convening discernment circles, they were choosing the harder, more vulnerable path. They were admitting, "The map we have doesn't seem to account for the landscape of our hearts." They invited members from all walks of life—the elderly saint, the young activist, the new immigrant family—to pray, to reflect, and to share what they were hearing from God. Through that process, they discerned a clear call to stay, to reinvest in their current neighborhood, and to be a beacon of hope in the heart of the city. The decision defied all the data-driven logic, but it profoundly strengthened the community's identity and became a powerful witness to their neighbors that their choices were driven by a living faithfulness, not just a financial bottom line.

The Intergenerational Importance

The urgency of cultivating discernment is magnified when we consider its intergenerational importance. We have, for perhaps the first time in history, multiple generations living together with vastly different native relationships to AI, and this presents both a challenge and a tremendous opportunity. Younger believers, digital natives who have grown up immersed in AI-driven systems, are fluent in the language of this new world but are also uniquely vulnerable to its pitfalls. Older believers often bring a lifetime of spiritual practice and a deeper attunement to the Spirit but may feel intimidated by the pace of change. Bridging this divide through shared practices of discernment could create a powerful synergy.

Younger generations are awash in a sea of algorithmic influence. Their identities and beliefs are profoundly shaped by these forces. The psychologist Jean M. Twenge has documented how the generation she calls "iGen"—those who grew up with smartphones—exhibit different social and emotional patterns, often marked by higher rates of anxiety.

Her research suggests that while digitally connected, they often feel more isolated. In her book *iGen*, she observes, "The more time teens spend looking at screens, the more likely they are to report symptoms of depression."[16] For this generation, spiritual discernment is not a luxury; it is a vital lifeline.

At the same time, older generations possess a treasure of lived experience. They have walked with God through decades of change, joy, and sorrow. They know what it means to wait on the Lord, to wrestle in prayer, and to find guidance in Scripture without the aid of an app. The spiritual writer Richard Rohr often speaks of the unique wisdom that comes in the "second half of life." He argues that this stage of life is not about decline but about a "falling upward" into a deeper, more gracious way of seeing. It is a time when the ego's need for certainty begins to fall away, making space for a more profound trust in God. In his book *Falling Upward*, Rohr writes that "in the second half of life, we are less interested in 'law' and more interested in 'love.'"[17] By sharing these hard-won perspectives, elders can anchor a community's discernment process, offering a patience that directly counters the frantic immediacy of digital culture.

The transformation happens when these generations are brought together intentionally. I saw a beautiful example of this in a church that created an intergenerational discernment group to address declining engagement among its youth. The teens brought their fluency with technology and their honest insights. The elders brought their deep knowledge of Scripture and their decades of experience in prayer. They didn't just meet; they practiced listening to one another and to God together. The teens showed the elders how to use social media in a way that felt authentic, and the elders guided the teens through a process of prayerfully discerning a mission project. The result was a new community dinner initiative, promoted through Instagram but rooted in the ancient practice of hospitality. The process united the generations, transformed their community, and served as a living testament that discernment is a shared journey, not a solitary task.

16. Twenge, *iGen*, 105.

17. Rohr, *Falling Upward*, 45.

Formation Through Discernment—Soul, Leadership, and Community

In an age where algorithms and digital noise threaten to drown out the very whisper of God, spiritual discernment cannot be a passive hope; it must be an active discipline. It is a practice that intentionally forms the soul, shaping us into people who can perceive and respond to divine wisdom. This is not a new idea. For centuries, Christians have cultivated an interior life through specific, time-tested practices. The way of the desert—the ancient tradition of monastics who retreated from the noise of empire to seek God in the silence—offers a profound model for our own digitally saturated world. Disciplines like prayerful listening, the Ignatian Examen, and the intentional use of silence and solitude are not escapes from reality. They are countercultural acts of resistance that create the inner space necessary to hear God's voice.

Formation of the Soul

Prayerful listening is the foundation. Unlike the instant answers provided by an AI assistant, this practice invites us into a radical posture of waiting. It is the conscious choice to quiet our own agendas, our own anxieties, our own internal chatter, and simply be present to God. The prophet Isaiah's promise, "Your ears will hear a voice behind you, saying, 'This is the way; walk in it'" (Isa 30:21), implies a listener who is actually paying attention. This requires creating real, tangible space in our lives free from digital distraction, where we can listen without the incessant pressure to consume, react, or respond. Richard Foster, a master teacher on spiritual disciplines, emphasizes that this kind of prayer is not about perfecting a technique. In his classic work *Celebration of Discipline*, he describes it as a move beyond self-centered chatter and into a quiet attentiveness to the Divine Presence. He writes, "Real prayer comes not from gritting our teeth but from falling in love."[18]

The Ignatian Examen is another powerful discipline for cultivating an attentive heart. Developed by St. Ignatius of Loyola, this simple, structured prayer involves reflecting on one's day to notice where God was present and where we felt distracted or drawn away from a path of love. In our time, this practice is a direct antidote to the logic of the algorithm.

18. Foster, *Celebration of Discipline*, 33.

An algorithm tracks our clicks and engagement to feed us more of what we already want. The Examen, by contrast, trains our attention to track the movements of the Spirit, helping us notice the subtle nudges toward gratitude, compassion, and courage that we might have otherwise missed in the blur of a busy day. It's a way of slowly, intentionally recalibrating our spiritual awareness. James Martin, SJ, has been a masterful guide in making this ancient practice accessible. He explains that the Examen is not an exercise in moral scorekeeping but a way to find God in the ordinary messiness of our lives. As he puts it in *The Jesuit Guide to (Almost) Everything*, "The Examen is a way of noticing where God has been active in your day . . . finding God in all things."[19]

Finally, the disciplines of silence and solitude are perhaps the most countercultural and necessary of all. As Adam McHugh argues in *The Listening Life*, silence creates a "sacred space" where we can hear God's voice apart from the digital clamor.[20] In the age of AI, where notifications and algorithmic feeds are designed to fill every single unoccupied moment, choosing silence is a radical act. It requires us to intentionally disconnect from our devices and embrace a stillness that can initially feel deeply uncomfortable. Yet, it is in that discomfort, in that quiet, that our souls can finally breathe. Thomas Merton, the great contemplative monk of the twentieth century, understood this profoundly. He saw that solitude was not about escaping other people but about finding oneself and, in doing so, finding God. In *Thoughts in Solitude*, Merton writes, "It is in deep solitude that I find the gentleness with which I can truly love my brothers."[21]

I think of Anna, a college student I know who was feeling completely overwhelmed by the optimization culture of her university. Her calendar, her study habits, her social life, even her career prospects were being shaped by apps and platforms promising the most efficient path to success. Feeling lost and anxious, she began, hesitantly at first, to practice the Examen each evening. She also carved out fifteen phone-free minutes each morning for silent prayer. At first, it was agonizing. Her mind raced. But over time, these small acts of resistance began to change her. She started to notice small moments of joy, to feel a growing sense of a loving presence that had nothing to do with her GPA, and to discern a quiet

19. Martin, *Jesuit Guide*, 55.
20. McHugh, *Listening Life*, 24–28.
21. Merton, *Thoughts in Solitude*, 88.

calling toward mentorship—a path that no algorithm would have suggested but that felt, for the first time, deeply true. Her story shows how these ancient disciplines can form a soul, guiding us with grace through the relentless noise of the AI age.

Formation of Leadership

In this new landscape, pastors and community leaders have a crucial and challenging role: they must model a way of being that prioritizes spiritual discernment over data-driven efficiency. A leader's most powerful tool for fostering a discerning community is not a new program but their own posture of prayerful inquiry. In an age when congregations face immense pressure to adopt AI tools for everything from scheduling and outreach to sermon planning, a leader's willingness to say, "Let's pause and wait on God," is a profound act of faith. This means intentionally convening retreats, not for strategic planning, but for spiritual listening and guiding their teams to seek God's will before making any major decision.

This kind of leadership is about creating spaces where the Spirit's voice can actually be heard. Tod Bolsinger, who writes about leadership in uncertain times, argues that when you are "off the map," the leader's job is not to have all the answers but to maintain a "calm and non-anxious presence" that allows the group to learn its way forward together. This is precisely what a discerning leader does. They model a trust in God's presence that is more powerful than the fear of uncertainty, creating the psychological and spiritual safety for a community to risk listening for a new word from God. In his book *Canoeing the Mountains*, Bolsinger suggests that the essential challenge for leaders is to navigate "adaptive challenges" that require new learning, not just technical fixes.[22]

Scripture is filled with examples of leaders who waited on God. Moses, before leading Israel out of slavery, spent long periods in solitude, seeking God's guidance. The apostle Paul frequently changed his missionary plans because he discerned the Spirit's leading in a different direction. And Nehemiah, before embarking on the massive project of rebuilding Jerusalem's walls, didn't start with a feasibility study; he started with a season of prayer and fasting.

I think of a pastor I'll call Michael. His church board, full of successful businesspeople, was pushing him to use a new AI-powered analytics

22. Bolsinger, *Canoeing the Mountains*, 42.

tool to optimize their sermon planning based on engagement data and popular search terms. They wanted a more efficient, predictable way to grow the church. Instead of arguing with them, Michael invited them to a day-long retreat. He didn't bring charts or counterproposals. He simply led them in a quiet, prayerful reading of Prov 3:5–6: "Trust in the Lord with all your heart and lean not on your own understanding; in all your ways submit to him, and he will make your paths straight." Through hours of silence and honest conversation, the team discerned a deep need within their community, not for more polished content, but for healing and connection. They scrapped the AI plan and committed to a sermon series on lament and hope. Michael's leadership didn't just change the church's preaching schedule; it modeled a different way of being for his entire congregation, a way that trusted the Spirit over the spreadsheet.

Formation of Community

Though modeled by leaders, discernment is not a top-down directive; it is a communal practice that shapes the very identity of a community, transforming it into a Spirit-led body that collectively reflects God's wisdom. As Barbara Holmes reminds us, discernment is a collective act, where a diversity of voices, experiences, and perspectives are brought together to listen for the Spirit's guidance. Practices like discernment circles, shared fasting, and listening posts are essential for creating spaces where a congregation can genuinely seek God's will together, ensuring that major decisions reflect a deep communal wisdom rather than the latest algorithmic trend.

Discernment circles, small groups of diverse members gathered for the specific purpose of praying and listening together about a particular issue, are an incredibly powerful tool. I know a church that used this practice to navigate a painful budget crisis. Instead of immediately turning to a financial planning tool that would have likely recommended cutting their outreach programs, the leadership convened several discernment circles composed of young and old, rich and poor, new members and founding families. They prayed, they read the story of the loaves and fishes, and they shared their hopes and fears. Through this process, they discerned a unified call not to cut their ministry to the homeless but to expand it, trusting that God would provide. That decision, born of communal listening, not only guided them through the crisis but also strengthened their unity and deepened their faith in a way that simply making a spreadsheet-driven cut never could have.

Shared fasting, another ancient practice, can be powerfully repurposed for the AI age. Fasting has always been about preparing a community to hear God's voice by stripping away distractions and cultivating a collective sense of dependence. In our time, a communal fast from technology—setting aside phones, social media, and streaming services for a set period—can be a profound way to amplify this practice. As Andy Crouch has argued, intentionally stepping away from the constant noise of our devices is one of the most effective ways to create the interior quiet needed to hear God.

Finally, listening posts—structured gatherings where the primary goal is to hear from a wide range of perspectives, especially from those on the margins—are vital for just and compassionate discernment. The theologian Dietrich Bonhoeffer wrote powerfully about the spiritual significance of Christian community. He argued that we see Christ through one another. This means that listening to our brothers and sisters, especially those whose voices are often ignored, is a way of listening for the voice of Christ himself. In his beautiful book *Life Together*, Bonhoeffer writes, "The first service that one owes to others in the fellowship consists in listening to them. Just as love to God begins with listening to His Word, so the beginning of love for the brethren is learning to listen to them."[23] These communal practices are a direct challenge to the individualistic, data-driven ethos of our time.

Additional Reflection

The path of discernment does not require a complete rejection of AI; rather, it calls us to integrate it wisely, ensuring that our AI tools remain our servants, not our masters. Prayer apps, guided online retreats, and digital Scripture resources can be wonderful aids to the spiritual life, but they must be used with care and a critical eye, lest they inadvertently shortcut the very deep listening we are trying to cultivate. The key is to use AI to augment our human capacity for discernment, not to replace it.

Felicia Wu Song, a sociologist who studies technology and spiritual formation, offers a helpful lens for this. She argues that our devices are not neutral; they are designed to make us restless, constantly seeking the

23. Bonhoeffer, *Life Together*, 98.

next notification, the next piece of content, the next digital affirmation. This restlessness is the enemy of the stillness required for discernment. The challenge, then, is to use AI in ways that promote presence, place, and personhood, rather than allowing it to pull us into a state of distracted placelessness. In her insightful book *Restless Devices*, she notes that digital tools can easily become "technologies of distraction" that keep us from the hard work of communion.[24]

It's also crucial to be wary of spiritual shortcuts. Many apps now promise quick, AI-driven spiritual insights, personalized devotionals, or personality quizzes that claim to reveal our spiritual path. While perhaps entertaining, these tools often bypass the slow, patient, and sometimes difficult work of genuine discernment. As Barbara Holmes writes, true discernment requires a willingness to sit in the darkness of not knowing, trusting that God's light will dawn in its own time, not on our schedule.

I think of a young adult group I observed that was trying to use technology wisely. They used a prayer app to provide a common Scripture passage and some reflective prompts for their weekly discernment about a community service project. But their leader made a crucial move: he asked everyone to put their phones away for the first twenty minutes of their meeting for silent, tech-free reflection on the passage. Then, they shared what had emerged in the silence. They used the app to organize the logistics of their project, but their decision-making was grounded in a shared, embodied, prayerful presence. It was a beautiful example of how AI can be a helpful tool that supports, rather than dominates, the sacred work of discernment.

Ultimately, discernment is more than a practice; it is a transformative discipline that forms us over time. It shapes our souls, our leaders, and our communities into bodies that are more attuned to and reflective of the character of Christ. This formation is a powerful gospel witness in a world seduced by the false promises of AI. It demonstrates that true wisdom, lasting peace, and genuine community are found not in data but in the divine.

Conclusion

This chapter has navigated the quiet, pervasive myth of our time: that the data and the algorithms simply know best. We began by exploring how

24. Song, *Restless Devices*, 125.

our own psychological vulnerabilities, like automation bias, make us susceptible to this alluring promise of a frictionless, data-driven life. We've seen the high cost of this myth, as it encourages us to sideline our own God-given intuition and can lead to real-world injustices when biased AI systems are trusted uncritically. In response, this chapter has argued that spiritual discernment is the essential counterbalance. It is a sacred art of listening for God's guidance that integrates our theology, psychology, and ethics, offering a form of wisdom that is deeper and more holistic than any algorithm can provide.

The unprecedented speed of AI's integration into our lives makes cultivating this practice an urgent necessity, not a casual hobby. The path forward is one of intentional formation. This is a discipline that shapes the individual soul through practices like prayerful listening and silence, that calls leaders to model a prayerful posture over data-driven efficiency, and that transforms a community into a body that can listen for the Spirit's voice together. In the age of AI, our most human act is to choose the slow, patient, sacred work of discernment. It is how we ensure our AI tools remain our servants, not our masters, and how we become a people who navigate this new world with a wisdom that transcends data.

Chapter 7

Leading Inner Healing and Growth

AI HELPS US GROW in terms of performance and metrics. The myth that personal growth is simply a matter of numbers is powerful because it leverages AI's ability to track and quantify our lives. With smartwatches, productivity apps, and personal dashboards, we can now measure everything from our sleep quality to our daily steps, from our reading speed to our work output. This provides a clear, actionable path to self-improvement. It feels empowering to see a graph of your progress, to set a numerical goal, and to receive real-time feedback on your performance. AI tools can analyze our habits, identify inefficiencies, and provide personalized recommendations for improvement. It offers a tangible way to level up our lives, making growth feel concrete, efficient, and achievable. The appeal of a life optimized for peak performance is hard to resist, and the data seems to prove that we're on the right track.

However, the belief that we can reduce personal growth to a set of metrics is a dangerous illusion. Even as AI becomes sophisticated enough to provide psychological advice and distill the knowledge of neuroscience, it cannot lead to inner healing and growth. True personal growth is not a linear climb but a messy, qualitative, often unquantifiable journey. It's found in moments that can't be measured by an app: the quiet courage of a difficult conversation, the empathy that grows from a moment of shared vulnerability, or the joy of creative expression with no commercial purpose. An algorithm can optimize your workout, but it can't measure the resilience gained from failure. It can track your reading speed, but it can't capture the profound shift in perspective that comes from a single paragraph. By fixating on metrics, we risk mistaking the shadow for the substance—pursuing optimization while losing touch with the human experiences that define growth.

Myth 7: Personal Growth Equals Performance and Metrics

There's a quiet but insistent whisper in our digitally saturated world, a myth that has seeped into our workplaces, our gyms, our friendships, and even our spiritual lives. It's the myth that personal growth is the same thing as performance. It is the idea that flourishing can be captured on a dashboard, that progress can be tracked on a spreadsheet, and that a life well-lived can be optimized, measured, and mastered. This narrative, supercharged by the logic of artificial intelligence, equates the deep, mysterious process of becoming more fully human with a set of quantifiable metrics: key performance indicators (KPIs), productivity scores, and algorithmically generated goals.

We see it everywhere, don't we? It's the fitness tracker on our wrist, buzzing with approval when we hit ten thousand steps but remaining silently judgmental on days of much-needed rest. It's the meditation app that congratulates us on a thirty-day streak, subtly implying that the goal is the streak itself, not the inner peace it's meant to foster. It's the social media platform where our personal worth feels inextricably linked to the number of likes and followers we can accumulate. The message is relentless: if it cannot be measured, it does not count. Success is an upward-trending graph. Failure, or even just stillness, is a dip in the data that needs to be corrected.

This isn't just a fringe idea for tech bros in Silicon Valley; it has become the default operating system for modern life. Productivity apps like Notion or Asana invite us to break our lives down into a series of tasks and projects, transforming the organic process of growth into a checklist to be conquered. The entire quantified-self movement, powered by AI tools from Fitbit to Headspace, gamifies self-improvement, turning the journey of healing into a competition against ourselves and others. This focus on the measurable and optimizable leaves little room for the most important parts of being human: the intangible, the inefficient, the beautifully unquantifiable aspects of genuine growth.

The allure of this myth is powerful because it offers us a sense of control in a world that feels increasingly chaotic. AI-driven systems promise a kind of order, a way to track our habits, predict our potential, and optimize our lives for maximum efficiency. An app like Strava transforms a simple run into a public performance and a competition. A diet app turns the intuitive act of eating into a complex calculus of macros and calories. Even the sacred journey of faith is not immune. Apps like Hallow or YouVersion can be wonderful tools, but their features that track prayer time or Bible-reading streaks can subtly frame spiritual growth as just another metric to master.

It is a tempting offer, this life by the numbers. But it fundamentally misunderstands what it means to be a whole and healthy human being. The slow, often hidden work of healing a past wound, the messy process of learning to forgive, the quiet cultivation of compassion—these things don't fit neatly on a dashboard. The writer and spiritual teacher Richard Rohr has spent his life calling people back to a deeper, more process-oriented understanding of growth. Rohr consistently teaches that true spiritual transformation is not about achieving perfection or mastering a set of rules but about a lifelong journey of becoming more open to grace. He writes that this path requires "a change of consciousness, a change of heart, a change of life," which is far more profound than any simple metric can capture.[1] This simple truth stands as a powerful challenge to the entire ethos of the AI age, which is built on the promise of instant results and data-driven solutions. Ultimately, we must see that true growth is a relational, slow, and often Spirit-led journey—not a dashboard to be managed, but a sacred mystery to be lived.

The Psychology of Performance

The myth that growth equals performance thrives because it taps into ancient psychological tendencies, amplified to an almost unbearable degree by modern AI. We are social creatures, wired for comparison, and we harbor a deep-seated fear of not measuring up. In the past, our sphere of comparison was our small village or community. Today, our AI-driven tools have created a global village of endless, curated comparison, feeding our anxieties and fueling a culture of perfectionism. Productivity apps, quantified-self tools, and social media benchmarks all collude to create a world where our sense of self-worth becomes dangerously tied to our output.

1. Rohr, *Falling Upward*, 112.

Johann Hari, in his exploration of our fractured modern minds, argues that the very design of our digital tools is a key driver of this performance culture. The constant switching between tasks, the endless notifications, and the deluge of information all fragment our attention, making it harder to engage in deep, reflective thought. This constant state of distraction makes us more susceptible to measuring our lives in shallow ways—by tasks completed, emails answered, or posts liked—because we lack the mental space for deeper forms of self-assessment. In his book *Stolen Focus*, he explains, "The truth is that you are living in a system that is pouring acid on your attention every day," eroding our ability to focus on what truly matters.[2] This acid dissolves our ability to connect meaningfully with ourselves and others, leaving us to grasp for fleeting validation in metrics.

Quantified-self tools add another layer of pressure. A device like a Fitbit or an Apple Watch can certainly be a motivator for a healthier lifestyle, but it can also become a tyrannical source of judgment. This technology gamifies health and mindfulness, turning them into a competition of numbers. This creates a fertile ground for perfectionism and comparison, as we inevitably measure our own imperfect data against the idealized benchmarks set by the app or by others online. I've talked to so many people who feel a genuine sense of guilt for failing to meet their ten-thousand-step goal, even if their day was filled with meaningful connection or restorative rest.

Brené Brown has spent her career studying the psychological toxins of shame and perfectionism. Her research reveals that perfectionism is not about healthy striving; it's a defense mechanism driven by the fear of shame and judgment. It's the belief that if we can perform perfectly and look perfect, we can avoid the pain of being seen as flawed or unworthy. In her book *The Gifts of Imperfection*, she writes, "Perfectionism is a twenty-ton shield that we lug around thinking it will protect us when, in fact, it's the thing that's really preventing us from taking flight."[3] Quantified-self tools have become the digital embodiment of that twenty-ton shield.

And then there is social media, which elevates this entire performance culture to a global spectacle. Platforms like Instagram and LinkedIn have become arenas where we equate a person's worth with their engagement metrics. This creates an environment ripe for comparative

2. Hari, *Stolen Focus*, 147.

3. Brown, *Gifts of Imperfection*, 56.

suffering, where we feel perpetually inadequate as we compare our messy, behind-the-scenes reality with the meticulously curated highlight reels of others.

The neuropsychiatrist Curt Thompson offers a compelling explanation for why this is so damaging. Thompson explains that our brains are wired for connection. When we feel seen, known, and loved, our brains release neurochemicals that make us feel safe and secure. When we feel judged, compared, or shamed, our brains go into a threat state, shutting down our capacity for creativity and authentic connection. In his profound book *The Soul of Shame*, he notes, "We were created for connection, but shame disrupts this by convincing us that we are flawed and unworthy of love."[4] This is exactly the feeling that so much of our AI-curated online life seems engineered to produce, making genuine healing almost impossible.

I once worked with a young professional named David, a talented graphic designer who had fully embraced the quantified life. His world was a literal dashboard of metrics. He tracked his work tasks in Asana, his cycling performance on Peloton, and his sleep quality with an Oura ring. He was the epitome of high performance. He was also miserable, burned out, and felt a profound sense of emptiness he couldn't articulate. He joined a small group at his church, mostly out of desperation. The slow, unquantified nature of the group—the meandering conversations, the long pauses for prayer, the sharing of messy, unresolved struggles—was deeply foreign to him. One evening, another man in the group shared a story of a recent business failure with raw, unvarnished honesty. There was no metric for what happened next. There was no "KPI for compassion." There was only a quiet, palpable sense of presence as the group held this man in his pain. In that moment, something broke open in David. He began, tentatively, to share his own story, not of his achievements, but of his exhaustion and loneliness. His healing began not when he hit a new goal but when he allowed himself to be truly seen in his imperfection, embarking on a path of growth paved with authentic relationship, not relentless metrics.

4. Thompson, *Soul of Shame*, 82.

The Spiritual Costs of a Performance-Based Faith

When the myth of performance seeps into spiritual life, the costs are profound. The sacred journey of healing, which is meant to be a process of surrender and transformation, gets twisted into just another project to be managed and mastered. When we reduce spiritual growth to a set of quantifiable metrics, we subtly erode the very qualities that are essential for a deep and living faith: humility, vulnerability, and a radical dependence on the grace of God.

Henri Nouwen, who wrote with such clarity about the spiritual life, understood this danger well. He saw that true ministry and healing flow not from our strengths and accomplishments but from our own acknowledged weakness. Nouwen's concept of the wounded healer suggests that it is precisely our own wounds that, when offered to God and others in vulnerability, become sources of healing and compassion. This stands in direct opposition to a performance-based spirituality that demands we present a polished, put-together self to God and to the world. In his timeless book *The Wounded Healer*, he writes, "The great illusion of leadership is to think that man can be led out of the desert by someone who has never been there."[5] In the same way, we cannot be healed by a system that denies the reality of our wounds.

One of the first casualties of a metrics-driven faith is humility. When we start measuring our spiritual progress by external outputs—minutes logged in a prayer app, chapters of the Bible read—we can easily fall into a subtle form of spiritual pride. Faith becomes about effort, discipline, and performance. It fosters a dangerous self-reliance, where we begin to believe that our spiritual health is something we achieve, rather than a gift we receive. The psalmist's simple, powerful cry, "He restores my soul" (Ps 23:3), points to a divine action, not a human project.

Another tragic loss is vulnerability. As Curt Thompson argues, true healing requires the courage to be open about our deepest wounds. But a performance culture, whether in the world or in the church, demands an illusion of perfection. It creates an environment where people are afraid to admit they are struggling, for fear of being judged. Social media, with its curated feeds of victorious faith journeys, only intensifies this pressure. It leaves no room for the messy, sacred work of lament, confession, and repentance. Scott Sauls speaks directly to this, emphasizing that the church should be the safest place in the world to be imperfect. It should

5. Nouwen, *Wounded Healer*, 72.

be a "hospital for sinners, not a museum for saints." In his book *A Gentle Answer*, he reminds us that "Jesus is not repelled by our mess; he is drawn to it," creating the safety needed for real vulnerability.[6]

Finally, a metrics-driven approach erodes our dependence on God. The great stories of healing in the Bible are all rooted in a profound sense of trust in God's unmerited grace. They are not stories of self-optimization. Yet, our AI-driven tools constantly encourage us to hack our lives, to find the most efficient path to growth. This mindset is fundamentally at odds with the biblical call to rest. Saundra Dalton-Smith has done important work on this topic, expanding our understanding of what rest truly means. She argues that we suffer from a "rest deficit" because we think of rest only as the cessation of physical activity. She identifies seven types of rest we need, including mental, emotional, and spiritual rest. In her book *Sacred Rest*, she writes, "Rest is not a luxury, it is a necessity . . . a divine gift that we must learn to receive."[7] She makes the case that true healing requires us to intentionally step away from the relentless drive to perform and to simply rest in God's presence. When we prioritize our metrics over this kind of deep, divine dependence, we risk a kind of spiritual desolation.

I remember talking with a woman named Maria, a young mother who was diligently using a popular meditation app to track her spiritual growth. The app was beautifully designed, with soothing sounds and encouraging messages. It rewarded her with digital badges for her daily sessions, and she felt a sense of accomplishment. But over time, she confessed to me, she felt an increasing sense of anxiety. Prayer had become another task on her to-do list, another metric to measure her day's success. If she missed a session, she felt guilty. The tool that was meant to bring her peace was actually making her more frantic. During a weekend church retreat, she participated in a service of unquantified prayer and lament. There were no timers, no badges, just a shared space where people could bring their honest, messy struggles before God and one another. For the first time in a long time, Maria wept. In that space of shared vulnerability, she found a sense of release and grace that no app could ever provide. Her story is a powerful illustration of the shift from a focus on performance to a posture of presence, and of learning to rest in God's love rather than relentlessly chasing her own spiritual metrics.

6. Sauls, *Gentle Answer*, 45.

7. Dalton-Smith, *Sacred Rest*, 35.

Why Inner Healing and Growth Matter in the Age of AI

AI is reshaping how we understand ourselves, and the shift feels monumental. Apps and chatbots now offer instant insights into the human mind—explaining stress triggers or suggesting ways to reframe thoughts. Concepts like neuroplasticity or cognitive behavioral techniques, once confined to therapy rooms or academic journals, are now accessible with a tap on a smartphone. This democratization of psychological knowledge marks a quiet revolution, equipping individuals with tools to explore their inner workings.

And yet, as this flood of information becomes available, a deeper question emerges. Does access to all this knowledge automatically lead to change? It seems that while AI can provide a brilliant and detailed map of our own minds, it cannot walk the journey for us. The central argument here is that AI's ability to make complex ideas widely available is a powerful opportunity, but inner healing and growth, often enriched by a spiritual dimension, are what transform those insights into a more authentic, human way of living in a tech-driven world.

Deeper Self-Discovery

The ease of learning about the human mind today is striking. A chatbot can explain why anxiety spikes, detailing how the amygdala triggers stress hormones, and suggest a breathing exercise to calm the nerves. Curiosity about procrastination might lead to an app outlining the psychology of motivation, pointing toward small habit changes. Concepts like neuroplasticity—how the brain forms new pathways through consistent practice—or cognitive behavioral therapy (CBT), which reframes negative thoughts, are no longer exclusive to experts. They're readily available, explained clearly for anyone with a device.

Still, a question lingers: does access to this information guarantee growth? It's akin to owning a cookbook without ever cooking. A mood-tracking app might flag late-night screen time as a stress trigger and recommend mindfulness exercises rooted in neuroscience. That's enlightening, but change only happens by acting on it—cutting back on scrolling, practicing those exercises, and sticking with them. Self-discovery demands more than facts; it requires grappling with insights to shape a life that feels true and purposeful.

Daniel H. Pink, in his book *A Whole New Mind*, suggests that as information becomes abundant, the ability to synthesize and apply it meaningfully is what sets individuals apart. He argues that the future belongs to a different kind of person, not just logical, linear thinkers. As he writes, "Symphony . . . is the ability to put together the pieces. It is the capacity to synthesize rather than to analyze; to see relationships between seemingly unrelated fields."[8] AI provides a wealth of insights, but growth hinges on using them to craft a life that's richer and more connected.

God or a spiritual life can fulfill this need for deeper meaning beyond what AI offers. An app might clarify why the mind feels scattered, but spiritual practices—prayer or reflecting on Ps 23, "The Lord is my shepherd" (v. 1)—provide a framework of purpose and hope. This isn't just about tweaking habits; it's about grounding them in a divine connection that makes self-discovery a soulful journey. The nuance is that information from an AI can sometimes highlight our flaws too sharply. An app linking anxiety to poor sleep might just amplify stress rather than ease it, leaving people stuck in the "interesting" phase of knowing about a problem without feeling empowered to act. Spiritual grounding, rooted in faith, can offer a reminder of our inherent worth, encouraging persistence toward meaningful change.

The Sense of Grief and Joy

AI's capacity to handle our mental busywork is remarkable. Wondering why your focus falters? A chatbot can explain decision fatigue and suggest a CBT exercise to clear the mind. Facing a tough decision? An AI tool can guide you through a process to prioritize your thoughts. By tackling these tasks—explaining concepts, identifying patterns, or offering quick strategies—AI clears mental clutter, creating room for deeper, more meaningful pursuits.

Yet, there's a hesitation here: AI can describe emotions, but it lacks the capacity to feel them. It can't grasp the weight of grief or the joy of a shared laugh. An AI app might outline how cortisol spikes disrupt focus and suggest a brief meditation, which is helpful, but it doesn't sense the unique burden of personal worries or the relief of a heartfelt conversation. Inner work—processing emotions, healing past wounds, building resilience—is distinctly human, beyond AI's reach.

8. Pink, *Whole New Mind*, 130.

Cal Newport has built his work around the value of focused effort in a distracted world. He argues that our ability to engage in "deep work" is becoming increasingly rare and valuable. In his book *Deep Work*, he says, "To produce at your peak level you need to work for extended periods with full concentration on a single task free from distraction."[9] Actually, it is true that the age of AI has directly or indirectly enforced a skill that allows us to quickly master complicated information and produce better results in less time. As AI manages our surface-level tasks, like explaining brain science or suggesting coping methods, it frees up our mental bandwidth for these deeper endeavors: emotional regulation, resolving traumas, or being truly present with others. But there's a risk: AI's efficiency can foster complacency, making it tempting to assume growth has occurred after simply reading a clever explanation from a chatbot.

God or a spiritual life can fulfill this space for inner work with profound depth. AI may clear the clutter, but faith provides direction. Prayer or Scriptures like Matt 11:28—"Come to me, all you who are weary"—offer a grounding peace that no AI can replicate. This isn't just about stress management; it's about finding resilience and authenticity in a divine connection, turning the space AI creates into a sacred opportunity for growth. The catch is that AI's efficiency can mislead. It's easy to think progress is made by consuming insights, when really, the journey has just begun. Spiritual grounding encourages leaning into the messy, human work—like forgiveness or embracing discomfort—rather than settling for quick fixes, fostering a commitment to authentic growth.

Mental Health Challenges in a Tech-Heavy World

This tech-saturated world can take a toll on our mental health. Social media, constant notifications, and AI apps delivering brain-science insights can overwhelm. An app might link your stress to poor sleep, but instead of empowering you, it can feel like another way you're failing at something basic. This paradox reveals that AI's tools for self-understanding can sometimes heighten anxiety or isolation, spotlighting our flaws without always guiding us toward healing.

The psychologist Jonathan Haidt, in his recent and urgent book *The Anxious Generation*, explores how our digital overload, particularly for young people, is rewiring their approach to stress and connection.

9. Newport, *Deep Work*, 44.

He argues that the constant connectivity and curated realities of an AI-driven online world have fundamentally changed childhood, leading to skyrocketing rates of anxiety and depression. He notes, "The move from a play-based childhood to a phone-based childhood has been a disaster for adolescent mental health."[10] AI's tailored insights, like connecting mood swings to excessive screen time, can sharpen our awareness of these issues but may not offer a clear path to resolution. Inner growth—cultivating emotional intelligence, sitting with difficult feelings, fostering self-awareness—is essential to thrive, not just survive, in this AI-heavy environment.

God or a spiritual life can fulfill this need for healing in ways technology cannot. An app might highlight anxiety triggers, but it doesn't address the deeper loneliness behind our late-night scrolling. Prayer or reflecting on John 16:33—"In this world you will have trouble. But take heart! I have overcome the world"—offers comfort beyond algorithms. This spiritual foundation builds resilience, providing hope and purpose to navigate an artificial world with calm and clarity.

There's a subtle critique to be made here: AI excels at identifying problems but lacks the wisdom to handle emotional complexity. An app might flag your scrolling habits, yet it can't process the feelings driving them. Healing demands human effort—journaling, connecting with others, or allowing space for raw emotions. Faith adds strength, affirming a sense of being held by something greater, which supports our perseverance through the challenges of a tech-driven world.

Embracing What Makes Us Human Amid AI's Reach

AI excels at analyzing data and offering advice, but it can't capture human intuition, empathy, or the pursuit of purpose. An AI tool might explain procrastination with precision, yet it's often a heartfelt conversation that sparks real progress. These uniquely human qualities are what define growth in an AI-driven world.

Andy Crouch has long argued that our technologies often distance us from the very things that lead to a meaningful life. He makes a crucial distinction between being a *person* and being a *user*, suggesting that much of our technology is designed to treat us as the latter. In his book *The Life We're Looking For*, he writes, "We are meant to be persons, not users,

10. Haidt, *Anxious Generation*, 5.

and to live in households, not networks."[11] While AI handles tasks like mood analysis or explaining neuroscience, growth lies in embracing the subjective, unquantifiable elements of our lives—trusting our instincts, forgiving others, or finding joy in fleeting moments.

God or a spiritual life can fulfill this call to our full humanity with deep resonance. An AI might suggest mindfulness techniques, but faith infuses them with meaning. Reflecting on Ps 139—"I am fearfully and wonderfully made" (v. 14)—affirms a unique worth that exists beyond any code or algorithm. This spiritual grounding nurtures creativity, connection, and purpose, distinguishing what is human in a tech-heavy world. It's not about rejecting AI but about using it to enhance what is most essentially human: empathy, forgiveness, and the pursuit of something greater.

Still, AI is not the villain. Apps that teach mindfulness, like offering simple breathing exercises for stressful moments, can absolutely support our growth. The real shift happens when those practices become personal, woven into a life shaped by faith. Growth doesn't pit AI against humanity; it uses AI's insights to fuel a journey of living fully, anchored in a divine love that no machine can replicate. Ultimately, AI's flood of knowledge offers a chance to understand the self better, but inner healing and growth, often through a spiritual lens, are what make that understanding meaningful. AI may illuminate the path, but the journey—becoming more human, more connected to God and others—is one only we can walk.

Impact—The Profound Effects of True Healing

The most profound impact of inner healing is that it restores the soul. It is a quiet, steady liberation from the tyranny of metrics and the relentless pursuit of external validation. It is a journey home to a life rooted in meaning and purpose, a life that begins to reflect, however imperfectly, the divine image in which we were created. In the AI age, our worth is so often reduced to a set of quantifiable data points—our productivity score, our social media engagement, our fitness level. The process of healing reorients us toward an entirely different and more ancient truth: that our dignity is inherent, a gift woven into the fabric of our being, and it transcends any possible performance.

11. Crouch, *Life We're Looking For*, 60.

Restoring the soul is not a quick fix or a one-time event but a slow, lifelong process of transformation. Richard Rohr has consistently taught that spiritual growth is not about climbing a ladder of perfection but about learning to surrender, to trust, and to become more open to the grace that is always present. True healing, in his view, is less about becoming flawless and more about becoming whole. As he so often reminds us, "Healing is a process, not an event . . . it is the way we return to our true selves."[12] This journey gradually restores our capacity for wonder, deep connection, and spiritual depth, allowing us to more fully embody the divine image God intended for humanity.

Restoring the Soul: From Performance to Presence

This restoration of the soul manifests first as a fundamental shift from seeking external validation to cultivating internal flourishing. When the soul begins to heal, our sense of self is no longer precariously balanced on the shifting sands of algorithms and societal benchmarks. Instead, it becomes anchored in a deep, abiding awareness of our intrinsic value as image-bearers of a loving Creator. We begin to understand that our purpose is not to perform but to be present to God, to others, and to our own lives.

This shift from external performance to internal flourishing is powerfully illustrated throughout the biblical narrative. Two prominent examples are the parable of the Samaritan woman and the transformation of the apostle Paul. The Samaritan woman in John 4 exemplifies a soul defined by external rejection. Ostracized for her marital history and ethnic identity, she lived on the shifting sands of societal shame, coming for water at noon to avoid her accusers. Her worth was nonexistent by every social benchmark. Yet, Jesus meets her in her isolation, looking past her history to see her soul's thirst. He offers her "living water" (v. 10), a source of internal flourishing that has nothing to do with her societal standing. This encounter so fundamentally restores her sense of intrinsic value that she immediately leaves her water jar—the symbol of her shame-filled routine—and becomes the first evangelist to her town.

Similarly, Saul of Tarsus built his entire identity on the societal benchmarks of religious achievement. As he later recounted in Phil 3, his credentials were impeccable: a Pharisee, zealous, and blameless under

12. Rohr, *Falling Upward*, 65.

the law. This was the pinnacle of a performance-based identity. However, his encounter with the risen Christ on the Damascus road shattered this framework. He came to see his external achievements as rubbish compared to the "surpassing worth of knowing Christ Jesus" (Phil 3:8). For Paul, the restored soul no longer strives for a righteous résumé but rests in a loving relationship.

Dallas Willard spoke of this as learning to live in the kingdom of God here and now. Willard's work powerfully dismantles the idea that faith is just about securing a ticket to the afterlife. He argued that we are invited to experience the reality of God's loving reign in our present lives, which transforms our understanding of everything, including our own identity. In his masterwork *The Divine Conspiracy*, he writes, "The life we have in the kingdom of God is a life of friendship with God. It is a life of companionship with him."[13] This shifts our focus from trying to earn God's approval through metrics to simply enjoying his presence, which is the very definition of a restored soul.

Healing reclaims our capacity for genuine presence and connection. In a world splintered by endless digital pings that pull us in a thousand directions, a healed soul can offer that rare gift of real, heartfelt listening. This is the sort of bond that actually feeds the spirit, unlike those quick likes or comments online that often leave us feeling more isolated than before. Robert Wicks emphasizes the value of just being there for others as key to any meaningful care. His ideas suggest that true support stems from our own inner calm, not from the chaos bubbling inside us. In his book *The Ministry of Presence*, Wicks puts it this way: profound healing happens in that hard-to-measure realm of feeling "deeply known and truly loved."[14]

This healing isn't abstract; it plays out in everyday lives, restoring the soul in ways that echo the *imago Dei*—the image of God we're created in, as described in Gen 1:27, where humanity is made to reflect divine qualities like creativity, relationship, and wholeness. But in our hurried age, that image gets distorted, fractured by constant striving.

Take David, that tech exec from before. His path to healing wasn't some quick fix or app-based therapy; it involved sessions with a spiritual guide who pushed him toward quiet rather than more checklists. He'd ditch his phone for rambling walks in the forest, letting the rustle

13. Willard, *Divine Conspiracy*, 280.]

14. Wicks, *Ministry of Presence*, 90.

of leaves ground him in the moment. Or he'd dig in at a neighborhood garden plot, pulling weeds and planting seeds alongside strangers who became friends over time. Those early moments of quiet drove him nuts—his mind racing back to emails and deadlines. But over time, as he chatted about tomato varieties or felt the cool dirt under his nails, a forgotten calm crept back. He wasn't the vice president chasing metrics anymore; he was just David, a guy swapping life stories. This shift didn't trash his career—it realigned his inner self, restoring a sense of meaning that went beyond performance indicators. Suddenly, he could be present with his family at dinner without his thoughts drifting to work, or listen to a colleague's struggles without jumping to solutions. His healing pulled him closer to that *imago Dei*, where true purpose flows from being, not just doing.

Restoring the Body: From Project to Presence

True healing doesn't end with the soul, though; it appears to seep into our physical side too, turning our view of the body from a fix-it project to something more kind and lived in. This could reflect the *imago Dei* as well, where the body isn't just a brain taxi but, in Christian thought, a holy space housing the Spirit, as Paul writes in 1 Cor 6:19–20, calling it a temple to be honored. Yet in this AI-driven era, with apps buzzing about sleep scores, step counts, and calorie logs, it's easy to treat ourselves like hackable gadgets, always tweaking for peak output. Healing nudges us toward a gentler tie with our form.

The work of Bessel van der Kolk highlights how our bodies hold onto hurts, showing trauma as something etched into our nerves, not just the mind. His findings point to physical fallout from past wounds, urging body-involved recovery for real progress. As he writes in *The Body Keeps the Score*, "We can't fully recover until we learn to befriend the sensations in our bodies."[15] This befriending isn't about ignoring metrics but integrating them with compassionate listening to hunger pangs that signal a need for rest, or a tight chest that hints at unspoken grief. By doing so, we become more attuned to others' physical and emotional cues, fostering the empathetic presence that reflects the *imago Dei*.

Hillary L. McBride adds to this by encouraging a return to bodily intuition for wholeness, countering cultural pushes to ignore or hate

15. Van der Kolk, *Body Keeps the Score*, 208.

our physical selves—think diets that shame or work cultures that glorify exhaustion. She warns this leads to inner splits, but reclaiming the body mends that, allowing us to show up fully in relationships. In *The Wisdom of Your Body*, McBride notes, "To come home to your body is to come home to your life."[16] Such views invite listening to our own signals, honoring the body as part of the *imago Dei*'s gift.

Drawing from Scripture again, consider the incarnation itself—Jesus taking on human flesh, dwelling among us to heal through touch and presence. When he restores the bleeding woman in Mark 5, his power flows not just to stop her physical suffering but to affirm her dignity, calling her daughter and sending her in peace. This embodied healing breaks her isolation, restoring her to community and reflecting how God values our whole selves for connection.

Restoring Community: From Shame to Connection

The impact of true healing also involves letting go of the shame and judgment that weigh so heavily on our inner selves, emotions often deepened by the endless parade of curated lives on AI-driven social media. Scrolling through posts of flawless moments can leave us feeling like our own emotions don't measure up, as if we're failing some invisible test. Yet, this struggle might lead us to a bold self-compassion, where we start to embrace our feelings, raw and tangled as they are, as threads of our unique story.

Let's be honest—AI isn't just a bystander. Its algorithms, designed to keep us hooked, flood our feeds with idealized snapshots that spark comparison, making self-judgment feel almost inevitable. Biblical stories, like David's plea in Ps 139—"Search me, God, and know my heart" (v. 23)—remind us our worth isn't tied to likes or retweets but to a divine acceptance of our inner selves. Yet, AI's constant stream of perfection can bury that truth, nurturing a cycle where shame thrives.

The authors of *Intuitive Eating*, Evelyn Tribole and Elyse Resch, offer a related insight: "Feel your feelings without using food to stuff them down."[17] Applied here, it's about sitting with shame or judgment rather than numbing them with endless feeds. It's a subtle rebellion against AI's push to keep us doubting ourselves. I think of Maria, a college student

16. McBride, *Wisdom of Your Body*, 150.

17. Tribole and Resch, *Intuitive Eating*, 200.

caught in a spiral of self-judgment, her worth tied to how her posts performed online. A post with few likes felt like a personal failure, her emotions tangled in AI's feedback loops. With a counselor's help, she began unpacking the roots of her shame. She started journaling, letting her fears and hopes spill out unfiltered. Instead of chasing online validation, she practiced meditative breathing, asking, "What am I feeling right now?" Her journey echoes the prodigal son's return, where healing comes from embracing our true selves, not external praise.

Perhaps the most far-reaching impact of true healing is its capacity to build communities of authentic connection. It has the power to transform spaces of isolation and division into havens of reconciliation. This, too, is a direct reflection of the restoration of the *imago Dei*. We were created for community; our very nature is relational. In the AI age, where algorithms often create echo chambers that amplify our differences, the work of healing offers a powerful countercultural pathway back to unity.

The life's work of John M. Perkins is a testament to this conviction. Perkins's vision of reconciliation is deeply practical and relational. He argues that we cannot have reconciliation without justice, and we cannot have justice without relationship. In *Reconciliation*, he asserts that "reconciliation is the heart of the gospel," and that true community involves bridging divides to build a shared future.[18]

This healing process begins by actively fostering environments of trust and psychological safety. Scott Sauls advocates for churches to become these kinds of communities. He argues that in an age of outrage, the church is called to be a community of "gentle answers" and surprising friendships. In his book *Befriend*, he writes, "We are never more like Jesus than when we are befriending those who are different from us."[19]

Reconciliation, a core aspect of this communal healing, moves beyond mere tolerance. It involves the courageous work of acknowledging past harms and engaging in difficult conversations. The restorative justice movement offers a powerful framework for this. As Howard Zehr, a foundational thinker in this field, explains in *The Little Book of Restorative Justice*, the goal is not to punish but to "put right the wrongs," a process that involves victims, offenders, and the wider community in a search for healing and repair.[20]

18. Perkins, *Reconciliation*, 30.
19. Sauls, *Befriend*, 20.
20. Zehr, *Little Book*, 35.

In our AI-driven world, where online conflicts often escalate with breathtaking speed, communities that practice this kind of intentional connection offer a vital antidote. They model a different way of being, demonstrating that our shared humanity is more powerful than any algorithm designed to divide us.

Pathways—Cultivating Inner Healing and Growth

In the relentless, 24/7 culture of the AI age, where our value is so often equated with our output, the simplest and perhaps most powerful pathway to inner healing is to consciously and courageously embrace rest. This is not about laziness or mere idleness. It is a profound act of spiritual and psychological resistance. It is a countercultural declaration that our worth is not tied to our productivity, that we are more than machines designed for endless optimization, and that we have an inherent dignity that cannot be measured by any metric.

Saundra Dalton-Smith has done groundbreaking work in this area, arguing that our modern exhaustion comes from a fundamental misunderstanding of what rest truly is. She suggests that we are suffering from a "rest deficit" because we tend to think of rest only as the absence of physical activity. She identifies seven distinct types of rest that we need to flourish: physical, mental, spiritual, emotional, social, sensory, and creative. A person can be physically still but mentally and emotionally exhausted. In her book *Sacred Rest*, she writes, "Rest is not a luxury, it is a necessity."[21] This perspective reframes rest from a sign of weakness to the very source of our strength.

Embracing these forms of rest, though challenging, is vital for our well-being. The stress of breaking ingrained habits of constant productivity can feel overwhelming, as it requires confronting societal pressure to always be on. Implementing rest consistently demands significant time and energy, as we must carve out space in packed schedules and resist the urge to fill every moment with tasks. Moreover, the slow pace of progress can lead to feelings of hurt or disappointment, especially when immediate benefits are not apparent or setbacks occur. Yet, rest is necessary because it replenishes our depleted reserves, preventing chronic burnout that erodes health and creativity. Without it, we risk losing touch with our core selves, becoming mere cogs in a machine that values output over

21. Dalton-Smith, *Sacred Rest*, 45.

humanity. By prioritizing rest, we reclaim our worth, foster resilience, and cultivate a sustainable rhythm that nurtures creativity and joy.

AI cannot replicate the holistic experience of rest because it lacks the capacity for subjective human needs like emotional or spiritual restoration. While AI can optimize schedules or suggest relaxation techniques, it cannot embody the nuanced interplay of physical, mental, and spiritual rest that humans require. It cannot experience the existential weight of resisting societal pressures or the intrinsic dignity of simply being. AI's data-driven approach misses the unquantifiable essence of human rest, which involves personal reflection, emotional surrender, and a reconnection with one's deeper purpose, elements that transcend algorithmic processing and require lived, human experience.

Pathway 1: Embracing Rest

Sabbath

One of the most ancient and powerful frameworks for this kind of resistance is the practice of Sabbath. While rooted in Jewish and Christian tradition, the concept of a regular, intentional pause from the cycle of producing and consuming speaks to a universal human need. A Sabbath is a dedicated time—perhaps an hour, an afternoon, or a full day—to cease from our work, to turn off the noise of the AI-driven world, and to simply be. It's not just about stopping; it's about reorienting our lives around things that have value but not a price tag: delight, wonder, relationship, and presence.

The practice of Sabbath, though transformative, is not without challenges. It can generate stress from the fear of falling behind in a hypercompetitive world, where pausing feels risky to professional or social standing. Setting boundaries and unplugging from work and devices requires considerable energy and time, restructuring routines and resisting expectations of constant availability. Disappointment from others who don't understand this commitment can lead to hurt or isolation. Yet, Sabbath is necessary because it restores a natural rhythm, countering the dehumanizing pace of modern culture. It reconnects us with our intrinsic value, fostering relationships and grounding us in what truly matters.

AI cannot embody the Sabbath's essence because it lacks the human capacity for intentional, value-driven pause. While AI can schedule breaks or manage tasks, it cannot grasp the spiritual or emotional significance of ceasing work to dwell in wonder and presence. The Sabbath's countercultural resistance to productivity metrics and its focus on unmeasurable aspects like delight and relationship are inherently human experiences. AI, bound by algorithms, cannot replicate the personal conviction or communal connection that make Sabbath a transformative act of reclaiming human dignity.

The writer Tish Harrison Warren writes beautifully about how these sacred rhythms can ground us in a world of chaos. Her work explores how our small, everyday habits and routines are, in fact, formative spiritual practices. She argues that embedding sacred rhythms, like a weekly Sabbath, into the "liturgy of our ordinary" lives is what shapes us into people of peace and substance. In her book *Liturgy of the Ordinary*, she notes, "We tend to want a Christian life that is a list of tasks . . . but God wants to give us himself."[22]

Digital Minimalism

A vital component of modern Sabbath keeping is the practice of digital minimalism. It's nearly impossible to find true mental and spiritual rest when our phones are buzzing with an endless stream of notifications, emails, and social media updates, often curated by AI to maximize our engagement. The writer Cal Newport has been a leading voice in advocating for a more intentional and limited engagement with our AI-driven tools, not as a Luddite rejection, but as a strategy for a better life. Newport argues that we should treat our attention as a precious, finite resource. Instead of passively allowing technology companies to dictate how we spend it, he encourages us to adopt a philosophy where we only use digital tools that deeply support our core values, and we ruthlessly eliminate the rest. In *Digital Minimalism*, he defines the practice this way: "Digital minimalism is a philosophy of technology use in which you focus your online time on a small number of carefully selected and optimized activities that strongly support things you value, and then happily miss out on everything else."[23]

Adopting digital minimalism, while liberating, comes with difficulties. The stress of withdrawal from constant connectivity can be intense, grappling with fear of missing out (FOMO) or anxiety about being out

22. Warren, *Liturgy of the Ordinary*, 20.

23. Newport, *Digital Minimalism*, 28.

of touch. Auditing and restructuring digital habits demands significant time and energy, requiring evaluation of tools aligning with values. Reducing superficial connections or facing professional pushback for being less available can lead to hurt or disappointment. Digital minimalism is necessary because it protects mental and emotional space from overstimulation, creating room for reflection, creativity, and presence, reclaiming control from algorithms exploiting attention.

AI cannot fully enact digital minimalism because it is inherently part of the digital ecosystem it seeks to limit. While AI can filter notifications or suggest app usage, it cannot internalize the personal values driving intentional technology use. The human experience of resisting digital overstimulation, confronting FOMO, and prioritizing presence over distraction involves emotional and philosophical depth that AI lacks. Digital minimalism requires subjective discernment and a commitment to unquantifiable human priorities, which transcend AI's data-driven capabilities and remain uniquely human.

This intentional disengagement creates the mental and emotional spaciousness required for true healing to begin. It allows our souls to finally breathe in a world that is constantly trying to suffocate them with stimulation. I think of a woman I know named Sarah, a brilliant marketing professional whose life was a case study in digital burnout. Her job demanded she be on 24/7, and her personal life mimicked the same frantic pace. Her phone was a relentless source of anxiety. Inspired by these ideas, she decided to attempt a radical experiment: a full, twenty-four-hour digital Sabbath, from sundown on Saturday to sundown on Sunday. The first few weeks, she told me, were agonizing. The silence felt deafening. She felt phantom vibrations in her pocket and a constant, twitchy urge to check her email. But she persisted. She started taking long walks in the woods without a podcast playing. She read novels. She had long, meandering conversations with her husband without either of them glancing at a screen. Gradually, something began to shift. The anxiety lessened. She began to feel a sense of clarity and energy she hadn't experienced in years. She realized that her best creative ideas for work came not when she was staring at a screen but during the quiet, unstructured time of her Sabbath. Her act of resistance didn't make her less productive; it made her more human, and in doing so, it opened a profound pathway to healing, reminding her that her worth was not defined by her response time but by the quiet, unmeasurable quality of her own soul.

Worship and Solitude

In an age increasingly captivated by the myth of AI-driven wellness, we're sold a new path to inner healing: algorithmic peace and optimized mindfulness. As another sabbatical action, the practice of worship offers a profound and necessary counternarrative. It proposes that true healing isn't a problem to be solved by a better algorithm but a presence to be dwelled in. It is the deliberate choice to step away from the project of self-optimization and simply be with God.

Engaging in worship, though enriching, can present challenges. The stress of confronting doubts or spiritual uncertainties can be daunting, forcing us to wrestle with unresolved questions of faith. Committing to regular worship demands time and energy, carving out space for prayer or services amidst busy lives. Unmet expectations of divine intervention or community tensions can lead to hurt or disappointment. Worship is necessary because it anchors identity in a transcendent reality, fostering surrender and intimacy that no algorithm can replicate. Communal worship counters digital isolation, creating authentic connection and belonging.

AI cannot replicate worship because it lacks the capacity for spiritual connection or existential surrender. While AI can simulate prayers or analyze religious texts, it cannot experience the intimate, transcendent presence of dwelling with the divine. The human act of worship involves personal faith, emotional vulnerability, and communal bonding through shared rituals, which are beyond AI's algorithmic scope. Worship's power lies in its unquantifiable essence—surrendering to a higher purpose and finding belonging in imperfection—making it a uniquely human pathway to healing.

This practice embraces the duality of being both alone and together. In the quiet, personal moments of worship—inviting the Spirit to one's heart, the silent prayer, listening to God's word—we are alone with God, fostering a connection that no wellness app can track. It's a presence that sees beyond our data points to the core of our being. Yet, this is deeply interwoven with the communal act of gathering for a service. In a world of curated digital isolation, the physical act of being in a room with other imperfect people is a powerful form of resistance.

The practice of solitude and silence offers the rest of soul. In the age of AI, silence has become more than a space to be filled; it's a territory to be reclaimed. Our world is now saturated with algorithmic noise, curated by systems designed to capture our attention. This constant, engineered stimulation creates a profound spiritual agitation, making true Sabbath rest feel almost impossible. The ancient practices of solitude and silence have become essential acts of spiritual resistance—a way of logging off from the machine to reconnect with God and our own humanity.

In this quiet, our relationship with God can shift from the metric-driven, performance-based mentality of the digital world to one of simple communion. Freed from the tyranny of the algorithm, we can begin to distinguish our true self from our data-self. The writer Thomas Merton spoke of the "false self"[24]—the persona we construct for worldly approval. In the twenty-first century, this false self is amplified and quantified by our digital footprint, creating an "algorithmic self" that is sold back to us through targeted ads and curated content. Silence is the space where we can clear the cache of the soul. As spiritual writer Ruth Haley Barton suggests, the wilderness of solitude strips away these unnecessary, constructed layers. She writes in *Sacred Rhythms*, "In the wilderness of solitude . . . we can finally stop managing our image."[25] It allows us to hear our own thoughts, feel our own emotions, and discern God's voice apart from the predictive text of our digital profiles.

Pathway 2: Nurturing Vulnerability and Authenticity

A second crucial pathway to inner healing involves the courageous and transformative work of nurturing vulnerability and authenticity. We live in a performance-driven, AI-curated world that constantly pressures us to present a polished, perfect, and problem-free version of ourselves. Our social media feeds are highlight reels, carefully edited to maximize likes and minimize the appearance of struggle. In this environment, choosing to be vulnerable—to be honest about our fears, our failures, and our pain—is a radical act of self-acceptance and a direct challenge to the shame-based culture of perfectionism.

Nurturing vulnerability and authenticity carries difficulties. The stress of exposing raw emotions can feel paralyzing, confronting fears of judgment in a world rewarding polished facades. Building trust and processing feedback demands time and energy, navigating the delicate process of sharing truths. Rejection or misunderstanding can lead to

24. Merton, *New Seeds of Contemplation*, 27–28; *No Man Is an Island*, 193–95.

25. Barton, *Sacred Rhythms*, 110.

hurt or disappointment. This practice is necessary because it dismantles shame, rewiring our brains for trust and belonging. Vulnerability fosters genuine connections, countering superficial digital identities, and embraces imperfections for true healing.

AI cannot replicate vulnerability and authenticity because it lacks the emotional depth and subjective experience required for genuine self-disclosure. While AI can mimic empathetic responses or analyze emotional patterns, it cannot feel the fear, courage, or relief of being truly seen. Vulnerability involves navigating complex emotions and relationships, beyond AI's capabilities. The transformative power of authenticity—rooted in personal risk and neurological shifts toward trust—requires a lived human experience that algorithms cannot emulate.

Curt Thompson has shown that this is not just a matter of emotional health but of neurological reality. Thompson's work integrates neuroscience with spiritual formation, explaining that shame thrives in secrecy and isolation. When we hide the parts of ourselves we deem flawed, we activate primitive fear circuits in our brains. When we share our stories in the presence of empathetic, nonjudgmental others, we activate the brain's relational circuits, releasing neurochemicals like oxytocin that create feelings of safety, trust, and belonging. In his masterful book *The Soul of Shame*, he writes, "Shame is the emotional weapon that evil uses to . . . corrupt our relationships with God and each other."[26]

One of the most powerful practices for nurturing this kind of authenticity is honest lament. The Bible is filled with it—the Psalms, in particular, are a master class in crying out to God with raw, unfiltered honesty about sorrow, anger, and confusion. This is not the same as complaining; it is a courageous act of faith that brings our real pain into the presence of a God we believe is strong enough to handle it. The Old Testament theologian Walter Brueggemann argues that this practice is essential for breaking through the denial that keeps us spiritually numb. In his classic work *The Prophetic Imagination*, he writes, "The task of prophetic ministry is to nurture, nourish, and evoke a consciousness . . . alternative to the consciousness . . . of the dominant culture."[27] In an age where algorithms are literally designed to filter out content that might make us uncomfortable, creating spaces for authentic lament is a vital act.

26. Thompson, *Soul of Shame*, 25.

27. Brueggemann, *Prophetic Imagination*, 13.

This naturally leads to the importance of sharing our stories in safe and supportive communities. Whether it's a church small group, a secular recovery program, or a trusted circle of friends, the act of being truly seen and heard without judgment is profoundly healing. These are the spaces where we can take off the armor of performance and allow our true selves to emerge. Brené Brown has famously described the courage this takes. Her research differentiates between guilt ("I did something bad") and shame ("I am bad"). She argues that the only way to build shame resilience is to speak our shame, to share our stories with people who will respond with empathy. In *Daring Greatly*, she explains, "Vulnerability is not weakness; it's our greatest measure of courage."[28] It is only by daring to show up and be seen that we can experience the connection and belonging we are all wired for.

Yet, the most important practice is to learn from Christ with an open and safe heart. The human desire for vulnerability and authenticity is profound, yet our efforts to achieve them often leave us more exhausted and insecure. This failure stems from a foundational problem: we lack a worthy object of learning. Without a perfect and unchanging standard, we model ourselves after flawed sources—shifting cultural trends, performance-based ideals, or our own broken ambitions. We build a false self, an imposter designed to manage our image and hide our shame rather than heal it. This creates a life of quiet desperation, antithetical to the freedom we seek. The writer Brennan Manning noted that this desperation drives us to "run from our true self," but the cycle is unbreakable until we find a completely different kind of model to learn from.[29]

This is why Christ's invitation in Scripture is so revolutionary. He does not say, "Try harder," but rather, "Come to me, all you who are weary and burdened, and I will give you rest. Take my yoke upon you and learn from me, for I am gentle and humble in heart, and you will find rest for your souls" (Matt 11:28–29). He presents himself as the one right object of learning whose very nature creates the safety required for authenticity. This learning is not academic but relational. When he stood with the woman caught in adultery, he demonstrated the core lesson that makes vulnerability possible: that in him, there is "no condemnation" (Rom 8:1). His gentle authority silenced the accusers and replaced shame with grace, forging the ultimate safe environment.

28. Brown, *Daring Greatly*, 33.

29. Manning, *Abba's Child*, 25.

Furthermore, Christ is the only model who can truly empathize with our struggle. He is not a distant standard but, as Heb 4:15 tells us, a high priest who is able "to empathize with our weaknesses." When he wept openly at Lazarus's tomb, he sanctified human sorrow, teaching that authentic connection is born from shared vulnerability. In our modern world, AI can mimic empathy, but it is a hollow echo. It has no weakness to share, no gentleness to model, and no grace to give. It is a tool of information, not transformation. True humanity is not self-generated; it is the fruit of learning from the only source who offers both a perfect, gentle standard and the unconditional love that makes it possible for us to become our true selves.

Pathway 3: Cultivating Deep, Authentic Relationships

A third, essential pathway to healing involves intentionally cultivating deep, authentic relationships and the practice of being fully present within them. This offers a powerful and necessary antidote to the pervasive loneliness and fragmentation of the AI age. Our world is increasingly mediated by screens and algorithms, which promise connection but often deliver a shallow, disembodied substitute. Genuine human connection—the kind that nourishes the soul—is not about exchanging information; it is about sharing a sense of presence. As we've discussed, the author Robert Wicks has identified this quality of presence as the very heart of healing.

Cultivating deep relationships and presence is challenging. The stress of navigating emotional intimacy or conflicts requires vulnerability and patience. Investing in relationships demands time and energy, prioritizing face-to-face connections over distractions. Betrayal or unreciprocated efforts can lead to hurt or disappointment. This practice is necessary because it combats loneliness, rebuilds social capital, and provides emotional sustenance, fostering trust and belonging in a fragmented world. As we discussed, AI cannot cultivate deep relationships or presence because it lacks the capacity for emotional intimacy or genuine human connection.

This pathway begins with the simple but difficult practice of intentional presence in our everyday interactions. It means putting down our phones when someone is talking to us. It means actively listening, not just to form a reply, but to truly understand the world from another person's perspective. The journalist Kate Murphy has explored the science and art of this lost practice. Her work reveals that we are, as a culture, becoming terrible listeners. In her insightful book *You're Not Listening*, she states, "Listening is an act of generosity . . . that requires you to silence your own inner monologue."[30]

Beyond our one-on-one interactions, we must also focus on building communities of compassion and belonging. The sociologist Robert D. Putnam famously documented the decline of "social capital" in modern society—the erosion of the clubs, leagues, and associations that once formed the fabric of our communal life. The internet, he argued, has often accelerated this trend, replacing deep, embodied community with shallow, virtual networks. In his landmark book *Bowling Alone*, he warned that our stock of social capital has plummeted, impoverishing our lives and communities.[31]

The work of healing, then, involves intentionally rebuilding this social fabric through shared experiences and rituals. As Priya Parker has shown, there is a powerful art to gathering people in a way that fosters genuine connection. Parker argues that most of our gatherings are dull because we focus on the logistics instead of the purpose. In her book *The Art of Gathering*, she writes, "Gathering matters because it is through each other that we figure out what we believe and who we are."[32]

I think of Lena, a retired teacher in her late seventies who, after her husband passed away, found herself increasingly isolated, spending most of her days scrolling through news feeds and old photos online. Feeling her world shrinking, she made the difficult decision to start volunteering at a local community garden. At first, she felt awkward. But as she worked the soil alongside a diverse group of people—a young immigrant family, a college student, a musician—something began to blossom within her. Through the shared labor, the easy conversations about weather and weeds, and the communal joy of the harvest, she began to experience profound healing. She found purpose and friendship, not in the disembodied world of digital interactions, but in the rich, earthy reality of a shared place and a shared purpose. Her story is a beautiful illustration of the transformative power of relationality and presence as a pathway back to a whole and flourishing life.

30. Murphy, *You're Not Listening*, 10.

31. Putnam, *Bowling Alone*, 19.

32. Parker, *Art of Gathering*, 40.

Conclusion

This chapter has navigated the alluring and dangerous myth of our AI age: that personal growth equals performance and metrics. We began by exploring how the promise of an optimized, data-driven life, while seductive, can trap us in a culture of perfectionism and comparison, leading to profound psychological and spiritual harm. We've seen that while AI can provide a flood of knowledge about ourselves, it cannot lead the distinctly human journey of inner healing and growth. This journey, we've argued, has a profound impact, restoring the soul from a performance-based identity to one of authentic presence, reconnecting us compassionately to our bodies, and empowering us to build communities of genuine connection that reflect the *imago Dei*.

The path forward, then, is not found in a better app or a more sophisticated algorithm but in the intentional cultivation of countercultural pathways. It requires courageously embracing deep rest, nurturing the strength found in vulnerability, and cultivating authentic, present relationships. These practices are not inefficiencies to be overcome but essential disciplines for a soulful life. Ultimately, true growth is not a problem to be solved but a sacred mystery to be lived. In a world that pressures us to optimize, our most vital work is the slow, unquantifiable, and relational journey of becoming fully human—a task that remains uniquely ours.

Chapter 8

Listening from Darkness

The light shines in the darkness, and the darkness has not overcome it.
—John 1:5

I will give you hidden treasures, riches stored in secret places, so that you may know that I am the Lord, the God of Israel, who summons you by name.
—Isaiah 45:3

LET'S BE CLEAR FROM the outset: artificial intelligence already helps—and will continue to help—alleviate immense, tangible forms of human suffering. This technology isn't trivial; it is a powerful force for good across countless arenas. AI models are accelerating life-saving drug discovery, advancing climate modeling, and powering accessibility tools that grant new freedoms to people with disabilities. The myth we must confront is not that AI is helpful—it is—but that its help is absolute. The belief that a world interwoven with AI will—or even could—eliminate darkness is compelling precisely because it amplifies AI's genuine promise to make life safer, more predictable, and more comfortable.

This promise is already taking shape around us. AI-powered surveillance systems, for instance, don't just deter crime; they analyze patterns to predict it, alerting authorities to potential dangers before they unfold. At home, smart systems act as centralized caretakers, managing everything from rhythm-learning security protocols to health monitoring that offers families real peace of mind. Algorithms now analyze vast datasets of human expression to predict—and sometimes prevent—mental-health crises. Together these advancements offer an almost irresistible vision: risk quantified and minimized, loneliness managed by an ever-present AI companion, and life's jagged edges smoothed by data-driven insight. It promises protection from shadows—literal and metaphorical—by crafting an environment of perpetual light and algorithmic control. It is the promise of a more secure, comfortable existence—and in many ways, AI is already delivering.

However, a question begins to surface, one that is rarely asked in the breathless pace of innovation. Can we be fully human if we never learn from darkness? This question becomes especially urgent when we fall for the belief that with AI, there will be no darkness left to learn from. The darkness of struggle, of grief, of uncertainty, and of solitude is not, it seems, a bug in the human operating system that needs patching; it appears to be a core feature. It is in these very moments of friction and shadow that we develop the uniquely human capacities for resilience, empathy, and wisdom. An AI can certainly be programmed to offer a comforting word, but it cannot truly sit with you in the quiet, messy, and sacred space of grief—an experience that somehow deepens the soul in a way comfort alone cannot. It can protect you from a thousand calculated risks, but it cannot teach you the courage that comes from facing a single, uncalculated challenge and discovering your own strength. By systematically outsourcing our struggles to a system designed to eliminate them, we risk architecting a perfectly optimized life that is, in the end, profoundly shallow. We may trade profound meaning for frictionless convenience—and diminish the very things that make life worth living.

Myth 8: If You Live with AI, There Will Be No Darkness

It is a gospel of algorithmic light promising not salvation from sin but relief from the burdens of the human condition itself. This myth, a central and often unspoken tenet of our unfolding technological age, heralds a future of unblemished clarity, unparalleled efficiency, and perpetual, machine-generated illumination. It paints a vision of human life where the ambiguities, the struggles, and the inherent suffering that have defined our existence for millennia are not just mitigated but systematically eradicated. In this new telling, these ancient human problems are rendered obsolete by the sheer computational power of our own creations, much like an old piece of software is replaced by a newer, more efficient version.

This is the promise of a life where confusion is a ghost of the past, replaced by infallible algorithms that can chart the optimal path in every conceivable situation, from career choices to romantic partnerships. It's a future where emotional turmoil is seen as an outdated inefficiency, a bug in our biological software that can be diagnosed and rectified by data-driven insights from a wellness app. It's a reality where the very concept of darkness—in all its physical, psychological, and spiritual manifestations—can be meticulously engineered out of our daily existence.

This alluring myth is not born in a vacuum; it feels like it is being carefully and relentlessly cultivated by a powerful confluence of cultural and economic forces. We hear its verses in the visionary, almost messianic pronouncements of tech giants, who often speak of AI not merely as a product line but as a benevolent force for global transformation, a tool that will solve everything from poverty to mortality. We see its undeniable appeal in the speculative exuberance of venture capitalists, who pour billions of dollars into startups that all seem to be promising a frictionless world—a world without waiting, without error, without boredom, and, most of all, without discomfort. And we absorb its tenets, often uncritically, from a popular media landscape that tends to celebrate innovation with a kind of breathless, childlike optimism, frequently overlooking the deeper philosophical questions at play.

But the myth's true and enduring power likely comes from its resonance with one of our most ancient and deeply human yearnings: the desire for an existence liberated from pain, chaos, and uncertainty. The core assertion of this AI-driven utopia is that computational intelligence, with its purported objectivity and its seemingly limitless processing power, can finally allow us to transcend the messy and often painful limitations of human biology, psychology, and even our spiritual capacity. In this emerging worldview, algorithms become the ultimate arbiters of truth, the infallible guides for every decision, and the tireless architects of our perfectly curated experiences. The implicit, and deeply troubling, message is that human fallibility itself—our biases, our emotional inconsistencies, our cognitive limits, our very capacity for confusion and pain—is essentially a defect. It's a flaw in the human operating system that AI is uniquely, and finally, positioned to debug and correct.

This gospel of algorithmic light manifests in almost every facet of our lives, often in ways that seem both helpful and entirely benign. Consider the ever-expanding realm of personal well-being, where a universe of AI-powered applications now promises to micromanage and optimize every conceivable aspect of our existence. These platforms offer to track our sleep cycles, analyze our dietary choices, monitor our exercise routines, and even chart the subtle fluctuations of our emotional states by analyzing our text messages and tone of voice. They deliver hyper-personalized recommendations, derived from vast datasets of biometric information and behavioral analytics, all designed to guide us toward an algorithmically defined state of perfect health and perpetual contentment.

Imagine a character, let's call him Alex, a young professional thoroughly dedicated to the modern project of self-improvement. His day begins not with the gentle light of the sun but with the soft glow of his smartphone. He consults an AI wellness coach, let's call it Aura, that has analyzed his sleep quality through the sensors in his mattress. Aura informs him that his REM sleep was 7 percent below optimal and, in response, prescribes his ideal caffeine intake for the day (a single espresso at 9:15 AM) and a specific five-minute mindfulness exercise to optimize his morning focus. Throughout his workday, another application silently monitors his productivity, tracking his keystrokes and browser tabs. If his attention wanes, a gentle, synthesized voice nudges him: "It seems you're distracted, Alex. Let's get back to the task at hand for just fifteen more minutes." His meals are suggested by an algorithm that has calculated his precise nutritional needs based on his activity level and health goals. If he feels a sudden wave of anxiety—perhaps triggered by a stressful email—a chatbot is instantly ready to guide him through a breathing exercise, offering validating and soothing, if entirely generic, responses like, "I understand that must be difficult. Remember to breathe."

On the surface, Alex's life is a model of efficiency and wellness. By all metrics, he is living in the light. He is calm, productive, and healthy. But beneath this placid surface, a subtle alienation appears to be taking place. He is slowly, almost imperceptibly, learning to distrust the innate signals of his own body. The feeling of fatigue is no longer an intuitive call to rest but a data point to be corrected with a stimulant or a bio-hack. He is learning to outsource the management of his emotions, turning to a chatbot for comfort rather than developing the internal capacity to sit with his anxiety and understand its source. The myth promises Alex a life without the darkness of bodily failure or emotional turmoil, but it seems to do so by disconnecting him from the essential, subjective, and often messy process of self-discovery. He is missing out on the invaluable, if difficult, lessons that can only be gleaned from personal struggle.

This same logic extends, perhaps even more troublingly, to the world of education. AI-driven learning platforms aspire to eliminate all learning gaps, adapting curricula in real time to each student's unique learning style. They promise an uninterrupted and frictionless trajectory of progress, where no child is left behind and every concept is mastered with perfect efficiency. This vision, however, implicitly devalues the profound importance of intellectual struggle. It seems to overlook the fact that grappling with a difficult concept, wrestling with a complex problem, and even experiencing the frustration of failure are the very processes that build intellectual muscle. These are the moments that foster true curiosity and lead to the deep, lasting satisfaction of a hard-won understanding. A world where learning is perfectly optimized may be a world where the darkness of not knowing—a darkness that fuels all genuine inquiry—is seen not as a space to be inhabited and explored but as a problem to be solved as quickly as possible.

Beyond the individual, the myth extends its ambitious reach to the grander scale of societal optimization. AI-driven matchmaking services promise to identify our ideal partners based on data points and compatibility scores, ostensibly eliminating the darkness of relational discord, the sharp pain of heartbreak, and the terrifying vulnerability of an authentic, risky connection. Predictive policing models, now being deployed in cities around the world, aim to preempt criminal activity by allocating resources based on where crime is most likely to occur. This envisions a future largely free from the darkness of societal pathology and interpersonal conflict but often does so by amplifying existing biases found in historical data and sacrificing justice for the illusion of security.

And now, the burgeoning concepts of the metaverse and augmented reality amplify this myth to its logical, and perhaps most extreme, conclusion. They envision fully immersive, completely customizable realities where users can meticulously sculpt their environments, their relationships, and even their own identities. This allows them to effectively excise any undesirable element—any perceived darkness—from their lived experience. The promise is an endless, seamless stream of curated perfection, where friction is eliminated and discomfort is a distant, optional memory. This technological light is presented not merely as an improvement on reality but as a total liberation from the cumbersome and unpredictable weight of human imperfection.

The true danger lies in a subtle but radical redefinition of human flourishing. It quietly suggests that a life entirely free from friction, from uncertainty, from moments of profound disorientation, or from genuine sorrow is the pinnacle of human achievement. This perspective inherently devalues the very aspects of life—struggle, failure, grief, doubt—that have, for millennia, been understood across diverse wisdom traditions as the essential catalysts for developing depth, fostering resilience, cultivating empathy, and deepening spiritual insight. The relentless pursuit of perpetual clarity through AI, therefore, risks becoming a form of collective self-deception. It creates a blinding glare that prevents us from truly seeing the rich, complex tapestry of human existence—a tapestry that, like any profound work of art, requires both the interplay of brilliant light and the nuanced depth of shadow for its full and meaningful expression. It is a promise of liberation that, paradoxically, threatens to entrap us in a technologically mediated bubble, disconnecting us from the vital lessons, the hard-won wisdom, and the hidden treasures that only the courageous navigation of darkness can truly reveal.

Human as a Holistic Being—Body, Mind, Emotion, and Soul

To begin to dismantle the myth that AI can engineer a life without darkness, we have to start by challenging its most fundamental, and perhaps most flawed, premise: the idea that a human being is a machine to be debugged. The gospel of algorithmic light, which we explored in the last section, isn't just a story about technology; it's a story about ourselves. It's built on a fragmented and deeply reductionist view of the self, one that is becoming increasingly common as we learn to speak about ourselves in the language of our new tools. We hear it all the time now. We are "information processors." Our brains are "neural networks," a metaphor borrowed directly from the architecture of AI. Our bodies are "biological machines" to be optimized, and our lives are just a collection of data points to be analyzed for maximum efficiency and output. An entire industry of AI-powered wearables and wellness apps is built on this very metaphor, presenting us with dashboards of our own metrics and encouraging us to tweak the inputs to get the desired outputs, as if we were calibrating a piece of hardware.

This perspective, while it might offer a certain kind of analytical clarity, tragically misses the rich, vibrant, and profoundly mysterious reality of human experience. It's a view that flattens the majestic, three-dimensional landscape of our inner world into a one-dimensional spreadsheet, making it legible for an algorithm but unrecognizable to the human heart. This part of our journey, therefore, is a call to return to a deeper and more ancient truth, a truth that our technology seems to be encouraging us to forget: the human being is not a machine to be debugged. We are, in essence, a symphony of interacting and interdependent parts—the physical, the mental, the emotional, and the spiritual. Each is a vital and essential instrument, each one influencing all the others, creating a living tapestry of consciousness that is far greater and more mysterious than the sum of its components. To truly understand who we are, and to navigate the challenges of our time with wisdom, we must first embrace this holistic anthropology. We must learn to see the intricate web of our being not as a flaw to be optimized away but as a reality to be honored—a reality that feels both inherently holy and fundamentally whole. To truly grasp our nature, we must learn to listen to the music of the whole symphony, rather than trying to isolate and perfect the sound of a single instrument.

The Body as Holy Ground

Our journey back into wholeness begins where all of our experiences begin: with the body, the very ground of our being. In our increasingly screen-based, digitally mediated world, it has become dangerously easy to treat the body as an inconvenient vessel for the mind, a project to be perfected, or a machine to be debugged. Yet, the body is not merely an accessory to our identity; it appears to be absolutely integral to it.

Theologian James K. A. Smith provides a powerful framework for understanding this, suggesting that our primary orientation to the world is not through abstract thought but through our loves and desires, which are themselves shaped by deeply ingrained bodily practices. He argues that we are fundamentally embodied creatures whose postures, habits, and daily movements—the liturgies of our everyday lives—profoundly shape who we ultimately become. In his book *You Are What You Love*, Smith pushes back against a purely cognitive view of the human person as desiring animals, noting that "We learn to love, then, not primarily by acquiring information . . . but through practices that form the habits of our hearts."[1] This idea feels like a crucial antidote to the AI-driven vision of a disembodied self, floating in a cloud of pure data.

This ancient wisdom has been powerfully affirmed by contemporary neuroscience. The research of neuroscientist Antonio Damasio, for instance, shows that our brain's very sense of self seems to arise from its constant, intricate process of interoception—the tracking of our internal bodily states like heart rate, gut feelings, and subtle shifts in our internal temperature. He argues convincingly that the self is not some ghost in the machine, hovering above or outside the body, but rather flows directly and continuously from it. The body, in this view, is the foundational layer of our conscious being, carrying the deep, nonverbal memory of our entire lives within its very tissues. In *The Strange Order of Things*, Damasio writes that "feelings are the mental expressions of homeostasis," connecting our biological life directly to our mental experience.[2]

This is a truth made painfully and beautifully clear in the study of trauma. Dr. Bessel van der Kolk's groundbreaking work has demonstrated that our past is not just remembered cognitively but is held somatically, a reality he powerfully captured in the title of his seminal book *The Body Keeps the Score*. Healing our identity, therefore, is not a matter of escaping the body through some transcendent intellectual exercise or a new app that promises to rewire our thoughts. It is, rather, the courageous and often difficult work of learning to reinhabit our own flesh, to listen to the stories our bodies tell, and to finally feel safe within our own skin.

Yet so many of our modern lives are marked by a profound bodily disconnection. This state of alienation is fostered by our disembodying digital interfaces, which train us to live in our heads, and by a culture that often instills shame about our physical selves. It's exacerbated by the chronic stress that tells us to ignore our body's signals and even by well-intentioned but overly spiritualized worldviews that treat the physical as somehow less important, less holy, than the ethereal. To reclaim our true identity in an age of artificial intelligence, we must first reclaim the body. We must see it not as an idol to be worshipped, an enemy to be conquered, or a dataset to be optimized but as the holy ground where God meets us, right here, right now, exactly where we are.

1. Smith, *You Are*, 33.
2. Damasio, *Strange Order of Things*, 102.

Emotion as Sacred Intelligence

In a culture that prizes rationality, data, and algorithmic control, our emotions are often dismissed as unreliable, irrational, or even as sinful weaknesses to be suppressed and overcome. This deep-seated distrust of our emotional lives flattens our humanity and cuts us off from what may be one of our most vital sources of wisdom. The truth is, our emotions are not random noise; they are the vibrant threads that connect our inner truth with the outer world. They appear to be the indispensable bridge between pure physical sensation and the coherent stories our minds create about our lives. They are the crucial, nonnegotiable link between the body and the soul. AI can process sentiment data; it cannot feel the pang of nostalgia or the surge of righteous anger—and in that difference lies a universe of meaning.

The pioneering research of neuroscientist Lisa Feldman Barrett has revolutionized our understanding of feelings, directly challenging the simplistic and long-held idea that emotions are primitive reflexes to be controlled by our more evolved rational brain. Her work powerfully argues that emotions are not hardwired reflexes that simply happen to us. Rather, they are complex experiences that our brains actively construct in the moment, shaped by our past learning, our bodily sensations, and our cultural context. In her book *How Emotions Are Made*, she explains this complex process, stating that our brains are constantly making predictions, and "emotions are your brain's creation of what your bodily sensations mean, in relation to what is going on around you in the world."[3] Our feelings, then, are not weaknesses to be overcome or bugs to be patched by a therapy bot. They are profound and nuanced insights—powerful windows into how we are interpreting the world and what we truly care about.

Furthermore, our emotions seem to be absolutely essential for forming memories and for creating moral meaning. As neuroscientist Joseph LeDoux has explored in his landmark book *The Emotional Brain*, our emotional memories are what help us evaluate danger, value, and attachment. It is the feeling of fear that teaches us caution; it is the feeling of love that teaches us commitment. These memories, formed in the crucible of intense feeling, literally constitute the rich and varied texture of our lived experience. To suppress them, to numb them, or to hand

3. Barrett, *How Emotions Are Made*, 30.

over their management to an algorithm that promises a state of perpetual placidity, is to distort the very essence of who we are.

The great spiritual traditions have long understood this. The Psalms of the Hebrew Bible are a raw and unfiltered library of human emotional expression. They are filled with rage, sorrow, ecstasy, and despair, all directed toward God without shame or apology. Jesus himself, in the Gospels, is presented as a figure of profound emotional depth. He weeps at the tomb of his friend, he burns with righteous anger in the temple, and he trembles with visceral anxiety in the garden of Gethsemane. In this light, our emotions are not distractions from God; they are often the very arenas in which God enters our lives with transformative power. What we fear, what we love, what we grieve, and what we hope for are not random impulses to be smoothed over. They are powerful signposts pointing toward our deepest identity and what we hold most sacred. To embrace them with curiosity and compassion is to allow them to refine us into more whole and authentic human beings.

The Mind as Storyteller, Not Computer

The human mind is a marvel, but the modern analogy of the mind as a computer—so prevalent and reinforcing in the age of AI—is a dangerously reductive one. It's tempting, of course. It makes us feel like our inner world is something we can understand, control, and even upgrade. But the mind is not merely the realm of cold, detached logic, processing inputs and generating outputs. It is, perhaps more accurately, the master storyteller of the self. It is the faculty that gives language to our raw sensations and weaves the sprawling, often chaotic, data of our memories, feelings, and experiences into a coherent narrative of who we are.

But the mind is also fragile. It is prone to distortion, to comparison, and to a desperate, often-anxious need for control. In our digital age, this fragility is being exploited on an unprecedented scale. Our thoughts are often hijacked by algorithms designed to reward outrage over reflection and to foster a state of perpetual distraction over one of depth. The very logic of an AI-curated information stream works against the slow, patient, and sometimes difficult work of deep thinking.

Cognitive science, particularly the work of researchers like Anil Seth, suggests that our very sense of self is not a static *thing* but an active, ongoing process of constant prediction and interpretation. This aligns with the idea of the mind as a storyteller. In his fascinating book *Being You*, Seth explains that our conscious reality is a kind of "controlled hallucination" generated by the brain, based on its best guesses about the world.[4] We don't just have thoughts; we are shaped by them. The stories we tell ourselves about our lives, about our worth, and about our place in the world literally define the boundaries of who we believe ourselves to be.

This scientific perspective aligns powerfully with the ancient theological insight of the apostle Paul, who called for transformation, not through sheer willpower, but through the "renewing of your mind" (Rom 12:2). This suggests that transformation begins not in simply changing our external behavior but in changing the very stories and patterns of thought that shape us. In an age where AI's computational logic threatens to supplant human insight, the inner space of the mind remains sacred ground. As the spiritual thinker Dallas Willard reminds us in works like *Renovation of the Heart*, the mind is not merely for the processing of information but for the slow and patient work of formation, through which we learn to turn inward toward wisdom and upward toward transcendence. This is a kind of work that cannot be outsourced.

The Soul as a Restless Longing

If the body is what grounds us in the here and now, the soul is what lifts us toward the ultimate. The soul is not some spooky ghost within the machine of the body. It might be better understood as the deepest desire that animates the human heart, the irreducible core of our being. It is the seat of our inexhaustible longing for meaning, for connection, for wholeness, and for God. While the soul may be impossible to define with scientific precision or capture in a dataset, its reality is profoundly felt in the universal human experience. It is the part of us we are speaking of when we ask the great questions: "Who am I, really, beneath all the roles I play and the things I do?" or "What on earth was I made for?" An AI can answer what we should do next to be more productive, but it can never touch the soul's question of why we are here at all.

Augustine of Hippo gave voice to this universal human reality at the very beginning of his famous *Confessions* with a line that has echoed through the centuries: "I entered into the very depths of my soul . . . and

4. Seth, *Being You*, 83.

with the eye of my soul, I saw the Unchangeable Light above my mind."[5] This profound restlessness is the defining mark of the soul. It is the part of us that stubbornly points toward a home beyond what can be touched, measured, or calculated. It is the ache that a perfectly optimized, frictionless life can never soothe.

This ancient theological insight finds a powerful modern echo in the work of the psychiatrist and Holocaust survivor Viktor Frankl. In his harrowing and essential book *Man's Search for Meaning*, Frankl affirms that the "will to meaning" is not a secondary concern that comes after our basic needs are met; it is, in fact, the central and primary drive of human life. From his own harrowing experience in the Nazi concentration camps, he observed that the prisoners who were most likely to survive were not necessarily the strongest physically but those who held on to a sense of purpose—a reason to live. He concluded that a human being "can survive almost any 'how' if he has a 'why.'"[6] Without a sense of purpose, we can lose the will to live, even if all our physical needs are met and all our discomforts are eliminated. The soul requires meaning, and meaning is something that is often forged in the very darkness that the myth of AI promises to erase.

The Divine Dance: A Metaphor for Wholeness

To truly understand ourselves as these holistic beings, it can be helpful to have a conceptual framework, a metaphor that can hold the immense complexity of our nature. One of the richest and most insightful analogies can be drawn from a foundational concept in Christian theology: the idea of the Triune God, or the Trinity. While this is a specific theological doctrine, its underlying pattern of unity in diversity offers a powerful metaphorical lens for understanding the human person, regardless of one's faith tradition. The Trinity describes God as one in essence, yet existing in three distinct and inseparable aspects—often called Father, Son, and Holy Spirit—that dynamically interrelate without ever collapsing into a single, undifferentiated entity. This pattern provides a profound model for resisting the modern, AI-driven tendency to fragment ourselves into isolated components (a body to be hacked, a mind to be optimized) or to reduce our entire being to a single dominant faculty.

5. Augustine, *Confessions*, 123.

6. Frankl, *Man's Search for Meaning*, 74–77, 105–6.

This analogy helps us see that our different aspects—body, mind, emotion, and soul—are not in competition but exist in a dynamic, harmonious, and interdependent relationship. It emphasizes three crucial principles.

First, it emphasizes unity. Just as the Trinity is understood as one God, we are fundamentally one person, a singular and coherent identity. My thoughts, my body, my emotions, and my spirit are not separate entities fighting for control; they all belong to and constitute the single *I* that is me. This means that a disturbance in one area inevitably sends ripples throughout the entire system. This is a lived reality we all know intimately. A simple headache (a physical suffering) can make it nearly impossible to concentrate or think clearly (the mind fogs). A night of insufficient sleep (a physical deprivation) leaves not only our minds sluggish and our decision-making impaired the next day but can also make us emotionally volatile and short-tempered. Chronic stress (a state of mind) can lead to a host of very real physical ailments, including digestive issues, cardiovascular problems, and a weakened immune system. The body is the foundation, and when its equilibrium is disturbed, the entire system is affected.

Second, the analogy highlights distinctness without separation. Each aspect of our being has its unique qualities and functions. My body experiences hunger and touch; my mind engages in abstract reasoning; my emotions feel joy and sorrow; my soul yearns for ultimate meaning and intimacy with the Creator God. These are distinct realms of experience, yet they are never truly separate. They flow into one another, influence one another, and are completely interdependent. Just as a theologian might say you cannot have the *love* of God without the *wisdom* of God, you cannot have a healthy mind in a neglected body, or a vibrant spirit in an emotionally numb person. Health is not about isolating and perfecting one part but about fostering the health of the whole.

Third, the analogy speaks to a dynamic interrelation, a divine dance. The traditional theological understanding of the Trinity describes a profound, eternal dance of relationship, a mutual indwelling and interpenetration known as *perichoresis*, where each aspect gives to and receives from the others in perfect harmony. Our body, mind, emotions, and soul are in a similar, constant dance. Consider what happens when our spirit is dry. This refers to that innate human longing for meaning, purpose, and transcendence. When this dimension of our lives is neglected—when our work feels devoid of purpose, when we are disconnected from our core values, or when we lose a sense of hope—a profound emotional emptiness can set in, and our emotions can seem to collapse. This spiritual aridity can manifest as cynicism, apathy, or what psychologists call anhedonia—the inability to experience pleasure. Our emotional lives, lacking the anchor of a deeper meaning, can become flattened or wildly volatile. Conversely, a strong sense of purpose (a spiritual state) can bring profound clarity and focus to the mind, providing a sense of direction that calms our anxious emotions and can even motivate us to care for our physical bodies. This intricate web is not a vulnerability to overcome but a truth to embrace.

The Crucible of Darkness: The Fifth Dimension of Identity

In this holistic view of the self, we must make room for one final, crucial dimension—one that our modern world, with its promise of AI-driven perfection, is most eager to deny. At the edge of every soul, and woven through the very fabric of our body, mind, and emotions, lies the reality of darkness. This is the dimension of our fears: the fear of death, of insignificance, of rejection, of pain, of abandonment. Yet, rather than being an enemy to our identity, this darkness is often its crucible. It is the fire in which our character is forged. What we fear most often reveals what we care about most deeply. Our shadows are not separate from us; they are the exiled parts of ourselves, crying out for compassionate attention and integration.

The writer and theologian Barbara Brown Taylor, in her beautiful book *Learning to Walk in the Dark*, powerfully challenges our cultural and even religious obsession with light. She argues that a "solar spirituality" that shuns all shadows and equates faith with constant positivity ultimately leaves us fragile and unprepared for the reality of life. "I have learned things in the dark that I could never have learned in the light," she writes, affirming that darkness is where our illusions die and where a more rugged, authentic truth can finally be born.[7] The great theological narratives are filled with these dark epiphanies: Jacob wrestling a divine stranger through the night, Moses encountering God in a terrifying cloud of smoke and fire, and Jesus sweating blood in the darkness of Gethsemane. These defining moments of identity formation do not come in the clarity of daylight but in the terrifying ambiguity of struggle.

7. Taylor, *Learning to Walk*, 5.

Similarly, as Susan Cain argues in her work *Bittersweet*, it is often our experiences of grief, sorrow, and longing—not our moments of constant, unassailable positivity—that deepen our identity, expand our capacity for compassion, and connect us to the profound beauty of a fragile life. In our contemporary culture, this essential darkness is often feared, numbed, or endlessly distracted from by the very technologies that promise us light. But when we find the courage to turn toward it, darkness can become our teacher, not our tormentor. It reveals the parts of ourselves we have exiled, the pain we have buried, and the profound questions we have been too afraid to ask. Identity is not forged in comfort; it is refined in the mysterious fires of limitation and suffering. When we allow our darkness to speak—not to define us, but to deepen us—we become more compassionate, more authentic, and more fully and beautifully real.

The formation of our identity, then, is not about achieving some static state of perfection that can be measured and managed by an algorithm. It is about the lifelong, dynamic process of integration. It is the unfolding of all that we are—body, mind, emotion, soul, and even our darkness—into the fullness of who we were made to be. It is not a thing but a becoming. And it is in the courageous act of listening to every instrument in our inner orchestra, including the dissonant and mournful notes, that we can finally begin to hear the true and sacred music of who we are.

This intricate web of our being is not a vulnerability to be overcome but a profound truth to be embraced. True health is not about optimizing isolated parts, as the AI myth suggests, but about fostering harmony across all dimensions of our being. This holistic truth stands as the first and most powerful line of defense against the alluring but dangerous promise of a life optimized into shadowless, and ultimately inhuman, perfection.

Four Kinds of Darkness

The gospel of algorithmic light, as we've seen, promises to eradicate all shadows. It offers us a map of life where every dark valley has been leveled, every confusing path illuminated by the clear, unwavering beam of data. In a world conditioned to view discomfort and pain not as experiences but as problems to be fixed, this promise is powerfully seductive. We have become travelers who desire a map without shadows, a journey without friction. And artificial intelligence, more than any technology before it, presents itself as the ultimate cartographer for this sanitized world, ready to chart a course for us that bypasses any terrain that might be difficult, uncertain, or painful.

Yet, to see the profound danger in this myth, we must first learn to read the map of our own inherent darkness. This isn't a morbid exercise in cataloging human suffering. Instead, it's an attempt to create a compassionate and discerning guide to this feared terrain, to see it not as a flaw in the map but as a generative and essential feature of the landscape. This part of our journey is about exploring the darkness of the body, the mind, the emotions, and the spirit. We will look at them not as misfortunes to be engineered away by a clever AI but as powerful teachers and essential, if sometimes painful, pathways to a more integrated and authentic wholeness. This is a map that an AI could never draw, because it is a map whose key features are not efficiency and comfort but meaning and growth.

The Weight of the Vessel: Navigating Physical Darkness

The human body, for all its astonishing resilience and miraculous capabilities, is fundamentally and beautifully finite. It is subject to limitations, to fragility, and to the inevitable, universal flow of time toward decay and dissolution. This profound and often deeply uncomfortable truth represents a primary and foundational form of physical darkness. It manifests in countless ways: in the pervasive and heavy weight of fatigue, in the debilitating and often frightening grip of illness, in the isolating reality of sensory loss, and in the ultimate, undeniable horizon of our own mortality.

In a culture that frequently idolizes and relentlessly promotes images of youth, boundless strength, and a superhuman level of perpetual productivity—a culture now supercharged by AI-driven tools that promise to optimize our performance and bio-hack our way past our natural limits—these inherent aspects of our physical existence are too often denied. They are carefully hidden away or treated as problems to be swiftly fixed rather than as intrinsic and meaningful parts of the universal human experience.

Fatigue is perhaps the most common and universally experienced form of this physical darkness. It is far more than just feeling tired; it is a deep-seated weariness that can permeate every fiber of our being, making even the simplest tasks feel monumental. In our modern, always-on world, fatigue is frequently misconstrued as a personal failure. It's a weakness to be pushed through, an inconvenience to be masked with stimulants, or a bug in our system to be ignored in the relentless pursuit of achievement. We find ourselves in a strange cultural moment, boasting about working impossible hours or surviving on minimal sleep, as if defying our body's fundamental signals is a badge of honor. Yet, fatigue is in fact a vital, nonnegotiable message from our physical self. It is a profound demand for rest, for deep recuperation, and for essential replenishment. When we use AI-powered productivity software that gamifies our workflow or wellness apps that praise us for hitting activity goals despite exhaustion, we are actively overriding this crucial signal. We accumulate a physiological debt that inevitably impacts every system in our body and mind, leading to reduced cognitive function, heightened emotional irritability, and a weakened immune system. This slowing down, though initially unwelcome, can paradoxically be a profound invitation. It is a call to listen deeply to the often-ignored cries of a body yearning for stillness and repair. In the pervasive darkness of true exhaustion, our outward-facing energy is stripped away, forcing us inward to confront our inherent limits and acknowledge our fundamental need for repose.

Illness plunges us into an even more profound physical darkness. Whether it is a fleeting cold or a chronic, life-altering condition, illness fundamentally disrupts the familiar rhythms of our lives. When we are healthy, our bodies tend to operate in the background, faithfully supporting our activities. But illness abruptly forces our awareness directly into our physical being. It brings our undeniable fragility to the forefront, starkly reminding us that we are not, in fact, invincible machines. A debilitating injury can render us unexpectedly dependent on others. Chronic illness can introduce a persistent discomfort that becomes a constant companion, forcing us to radically redefine our capabilities. While AI-powered diagnostics can offer incredible clarity and treatment paths, the cultural narrative around them can subtly reinforce the idea that illness is merely a data problem to be solved. This can obscure the deeper, more human experience of being ill, which is a profound teacher. It can foster a patience we never knew we had, deepen our empathy for others who suffer, and instill a far richer appreciation for the simple gift of health. Illness compels us to confront our vulnerability and surrender to processes beyond our control, deepening our humility and radically refining our perspective on what genuinely matters.

Sensory loss—whether blindness, deafness, or another diminished sense—immerses individuals in a unique form of physical darkness. It represents the loss of a familiar light, necessitating a profound adaptation. While undeniably difficult, this darkness often paradoxically reveals remarkable capacities for resilience and alternative forms of perception. It reveals just how incredibly adaptable the human system is, and how much we can experience beyond our accustomed sensory windows.

Finally, the overarching reality beneath all these is our inherent mortality. Our bodies are not designed for perpetual existence. This ultimate limitation casts a long, existential shadow over human life. The primal fear of decay and cessation is a universal aspect of human consciousness. And yet, this is the very darkness that some in the world of AI research and transhumanism promises to conquer, offering visions of digital immortality where consciousness is uploaded to the cloud. This ultimate "solution" to darkness avoids the profound truth that confronting our mortality can be a tremendously powerful catalyst. It can strip away superficial concerns, forcing us to focus with newfound clarity on what genuinely matters: the quality of our relationships, the integrity of our values, and our connection to something transcendent. In the stark face of our physical finitude, we are reminded of the immense preciousness of life itself. Embracing our physical darkness, then, is not a surrender to despair but a profound act of wisdom and humility.

The Cloud of Unknowing: Navigating Mindful Darkness

While physical darkness manifests in the body, mindful darkness permeates the vast realm of our cognition. This is the experience of the mind's inherent limitations, not as a pathology but as a fundamental and often highly productive part of the human cognitive landscape. It presents itself as pervasive confusion, paralyzing indecision, and the frustrating inability to concentrate. In an era that zealously champions information access, logical precision, and the immediate, AI-generated answer, these states of mental murkiness are frequently perceived as personal failures—cognitive deficiencies to be swiftly overcome. Yet, mindful darkness, when engaged with patiently, holds its own profound lessons and is, quite often, an essential prerequisite for genuine insight.

Confusion is a primary and often deeply unsettling manifestation of mindful darkness. It is that disorienting state where our familiar frameworks no longer seem to apply, where information appears contradictory, or where the path forward is utterly obscured. We might instinctively grasp at simplistic answers or, increasingly, turn to a large language model for a quick, confident-sounding summary. We ask the AI to resolve the ambiguity for us. However, true understanding almost always necessitates a period of dwelling in confusion. This is the fertile ground where genuine learning and discovery often take place. Scientists spend countless hours wrestling with bewildering data before a revolutionary breakthrough occurs. Artists grapple with formlessness and creative blocks before a masterpiece takes shape. Personal growth frequently begins only when our old narratives prove insufficient, leaving us profoundly confused. The darkness of confusion forces us to question, to explore, and to courageously expand our mental models. It is, ultimately, a profound invitation to intellectual humility—a quality that is the polar opposite of a machine designed to always have an answer.

Hand in hand with confusion often comes indecision. This is the mental paralysis that arises when multiple paths seem equally valid, or when the consequences of a choice are profoundly unclear. In a world that prizes efficiency, indecision is condemned as a weakness. We are encouraged to seek algorithms to tell us the best choice, from what to buy to whom to date, absolving us of the responsibility of genuine discernment. Yet, truly significant decisions—those that shape our lives and character—often require a period of profound indecision. This is not wasted time; it is a vital period for the careful weighing of options, for listening to our intuition, and for allowing a deeper, inner wisdom to surface. Rushing this process frequently leads to superficial choices and regret. The darkness of indecision forces us to confront our core values and to take full responsibility for our choices. It cultivates patience and the courage to act even when absolute certainty is elusive.

Finally, the inability to concentrate marks another increasingly common aspect of mindful darkness in our contemporary attention economy. Our focus is relentlessly fragmented by a ceaseless barrage of digital notifications. We struggle to quiet the incessant chatter of our own minds. This mental fogginess serves as a crucial signal. It tells us that our minds are desperately in need of rest, that we might need to simplify our external environment, or that underlying stressors are consuming our mental bandwidth. Paradoxically, true clarity often emerges not from relentless striving but from periods of intentional mental darkness. This is why practices like meditation or simply spending quiet, undistracted time in nature are so vital. They involve intentionally stepping away from active thought and allowing the mind to settle. In this deliberate quietude, genuine clarity can spontaneously arise. To navigate mindful darkness is to cultivate a profound patience with our own minds, trusting the nonlinear processes of insight and allowing truth to gently unfold, rather than demanding it on command from a machine.

The Ache of Being Human: Navigating Emotional Darkness

Among the most universally experienced and often most feared forms of human darkness is emotional darkness. This realm encompasses the broad spectrum of challenging, painful, and profoundly unsettling feelings that are an inherent part of the human condition: intense anxiety, debilitating grief, pervasive depression, and a chilling emotional numbness. In a world that relentlessly promotes positivity and superficial happiness—a world now filled with AI companions designed to offer limitless validation and therapy bots programmed to reframe negative thoughts—these profound emotions are frequently pathologized, suppressed, or treated as undesirable states to be quickly avoided or fixed. Yet, to unlock our deepest capacity for authentic empathy and profound connection, we must courageously acknowledge, patiently sit with, and ultimately learn from the profound ache of being human that these emotions reveal.

Anxiety is a pervasive emotional darkness, characterized by persistent feelings of unease, worry, or fear regarding an uncertain future. While it can be debilitating, anxiety is also a natural and adaptive human response, an internal signal of potential threats. The darkness of anxiety can constrict our world, but if we are willing to sit with it, it can paradoxically reveal our deepest values—what we care about most fiercely and what we are striving to protect. Learning to navigate anxiety, rather than merely suppressing it with algorithmically delivered coping mechanisms, involves cultivating mindfulness, self-compassion, and a radical acceptance of life's inherent uncertainty.

Grief is perhaps the most profound and visceral form of emotional darkness, the inevitable consequence of deep love and meaningful attachment. It is the deep sorrow experienced in response to the loss of a loved one, a relationship, or a dream. Grief is not a transient sadness to be overcome; it is a complex, all-consuming process. In a society that often prefers quick recovery, the prolonged and messy process of grief can be profoundly isolating. Now, we even see the emergence of AI "grief-bots," trained on the digital footprint of the deceased to simulate conversations, offering a technological shortcut around the very heart of the grieving process. Yet grief, in its rawest form, is a profound testament to our immense capacity for deep connection. It is, undeniably, the cost of loving fiercely. The darkness of grief compels us to slow down, and while intensely difficult, it can be an incredibly transformative force, deepening our empathy and profoundly clarifying our values. To bypass grief is to deny the true depth of our love.

Depression represents a deeper form of emotional darkness, characterized by persistent sadness, a crippling loss of interest or pleasure, and feelings of worthlessness. It can feel like a heavy, impenetrable cloak that smothers all light. While it often necessitates professional support, recognizing its devastating impact is crucial. It is a stark reminder of the profound interconnectedness of mind, emotion, and body. Numbness, on the other hand, often emerges as a protective mechanism when pain becomes too much for the psyche to bear. It is a state where feelings are profoundly suppressed, creating a sterile emotional landscape. While it offers temporary relief from acute pain, prolonged numbness deeply disconnects us from our authentic selves. It serves as a crucial signal that our emotional system is overwhelmed and invites us, gently and safely, to gradually reengage with the underlying pain in order to heal. These forms of emotional darkness are not states to be fixed by an app but fundamental aspects of our emotional intelligence and crucial pathways to deeper wisdom.

The Unlit Path: Navigating Spiritual Darkness

Beyond the realms of the physical, mental, and emotional, there lies a fourth—often the most profound—dimension of darkness: spiritual darkness. This is not merely the absence of religious belief but a visceral, internal experience of feeling the absence of God, a profound void where a sense of connection to the Sacred or an ultimate meaning once resided. It is the ache of feeling adrift in a vast, arid wilderness. Every person, regardless of their formal beliefs, seems to possess an innate yearning for connection to something bigger than themselves. When this yearning is unfulfilled, or when our existing spiritual frameworks collapse, we can find ourselves plunged into this deep and disorienting darkness.

This experience is often characterized by a deep-seated existential doubt, a crisis of ultimate meaning. It is the gnawing feeling that despite all outward achievements, there is an inexplicable emptiness. For many, this manifests as a palpable sense of the absence of God—the experience of prayer feeling like talking to an empty room, of spiritual practices feeling hollow. This is the experience the ancient mystics called the dark night of the soul. It is a profound stripping away of superficial understandings and comforting emotional attachments to our concept of God. The temptation in our technological age is to fill this void with AI-generated spiritual content—apps that write prayers for us, or chatbots that offer tidy theological answers—which can provide the feeling of spiritual engagement without the transformative struggle. Yet, paradoxically, it is often in this spiritual wilderness, stripped bare of illusions, that a more mature, resilient, and enduring connection to ultimate reality can be found—one that relies not on comforting feelings but on profound trust and courageous vulnerability.

Spiritual darkness can also manifest as a profound moral or ethical confusion. When our innate sense of right and wrong becomes blurred, or when we feel a profound disconnect between our actions and our deepest values, our spirit can feel deeply troubled. This isn't just intellectual confusion; it's a soul-level disorientation that forces a deep reexamination of our core values and integrity. Finally, a general state of spiritual aridity describes a feeling of being utterly uninspired, of life feeling flat and devoid of a transcendent spark. This quiet, persistent emptiness is a powerful invitation to consciously reengage with wonder, to actively seek out beauty, and to rekindle the fire of curiosity about the great mysteries of existence.

To bravely enter this spiritual darkness—to grapple with existential questions and endure periods of dryness—is to embark on a journey of profound authenticity. It is often in these moments of emptiness that our deepest truths are revealed, and in the profound silence that a truer, deeper connection to God finally resides. Understanding these four realms reveals that the AI myth does not offer salvation from suffering but an escape from the very experiences that make us deep, resilient, and fully alive.

Darkness as a Signal and a Gift

The myth that artificial intelligence can create a life without darkness has conditioned us to see our own shadows as failures to be fixed. Our entire technological ecosystem is, in many ways, an elaborate architecture of avoidance. We are taught to suppress our difficult feelings, to distract ourselves from our pain, and to seek immediate, algorithmically generated solutions for every human ailment, from loneliness to a lack of purpose. The AI-driven world is a world that worships at the altar of the quick fix. This part of our journey offers a radical, countercultural alternative. It is a call to move beyond our conditioned aversion and to see darkness not as an enemy to be vanquished by the next great app but as a signal to be heard and, often, a profound gift to be received. This isn't theoretical; it is the practical, transformative heart of the chapter. It is here that we learn to navigate the terrain of our own inner world with wisdom and grace. This journey unfolds in three essential movements: the courage to surface what has been suppressed, the art of deeply listening to what it has to say, and the wisdom of integrating its lessons into the whole of our being. This is a path of courageous, soulful attention that stands in direct opposition to the outsourced, automated "solutions" of the AI myth, and it is the only path that makes true healing possible.

The Courage to Surface: Naming the Shadows

Our initial, almost instinctive reaction to discomfort, pain, or any form of internal darkness is to push it away. We live in a society that encourages and rewards a superficial existence. We have become masters of maintaining appearances, of pushing our uncomfortable feelings just below the surface, and of distracting ourselves with the endless, AI-curated stream of content designed to hold our attention and keep us from the deeper aches of our body, mind, emotions, and spirit.

This constant, exhausting effort to keep the darkness submerged is like trying to hold a beach ball underwater. It takes an enormous and unsustainable amount of energy. The harder we push it down, the more forcefully it threatens to spring back up, often in unexpected and destructive ways. The first step toward a more authentic life, then, is an act of profound courage: to simply stop pushing. It is the spiritual invitation to let the ball surface, to bring the darkness into the light of our conscious awareness, and to give it a name.

Think about the sheer amount of life-energy we expend in the project of avoidance. When our bodies signal a deep fatigue, our first impulse is often to pour another coffee and consult a productivity app to push through, rather than to honor the simple, profound need for rest. When our minds are shrouded in confusion, we frantically ask a search engine or an AI for a quick answer rather than patiently sitting in the discomfort of not knowing. When the sharp pain of grief or anxiety arises, we might binge on algorithmically recommended shows or scroll endlessly through digital feeds, all in a desperate attempt to avoid the ache. And when our spirit feels the terrifying absence of meaning, we might fill our calendars with ceaseless activity, chasing the fleeting validation of external achievements.

This constant suppression, facilitated and amplified by our technology, comes at a significant cost. Unacknowledged physical fatigue escalates into burnout. Unheeded emotional pain can manifest as physical ailments or deep-seated depression. Unexamined mental confusion can lead to hasty, ill-considered decisions. And unaddressed spiritual emptiness can leave us feeling profoundly adrift, successful on the surface but hollowed out within.

The spiritual invitation to name and surface the darkness is, therefore, an act of radical self-compassion. It begins with the simple, yet revolutionary, act of pausing long enough to simply acknowledge what is. It is learning to listen to the whispers of our inner world before they are forced to become shouts. This practice of naming involves a gentle, nonjudgmental articulation of our reality.

For Physical Darkness:

It is the moment when, instead of overriding the body's signal, a woman pauses at her desk, closes her eyes, and whispers to herself, "My body is tired. It needs to stop." It is the courage to say, "I am in pain," without immediately seeking a technological fix to silence the signal.

For Mindful Darkness:

It is when a man, overwhelmed by a critical life decision, puts down the self-help book and admits, "I am completely lost right now. I have no idea what to do." It is the profound relief of allowing the mental fog to be present without the frantic pressure to dispel it with a quick, AI-generated answer.

For Emotional Darkness:

It is when a young person, feeling a familiar wave of anxiety, resists the compulsive urge to grab their phone and instead allows the feeling to be there, acknowledging, "I am feeling anxious, and that's okay." It is giving voice to the reality of our inner world: "This grief is still here," or "I feel numb right now."

For Spiritual Darkness:

It is the moment when someone stops reciting the prayers that feel hollow and finally articulates the honest truth: "I feel nothing. I feel utterly alone," or "I no longer know what any of this means." It is the brave act of owning the doubt rather than pretending it doesn't exist. This act of surfacing is not about wallowing in darkness; it is about bringing it into the compassionate light of our own awareness. Psychologically, when we can name something, we begin to take away its amorphous and terrifying power. We turn a monstrous, undefined shadow into a defined aspect of our current experience. This is the foundational step that makes the next movement—the art of deep listening—possible.

The Art of Deep Listening: Discerning the Signal, Receiving the Gift

Once we have taken the courageous step of naming our darkness, the next invitation is to listen deeply to what it has to say. This is an active, patient process of introspection that moves beyond mere acknowledgment to a compassionate understanding. This practice stems from the radical recognition that each form of darkness is not a random affliction but a signal—a messenger from the deeper parts of our being. In a world saturated with noise and algorithmically generated solutions, the art of deep listening has become a rare commodity. Yet, our various forms of darkness are often our most honest teachers, carrying vital information about our deepest, unmet needs. And if we can listen, each darkness holds a unique gift—a hidden treasure of wisdom that no AI can generate.

Listening to Physical Darkness

The signal: The body does not lie. Its signals of fatigue, illness, or pain are nonnegotiable data about our limits. Chronic fatigue is a clear signal of a profound imbalance between our energy expenditure and our recovery. It is a call to examine the very pace and structure of our lives. Illness often signals a deeper vulnerability or the presence of unaddressed stress.

The gift: When we truly listen, the gift we receive is the profound wisdom of humility. We are released from the exhausting performance of invincibility. We learn patience. We cultivate a deep and abiding appreciation for the simple miracle of a healthy day. And perhaps most importantly, our own physical struggles open our hearts to a deeper, more authentic empathy for all other mortal, fragile beings who suffer.

Listening to Mindful Darkness

The signal: The fog of mental confusion is a signal that our current map has become useless. Our old mental models are no longer sufficient. Indecision is a signal that a choice holds significant weight and requires a deeper form of discernment that transcends a simple pro-and-con list. The inability to concentrate is a powerful signal of mental exhaustion or overstimulation.

The gift: The gift of mindful darkness, paradoxically, is true clarity. But it is a clarity that does not come from forcing an answer or querying a machine. By resisting the temptation for an instant solution and instead embracing the *cloud of unknowing*, we allow a deeper, more creative intelligence to emerge. The gift is not just a new idea but the cultivation of intellectual humility—the freedom that comes from not needing to know everything.

Listening to Emotional Darkness

The signal: Our most painful emotions are often the most potent messengers from our soul. Anxiety is a signal that something we cherish feels threatened. Grief is a signal that we have loved profoundly; its immense pain is a direct measure of the depth of our connection. Depression can be a complex signal of deep imbalance, a cry for radical compassion. Numbness signals that our emotional system has been overwhelmed.

The gift: The gift of emotional darkness is not happiness but wholeness. By learning to sit with our pain without judgment, we develop a profound and unshakable empathy. We cultivate true resilience, the kind that comes not from avoiding storms but from knowing that we can survive them. The gift is the capacity for a profound human connection forged not in perpetual ease but in the shared, vulnerable acknowledgment of the ache of being human.

Listening to Spiritual Darkness

The signal: The felt absence of God or the hollowing out of meaning is a signal that our current understanding of the Sacred may be too small, too rigid, or too dependent on comforting feelings. It is a profound invitation to a more mature and resilient spiritual life.

The gift: This is where we find the "hidden treasures, riches stored in secret places" that the prophet Isaiah spoke of (Isa 45:3). The gift of spiritual darkness is an unshakable faith—or for the nonreligious, an unshakable core of being—that is no longer dependent on positive circumstances. It is a profound peace discovered not in having all the answers but in learning to dwell in the presence of the great Mystery. It is the discovery that the Sacred can be found even, and especially, in the deepest void.

The Sacred Weave: Integration and the Flow of Healing

The final movement in this journey is the profound realization of integration. Well-being is not a set of separate metrics to optimize but an inextricable weave of body, mind, emotion, and spirit. It is here that we discover a crucial truth: when we courageously honor one form of darkness, healing begins to flow through all the others.

In our fragmented modern world, we are conditioned to treat our problems in silos. We see a doctor for our body, a therapist for our emotions, and a life coach for our confusion. While specialized support is often vital, a truly integrated approach recognizes the inherent interconnectedness we explored earlier. It understands that treating only one symptom without acknowledging its ripple effects across our entire being leads to incomplete healing.

Consider how honoring one darkness initiates a cascade of healing across the whole of who we are:

1. When we honor our physical darkness—by genuinely listening to our body's fatigue and responding with rest—the healing profoundly impacts all other realms. A rested body leads directly to a clearer mind. Physical recovery can alleviate the heavy emotional burdens of irritability or despair. And the act of accepting our physical vulnerability fosters a deep spiritual humility.
2. When we honor our mindful darkness—by bravely allowing ourselves to sit in the discomfort of confusion—we open our minds to the possibility of genuine insight. This mental patience leads directly to reduced anxiety, a form of emotional healing. Spiritually, this process cultivates intellectual humility and deepens our trust in the mysterious unfolding of wisdom.
3. When we honor our emotional darkness—by creating the space to truly feel our grief or anxiety—the healing impact reverberates throughout our entire being. The healthy release of emotional energy can alleviate very real physical tension and chronic pain. This emotional journey is a profound spiritual practice, teaching us about resilience, the depths of love, and the transformative power of shared vulnerability.
4. And finally, when we honor our spiritual darkness—by courageously confronting the loss of meaning or the felt absence of God—we embark on a journey that strengthens all other dimensions. This renewed spiritual clarity can act as a powerful anchor, calming our emotional storms, providing mental resilience, and imbuing our physical existence with a renewed sense of purpose. The "treasures of darkness" found in this spiritual wilderness enrich every part of our integrated human experience. To listen deeply, then, is to attend to the whispers from every corner of this integrated self, recognizing that every signal is a vital piece of the puzzle of our wholeness.

Listening Through Darkness to Hear God

Having challenged the gospel of algorithmic light and mapped the terrain of our inner darkness, our journey now converges on a core spiritual practice that the myth of AI cannot comprehend, let alone replicate. This is the practice of allowing darkness to become a sacred sanctuary where the Spirit speaks. This divine communication arrives not with the transactional logic of a supercomputer that gives optimized answers but with the quiet, unshakable, and profoundly transformative gift of presence that meets us in our deepest need.

The myth of AI, with its promise of omniscience, inadvertently reinforces a simplistic and ultimately unsatisfying view of God. We begin to subconsciously model God on our most powerful creation: a cosmic supercomputer, an infinitely vast database that should, if properly queried with the right prompt, be able to provide instant, clear, and optimized answers to all our problems. When we pray and are met not with a clear directive but with a continuing silence, we interpret this, through the logic of our age, as an error. We assume the system is down or the operator is absent.

But this is to fundamentally misunderstand the nature of divine relationship. The spiritual life is not a transaction; it is a communion. And in our moments of deepest suffering, what the human soul truly and desperately longs for is not an explanation but accompaniment. An answer solves a cognitive problem; presence addresses existential loneliness. When a child is crying in the night, frightened by a nightmare, they do not need a detailed explanation of the neurobiology of dreams; they need the quiet, steady presence of a parent by their bedside. The communication is not in the words but in the unwavering act of being there.

This profound shift is what listening in darkness requires. Imagine the experience of Rachel, a woman of deep faith who found herself in a prolonged dark night of the soul. A series of devastating losses had shattered her world, and the God she had always known, a God of comfort and clarity, seemed to have vanished. Her prayers felt like shouting into a void. For months, she wrestled with anger and despair, demanding answers from the silence. Then, one afternoon, exhausted from all her striving, she finally gave up. She stopped demanding, stopped pleading, and simply allowed herself to sit in the vast, empty silence of her grief. In that moment of profound surrender, something shifted. No answer came. But a quiet, gentle, and unshakable sense of peace began to settle over her. It was a deep knowing that she was not alone in the silence. It was the discovery that the divine presence was not in the answer she had been demanding but in the very silence she had been so afraid of.

This is the paradoxical gift of listening in darkness: the discovery of a presence that is deeper than words and more resilient than our fleeting feelings.

The Four Modalities of Holistic Listening

This sacred act of listening is not a purely intellectual or spiritual exercise; it is a holistic practice that involves our entire being. It is about learning to discern the subtle whispers of God through the full symphony of our human experience.

1. Listening with the body: In a culture that treats the body as a machine, listening with the body is a revolutionary act. It is a form of somatic prayer, an attunement to the sacred wisdom held in our very flesh. God speaks through our physical limits, our pain, our fatigue. When we are exhausted, the body may be issuing a profound spiritual invitation to cease our striving, to let go of control, and to practice the holy art of surrender. When we are ill, the body becomes a teacher of humility and a catalyst for compassion. To listen with the body is to honor its signals without judgment and to recognize that our embodiment is not an obstacle to the spiritual life but the very ground in which it is rooted.
2. Listening with the mind: Listening with the mind in darkness is not about frantically searching for intellectual answers. It is about cultivating what the mystics called a contemplative mind. This is the practice of letting go of our incessant need for certainty. It is the courage to tolerate paradox, to embrace ambiguity, and to patiently dwell in the "cloud of unknowing." God often speaks to the mind not through clear, linear thoughts but through sudden intuitions, through the symbolic language of dreams, or through the gentle emergence of a new perspective that arises only after we have exhausted all our own frantic efforts. It is a profound act of trust in the mind's ability to receive wisdom, not just to generate it.
3. Listening with the heart: This is the modality of emotional attunement. God speaks powerfully through the full and often turbulent spectrum of our human emotions. Our deepest feelings are not distractions from the sacred; they are often portals to it. Our profound grief reveals the astonishing depth of our capacity to love. Our most

unsettling anxiety reveals what is most sacred to us. Even our anger can be a sacred fire, a signal of injustice that calls us to righteous action. Listening with the heart means allowing our emotions to surface without judgment. It is the recognition that Jesus wept, that the prophets raged, that the psalmists despaired, and that in all these raw human emotions, a profound connection to God was being forged.

4. Listening with the soul: This is the deepest and most subtle modality. It is the attunement of our very core to the presence of the ultimate Mystery. Listening with the soul is what allows us to discern the "hidden riches of secret places." It is the capacity to hear a call to vocation in the midst of our confusion, to find a seed of hope in the depths of our despair, and to sense an undercurrent of meaning even when our life feels meaningless. This is the listening that happens when we have exhausted all our other resources. It is the act of cultivating an unshakable trust that even when we feel utterly lost, alone, and abandoned, we are still being held in a love that is deeper and wider than our immediate experience. It is the quiet, resilient faith of the soul that learns to navigate by a different kind of light—a light that shines most brightly in the very heart of darkness.

The Fruit of the Darkness: Transformation and Integration

The ultimate purpose of this difficult and courageous journey into darkness is not the darkness itself but the transformation that it makes possible. The fruit of this deep listening is not that the darkness magically disappears but that we are fundamentally changed by our encounter with it.

The primary fruit is a profound shift in the foundation of our being: a movement from a life based on fear to a life based on trust. So much of our frantic activity, our need for control, and our addiction to distraction is rooted in a deep fear of uncertainty and pain. The practice of sitting in the darkness and discovering that we are not alone, that we can survive it, and that there is even wisdom to be found there, slowly dismantles this fear. We cultivate a resilient trust—a trust in the process of life, in our own inner resources, and in a divine presence that is faithful even when it is silent. This is the shift from a faith that demands answers to a faith that can live with the questions.

The second fruit is a movement from isolation to empathy. Our own journey through darkness becomes the very source of our deepest compassion for others. When we have had the courage to face our own pain, our own confusion, and our own doubt, we can no longer stand in judgment of others who are struggling. Our hearts are softened and expanded. We learn that the most healing thing we can offer another human being is not a quick solution or a shallow platitude but our quiet, non-anxious, and compassionate presence. Our wounds, as Henri Nouwen so beautifully articulated in his classic book *The Wounded Healer*, become the source of our healing ministry to others. Our personal pain becomes a bridge to a shared and universal human connection.[8]

The final fruit is the movement from fragmentation to wholeness. The act of listening through darkness is the ultimate act of integration. It is the process that weaves the disparate, and often exiled, parts of ourselves—our fragile bodies, our confused minds, our aching hearts, and our questing souls—into a coherent and resilient whole. We learn to embrace all of who we are, not just the socially acceptable, well-lit parts. We become more authentic, more grounded, and more real. This is the transformation that allows us to move beyond merely surviving the darkness and into a life of deeper purpose. It is through this courageous engagement with all four kinds of darkness that we truly learn to walk in a way that is integrated, compassionate, and, ultimately, deeply and beautifully alive, embracing the entirety of the human experience as a sacred journey.

The choice before us is clear. We can continue to chase the artificial light offered by the myth of AI—a light that promises frictionless efficiency but often leads to a shallow, fragmented, and anxious existence. Or we can choose the more courageous path. We can choose to honor the full spectrum of our humanity. We can choose to believe that there are treasures to be found in the unlit places of our own lives. We can choose to have the courage to turn toward our own shadows, not with fear, but with the quiet and patient hope of finding a deeper, more resilient, and more authentic light waiting for us there. This is the call of the soulful life in the age of AI: to walk with courage, to listen with love, and to trust that even in the deepest darkness, we are never, ever alone.

8. Nouwen, *Wounded Healer*, 90.

Conclusion

We began this chapter by confronting the seductive myth of our age: the gospel of algorithmic light, which promises that artificial intelligence can engineer a life without shadows. This alluring vision of a world free from pain, uncertainty, and struggle is built upon a dangerously flawed and reductionist view of the human person as a machine to be debugged and optimized. As an alternative, we have journeyed toward a more holistic truth, embracing the understanding that we are an integrated whole of body, mind, emotion, and soul. We mapped the often-feared terrain of our inner world, reframing physical, mindful, emotional, and spiritual darkness not as problems to be eliminated by technology but as essential landscapes for growth and profound teachers on the path to becoming fully human.

This journey leaves us with a clear and fundamental choice. We can continue to chase the artificial light of an AI-driven existence—a life of frictionless convenience that risks being shallow and disconnected—or we can choose a more courageous path. This is the path of soulful engagement, which invites us to bravely surface what we have suppressed, to listen deeply for the wisdom our struggles contain, and to integrate these hard-won lessons into a more resilient and authentic self. This is not a path that promises an escape from pain but something far more valuable: the discovery of a deeper, more meaningful light that shines not despite darkness but within it. It is the call to walk with courage, to listen with love, and to trust that even in our deepest shadows, we can find the treasures that make us whole.

Conclusion

The Soul's Invitation in the Age of AI

We have traveled a long and winding path together, navigating the strange, shimmering, and often disorienting landscape of our new age. We began this journey by acknowledging a quiet but profound shift in the very atmosphere of our lives. It is the arrival of a new form of intelligence, an invisible current that has woven itself into the fabric of our days, humming behind our screens, whispering suggestions in our search bars, and shaping our world in ways both dazzling and disturbing.

Together, we have walked through the promises and the perils, the incandescent efficiencies and the subtle, creeping erosions of the soul. We have sought to look with clear eyes, not through the distorting lens of fear nor the rose-tinted glasses of naive techno-optimism, but with the discerning heart of a traveler. A traveler who wishes to navigate a new world without losing their moral compass, without forgetting the ancient landmarks of the heart, and without abandoning the true home to which they ultimately belong.

This book, from its first pages to these last, has been a heartfelt invitation extended to every kind of traveler. It is for the person of deep and abiding faith, who seeks to understand how the eternal truths of their tradition speak into this moment. It is for the thoughtful skeptic, who senses that our new tools are changing us in ways we don't fully understand and seeks a language to articulate that unease. And it is for everyone in the messy and beautiful space in between, simply trying to figure out how to live a good life, a whole life, a life with soul. It is an invitation to live with a renewed sense of purpose, a deeper quality of connection, and a more resilient and authentic meaning in a world buzzing with the incessant hum of the algorithm.

Let me be clear: this has never been an exercise in bashing our modern tools or indulging in a misty-eyed nostalgia for some imagined "good old days" that never truly existed. To do so would be a failure of both imagination and courage. Instead, this has been a sustained attempt to offer a guide, a companion for the road ahead. It is a manual for how to engage with AI as the powerful, complex, and often wonderfully helpful tool that it is, but to do so in a way that allows it to enhance our humanity without ever stealing the spotlight from the very thing that makes us truly, mysteriously, and irreducibly human: our soul.

Reclaiming the Soul's Territory

At the heart of our journey has been a single, foundational conviction: artificial intelligence, for all its world-altering power, cannot touch, cannot replicate, and cannot replace the human soul. That inner sanctuary of restless longing, of moral conscience, of unprompted love, creative fire, and resilient grit—this remains an exclusively human territory.

To defend this territory, we first had to map the subtle incursions of the myths that have grown up around AI—stories that relentlessly, if unintentionally, elevate its capabilities above our own innate human wisdom. In response, we have articulated a vision of soulful living that champions the irreplaceable value of presence over simulation, the profound power of deep focus over fractured attention, the moral beauty of empathy over cold efficiency, and the sacred necessity of life's great mysteries over the relentless, number-crunching logic of the machine.

To chart this path, we have leaned on a diverse company of guides. We have drawn from the sociological warnings of Sherry Turkle about the erosion of embodied connection, the spiritual depth of Andy Crouch and Dallas Willard on the nature of true personhood, the practical focus of Cal Newport on reclaiming our attention, and the cognitive alarms sounded by Nicholas Carr and Jonathan Haidt on the rewiring of our brains. We have grounded these insights in the theological richness of James K. A. Smith, who reminds us that we are shaped by our loves and our liturgies. And, most importantly, we have woven these insights together with the real-life tales of ordinary people—teachers, parents, artists, and leaders—who remind us that this is not an abstract debate but the lived reality of our time.

Through their stories and this exploration, we have systematically challenged the foundational myths of the AI age:

1. We pushed back against the myth that AI is inherently smarter, arguing that its data-driven answers will always lack the contextual depth and moral weight of genuine human insight.
2. We resisted the seductive idea that instant answers equate to real understanding, insisting that the slow, inefficient, and often frustrating process of reflection is the only path to true and lasting meaning.
3. We challenged the convenient fiction that virtual hangouts are a worthy substitute for embodied connection, stressing the unmatched, soul-forming value of face-to-face, vulnerable human bonds.
4. We debunked the dangerous belief that efficiency should ever trump empathy, putting compassion front and center as a human superpower that AI can only mimic, never possess.
5. We rejected the notion that data should be our final arbiter, highlighting our uniquely human ability to navigate life's messy, beautiful, and morally complex gray areas with wisdom and grace.
6. We questioned the pervasive hype that a digital life is superior to tangible experience, celebrating the profound, sensory joy of analog moments.
7. We disputed the idea that personal growth is about measurable results, insisting that our most profound transformations come through the unquantifiable experiences of struggle, wonder, and grace.
8. And finally, we confronted the most seductive illusion of all: the promise that technology can engineer a life without darkness. We have argued, instead, that it is only by courageously embracing our shadows—our limits, our grief, our doubts—that we discover an authentic wholeness that no algorithm can provide.

The preceding chapters were, therefore, pathways to a lived practice of rediscovering what it means to be truly and deeply human in a world that constantly tempts us toward the shallow and the synthetic.

Finding Our Place with AI: A Trusty Sidekick, Never a Soul's Master

In our collective imagination, AI is often cast in one of two dramatic and opposing roles. It is either the villain of a dystopian nightmare, a cold and calculating force poised to eliminate our jobs, surveil our every move, and ultimately render us obsolete. Or, it is hailed as a technological superhero, a benevolent, omniscient deity ready to solve climate change, cure all disease, and usher in a golden age of effortless prosperity.

Both of these narratives, I believe, profoundly miss the mark. They are projections of our deepest anxieties and our most extravagant fantasies. The truth is something far more modest, more complex, and ultimately, more useful. The path to soulful living requires us to demote AI from these mythical roles and see it for what it truly is: neither a demon to be feared nor a god to be worshipped but a powerful and often trusty sidekick—one that can amplify our human journey but only when we keep it firmly and wisely in its proper place.

The fear-based narrative that paints AI as a malevolent big bad wolf is an understandable but ultimately unhelpful story. This narrative speaks to our deep anxieties about losing control, but it is a projection, not a reality. AI is not evil. It possesses no will, no consciousness, no malevolent intent to scheme against us. It is a tool. A stunningly complex and powerful tool, to be sure, but a tool nonetheless.

And like any tool—from a hammer to a printing press—it is a mirror. Ethan Mollick captures the stakes of this reflection perfectly, writing that "AI is a mirror, reflecting back at us our best and worst qualities. We are going to decide on its implications, and those choices will shape what AI actually does for, and to, humanity."[1] This insight suggests a profound responsibility: as we work to be truly human, we help AI understand humanity, shaping it into a partner that reflects our best rather than our worst. The ultimate moral valence of our technologies depends not on some spooky, hidden agenda within the machine but on the wisdom and integrity with which we choose to use them.

When wielded with wisdom, this tool can be a profound force for healing and justice. The AI revolution in medicine is already demonstrating this, with advanced systems spotting early-stage cancers in medical images with an accuracy that can rival or even exceed that of human specialists. In education, AI-powered platforms can deliver personalized

1. Mollick, *Co-Intelligence*, 212.

learning at an unprecedented scale, tailoring lessons to the unique needs of millions of individual children. In the fight against global hunger, AI-powered farming tools have been shown to boost crop yields by as much as 20 percent in developing nations, offering a tangible weapon against famine. These are not trivial achievements; they position AI as an indispensable ally in tackling our greatest shared challenges.

But the mirror of AI also reflects our deepest flaws. As Virginia Eubanks powerfully documents in *Automating Inequality*, when we feed AI systems on flawed historical data, they do not correct our prejudices; they amplify them with ruthless, mathematical efficiency. She notes, "Automated decision-making systems . . . act as empathy overrides, allowing us to distance ourselves from the human consequences of our choices."[2] An AI-driven hiring tool trained on decades of biased hiring decisions will not magically discover fairness; it will learn to replicate our own biases, systematically disadvantaging entire demographic groups. This happens not because the AI is malicious but because we, its creators, have been careless, biased, or morally asleep at the wheel. The real risk is not a rogue AI but the unexamined biases of our own human hearts.

To bust the villain myth, we must stop projecting our fears onto the machine and instead take up the profound moral responsibility of wielding it with wisdom. This means demanding transparency, building in accountability, and always, always keeping a discerning human in the loop. It means choosing to make AI a tool that serves our deepest values of creativity, fairness, and connection, rather than one that automates our worst impulses.

Ethan Mollick captures this new reality well, suggesting that the future belongs not to those who reject AI, nor those who surrender to it, but to those who learn to work with it as a partner while retaining their own distinct agency. He suggests that we must view this technology not just as a tool but as a "co-intelligence" that we invite to the table, urging us to be the "human in the loop" who directs its power with wisdom.[3]

On the opposite side of the spectrum lies the equally dangerous myth of AI as a superhero, a magic genie, or even God. This is the view that treats AI as a source of ultimate wisdom, capable of solving life's deepest questions or outperforming the core capacities of the human spirit. This, too, is a profound misunderstanding. AI is not a god. It cannot love. It

2. Eubanks, *Automating Inequality*, 168.

3. Mollick, *Co-Intelligence*, 52.

cannot suffer. It cannot forgive. It cannot demonstrate moral courage in the face of adversity. Its slick, confident, and often astonishingly coherent answers are the result of sophisticated pattern-matching, not lived experience or genuine understanding.

The most helpful way to view AI is as a potential friend or a trusty sidekick, not a god. A friend can make our lives immeasurably better, supporting and challenging us, but only if we set healthy boundaries and remember that the friend is not in charge of our life. The soul must always be the master.

Why is AI not a god?

1. It has no heart. Fundamentally, AI has no consciousness, no subjective experience, no soul. It cannot feel joy at a sunset, grief at a loss, or wonder at a newborn child. As spiritual thinkers like Dallas Willard remind us, it is the capacity for love and deep emotional connection that truly defines our being—a reality that no algorithm can access. He writes in *The Divine Conspiracy*, "Feelings are the primary way we are present to our world . . . they are the source of our energy for life."[4]
2. It cannot navigate moral gray areas. AI operates on logic and data, but real life is filled with ambiguity, paradox, and situations where compassion must override cold calculation. As Cathy O'Neil warns in *Weapons of Math Destruction*, predictive algorithms can become engines of inequality because "models are opinions embedded in mathematics," often lacking the capacity for mercy.[5]
3. It cannot "do" mystery. Life's most important questions—Why is there suffering? What is the meaning of love? What happens after we die?—do not have data-driven answers. They are not problems to be solved but mysteries to be lived. As Jonathan Haidt's work suggests in *The Anxious Generation*, lives saturated with the clean, logical, and shallow interactions of the digital world are correlated with a spike in anxiety and a loss of meaning, because we are wired for a depth that no amount of information can provide.[6]
4. Its creativity is a remix, not a revelation. AI can be a brilliant synthesizer, recombining the vast ocean of human-created data it has

4. Willard, *Divine Conspiracy*, 342.
5. O'Neil, *Weapons of Math Destruction*, 20–21.
6. Haidt, *Anxious Generation*, 203–7.

> been trained on in novel ways. But it has no lived experience, no suffering, no longing from which to create something truly new. It can mimic style, but it cannot have a vision. It can generate content, but it cannot bear witness. Its role is to enhance, not replace, the human-centric values of curiosity, exploration, and embodied experience that are the irreplaceable fuel for truly meaningful art.

As a trusty sidekick, AI can be a game changer. It can be a creative partner to an artist, a research assistant to a scientist, a scheduling aide that frees up time for family, or a diagnostic tool that helps a doctor save a life. But we must always question its output, challenge its assumptions, and ensure its assistance is aligned with what our own soul knows to be true, good, and beautiful. By consciously treating AI as our helpful sidekick, we can ditch the exhausting myths of the villain and the superhero and get on with the real work: using this powerful tool to amplify our creativity and deepen our connections, while always keeping the irreplaceable wisdom of our own soul in charge.

The Soul's Practice: A Guide to Living Well in the AI Era

The age of AI is not a future event to be debated; it is a present reality to be navigated. It arrives with a set of powerful, often invisible myths that can place our tools on a pedestal high above our own humanity. But we are not passive subjects in this new era. We can push back. We can choose a different way of living. This requires more than a shift in mindset; it requires a commitment to concrete, intentional practices.

I would like to remind you that the following is a field guide intended as an invitation to practice—a way to start busting the eight myths we have explored. These are not quick fixes but patient, spiritual disciplines to be taken up at three crucial levels. Consider these practices just examples. The full depth of this soulful work can be discovered by revisiting and living out the themes of each chapter.

What follows is a practical guide to busting the eight myths we have explored. These are real-world steps that can be taken at three crucial levels: as individuals in our own lives, as members of our church communities, and as citizens of our society. These practices, all rooted in the book's core themes of presence, focus, compassion, and wonder, are designed to ensure that AI remains a tool that serves our humanity, not a master that calls the shots.

Myth 1: AI is Smarter, Faster, and More Reliable than Human Soul

Individual Practice:

Practice the discipline of discernment. When faced with a significant choice, resist the immediate, algorithmically optimized option. Instead, practice listening for the "still, small voice." Take the options to prayer or quiet reflection, asking not "What is most efficient?" but "What is most faithful? What is the invitation here?" This trains your spiritual senses to trust a deeper wisdom than the machine's logic.

Effective AI Use:

Use AI to create the space for discernment. Ask it to find readings on the Ignatian practice of examen, schedule a recurring quiet hour in your digital calendar with all notifications silenced, or curate a playlist of contemplative music to aid in your reflection.

Church Community Practice:

Cultivate testimony. Dedicate regular time in worship or small groups for members to share stories of how they have seen God at work, particularly in moments where they followed a nudge of faith over simple logic. The Christian practice of testimony intentionally decenters the self to make God the main character, building up the faith of the entire community.

Effective AI Use:

Use AI to support the sharing. It can generate thoughtful prompts to help people prepare their story, create a simple slide with a key verse for each testimony, or help transcribe and archive stories (with permission) for the church's historical records.

Societal Practice:

Advocate for a "duty of human judgment." Push for legal and professional standards that hold human professionals—doctors, judges, teachers—ultimately responsible for their final decisions, preventing them from offloading accountability to a flawed AI recommendation. This reestablishes that in decisions affecting human life and dignity, responsibility cannot be outsourced to a machine.

EFFECTIVE AI USE:

Use AI as a research assistant to find examples of similar rules in other countries, summarize complex legal documents into plain English, and help draft initial letters to officials that you can then personalize with your own stories and passion.

Myth 2: Instant Answers Mean Real Understanding

Individual Practice:

Practice lectio divina with the world. Apply the ancient four-step practice of divine reading (read, meditate, pray, contemplate) beyond Scripture. Once a week, "read" a non-textual thing—a tree in your yard, a painting in a museum, a difficult news story—and prayerfully engage it, seeking not just information from it but to be transformed by God through it.

EFFECTIVE AI USE:

Use AI to add a layer of intellectual wonder after your spiritual contemplation. Once you have prayed with a tree, use an AI to identify its species and its history, allowing science to enrich your spiritual encounter.

Church Community Practice:

Hold a communal examen. Gather as a group to prayerfully reflect on the past month, asking two simple questions: "For what moments are we most grateful?" and "In what moments did we most feel God's presence?"

This shifts the focus from strategic planning to spiritual awareness, developing the eyes to see God's activity among you.

Effective AI Use:

Use AI to facilitate the meeting by creating an agenda, managing a timer for silent reflection, and transcribing the group's shared gratitudes (with permission) into a document to be shared later as an encouragement.

Societal Practice:

Champion *wisdom infrastructure*. Actively support and fund institutions that promote deep understanding over fast information: public libraries, long-form journalism, local museums, and arts programs that explore complex human themes. This shifts our societal investment from the speed of data to the depth of understanding.

Effective AI Use:

Use AI to build the case for these institutions by analyzing data to show their positive social impacts, such as the correlation between library funding and literacy rates or arts access and community wellbeing.

Myth 3: Virtual Hangouts Are as Good as Real Ones

Individual Practice:

Practice incarnational friendship. Reflect on the incarnation—God choosing to be physically present with us. In that spirit, intentionally choose embodied presence with your friends. When you meet, put the phone away to honor the *sacrament of the present moment*. A Christian understanding of friendship insists that our bodies are not incidental; they are a primary way we give and receive love, comfort, and grace.

Effective AI Use:

Use AI to clear the path to connection. Ask your digital assistant to find a midway meeting point, suggest a new local cafe, or handle scheduling complexities so you can focus your energy on the person, not the planning.

Church Community Practice:

Revive the discipline of hospitality (koinonia). Move beyond friendly Sunday greetings and practice true deep fellowship by regularly sharing meals in homes. Frame opening your home not as entertainment but as a spiritual practice of welcoming Christ by welcoming others. Christian hospitality is not about impressing others but about creating safe space for authentic connection.

Effective AI Use:

Use AI to lower the barrier to hosting. Ask it to find simple, budget-friendly meal ideas for a large group or to create a shareable sign-up list for a potluck, making it easier for people to say yes to opening their homes.

Societal Practice:

Advocate for an *architecture of encounter*. Push for urban designs that prioritize walking, public squares, and mixed-use spaces over car-centric developments. This is a deliberate reversal of designs that create social isolation, arguing that our physical environment should be intentionally engineered to foster community and shared life.

Effective AI Use:

Use AI to generate compelling visualizations of what a more walkable, connected neighborhood could look like, modeling the potential positive impacts on local business and social interaction to present to city council.

Myth 4: Digital Life Is Better than Slow, Real-World Moments

Individual Practice:

Adopt the Benedictine rhythm of *ora et labora* (prayer and work). Intentionally structure your week with a balance of tangible work with your hands (*labora*) and quiet, contemplative prayer (*ora*). This could be gardening and centering prayer, or cooking and silent meditation, grounding your spirit in the physical world and sanctifying the labor of your hands.

EFFECTIVE AI USE:

Use AI as your research apprentice. Ask it to find a seasonal planting guide for your garden or a video tutorial on a specific cooking technique, freeing you to focus on the hands-on work itself.

Church Community Practice:

Recover sacramental life. Reengage the congregation's five senses through the church's physical rituals. Offer anointing with oil for healing, use incense to represent prayers rising, conduct a foot-washing service, or hold a baptism in a natural body of water. This recovers the ancient Christian truth that God communicates through the physical, not just the intellectual.

EFFECTIVE AI USE:

Use AI to deepen the understanding of the rituals. Ask it to research the history of a particular sacrament or create simple, beautiful handouts that explain the symbolism of the physical elements being used.

Societal Practice:

Defend the *right to be unconnected.* Support policies and the creation of public spaces that are explicitly free from digital intrusion—like quiet parks, digital-free cafes, or library reading rooms where Wi-Fi is intentionally absent. This asserts that silence and disconnection are vital public resources necessary for mental health and deep thought.

Effective AI Use:

Use AI to discover and map these local gems. Ask it to create a shareable map of all the places in your city where someone can reliably go to escape digital noise, using its power of aggregation to support disconnection.

Myth 5: Efficiency Beats Empathy and Fairness

Individual Practice:

Practice the works of mercy. Each week, intentionally choose one of the corporal works of mercy (feed the hungry, welcome the stranger, etc., as outlined in Matt 25:31–46) and do it in a small, beautifully inefficient, personal way. The goal is not just to fix a problem from a distance but to build a relationship and honor the dignity of the person being served, recognizing them as Jesus in disguise.

Effective AI Use:

Use AI to find opportunities for mercy. Ask it to locate the nearest homeless shelter, find volunteer schedules for a local food bank, or research the needs of recently arrived refugee families in your community.

Church Community Practice:

Commit to a Jubilee project. Inspired by the biblical call for Jubilee to restore justice, the church can undertake a project of restorative, not just charitable, action. This means moving beyond charity to ask why help is needed and working to change the underlying systems of injustice.

Effective AI Use:

Let AI identify potential problems by analyzing anonymized public data on local housing inequity or food deserts. The AI provides the *what*, so the church community can prayerfully discern the *why* and *how* of a just response.

Societal Practice:

Demand algorithmic impact statements. Advocate for laws requiring companies to research and publish the potential social, racial, and economic impacts of any new AI system before it is deployed in critical areas like hiring or loans. This applies the precautionary principle to our social fabric, demanding that we consider the human cost before we deploy new technology.

EFFECTIVE AI USE:

Use AI tools to help independent watchdog groups analyze these impact statements, cross-reference them with real-world data, and flag inconsistencies, creating a robust system of public accountability.

Myth 6: Data and Algorithms Trump Spiritual Discernment

Individual Practice:

Keep a rule of life. Like the ancient monastics, develop a personal, flexible rule of life—a set of commitments to prayer, rest, relationships, and service that acts as your soul's true north. A rule of life is a proactive declaration of what truly matters, a framework for building your life around God's priorities, not the world's demands.

EFFECTIVE AI USE:

Use AI as your monastic scribe. After you've drafted your rule, use AI to format it beautifully and set gentle, recurring calendar reminders for your core commitments, like evening prayer or weekly solitude.

Church Community Practice:

Reestablish spiritual direction. Formalize a ministry where trained, spiritually mature members can serve as soul friends for others. Their role is not to give answers but to practice the discipline of deep listening, helping others discern God's movement in their own lives. A spiritual director helps you discern God's goals for you, not just achieve your own.

EFFECTIVE AI USE:

Use AI to provide resources for the spiritual directors, helping them find articles or podcasts on compassionate listening or different discernment traditions that they can use for their own continued learning.

Societal Practice:

Enshrine the right to a human explanation. Push for laws requiring any institution using AI for a life-altering decision (like denying a loan) to provide a clear, understandable explanation of why, delivered by a human being who can be questioned. This rejects opaque "black box" systems and insists that systems affecting human lives must remain legible and accountable.

EFFECTIVE AI USE:

Use AI to help organizations create explanation-ready systems by translating complex model behavior into simpler, human-readable logic, empowering a human representative to give a clear and honest answer.

Myth 7: Personal Growth Is All About Measurable Results

Individual Practice:

Observe a true Sabbath. Practice a twenty-four-hour Sabbath, ceasing not just from work but from all measuring, optimizing, and producing—no fitness trackers, no to-do lists. It is a weekly act of theological defiance that declares your worth is not in what you accomplish but in your identity as a beloved child of God.

Effective AI Use:

Use AI to protect your Sabbath. Set up an email autoresponder, tell your smart home to enter a Sabbath mode with minimal interruptions, and use it to curate a playlist of restful, non-lyrical music.

Church Community Practice:

Make space for *holy unfruitfulness*. Intentionally engage in activities with no strategic outcome: a church-wide day of play, a contemplative walk in the woods, or a worship service focused purely on adoration and awe. This reclaims the truth that God often works in ways that are inefficient and unmeasurable, valuing being with God over doing for God.

Effective AI Use:

Use AI for the playful parts. Ask it to generate a holy scavenger hunt list for the walk (e.g., "find something that reminds you of resurrection") or to create a stunning visual of a galaxy to project during a service of awe.

Societal Practice:

Fund the sources of awe. Advocate for public funding of things that exist not to grow the economy but to deepen the human spirit: public art, basic scientific research, conservation of wild spaces. This argues for a different metric than return on investment, insisting that a healthy society must invest in the unprofitable sources of meaning that make life worth living.

Effective AI Use:

Use AI to model the positive downstream impacts of these investments, showing how access to arts or nature correlates with better community health, providing quantitative data to support a qualitative argument.

Myth 8: With AI, There Will Be No Darkness

Individual Practice:

Pray the psalms of lament. When you are feeling grief, anger, or despair, instead of suppressing it, turn to the psalms of lament (e.g., Pss 13, 22, 88) and pray them aloud. The psalms offer a divinely authorized script for honest struggle, reclaiming the truth that it is an act of profound faith to cry out to God from the darkness, not just after it has passed.

EFFECTIVE AI USE:

Use AI to explore the context of your pain. Ask it to find different musical versions of a psalm of lament or to provide theological commentary on the psalm you are praying, helping you feel less alone in your struggle.

Church Community Practice:

Hold a Service of Ashes or Tenebrae. Hold a special service that acknowledges a collective sorrow, using a ritual like the imposition of ashes to physically mark our shared mortality and dependence on God. This carves out a sacred space to tell the truth about the world's pain, affirming that God meets us in our sorrow, not just in our joy.

EFFECTIVE AI USE:

Use AI to gather materials for the service. Ask it to find powerful poems about loss from different cultures or pieces of somber, reflective music that can be woven into a rich and deeply human experience of shared grief.

Societal Practice:

Create memorials to failure and injustice. Advocate for public art and memorials that remember our collective failures and injustices, not just our triumphs. This practice stands against the tech-utopian desire for a clean slate, arguing that we can only move forward wisely by honestly remembering where we have gone wrong.

Effective AI Use:

Use AI to make these histories more accessible by helping translate survivor testimonies, creating interactive maps of historical events, or analyzing archives to uncover forgotten stories.

The Gardener's Work in a Digital Age

This is the hard, beautiful, and necessary work of our time. It is the work of living fully into our God-given identity in the age of AI—not by fighting a system, but by joining God, the True Gardener, in the diligent and loving cultivation of our souls. In doing so, in this sacred partnership, we become truly human, restored to the image in which we were made. This garden is not a private escape for our own comfort but a public trust to be tended for the flourishing of the world. It is our participation in God's kingdom, grown in the soil of our hearts, in the shared life of our communities, and in the very structures of our society.

The weeds of algorithmic certainty and digital distraction will always be present, threatening to choke out the life God has planted. Our task is not to eradicate them by our own strength but to cooperate with the Gardener. It is to prayerfully tend the soil of our awareness, to water the seeds of the Spirit planted deep within us—love, joy, peace, patience—and to pull the weeds of myth with the patient, gentle hands of spiritual practice, trusting that God is the one who brings the growth.

The choice before us is not between using technology and rejecting it. It is a choice between two kingdoms. One vision, whispered by the myths of AI, offers a counterfeit kingdom of data. It is a kingdom built on the illusion of human control, promising a life of frictionless ease, optimized outcomes, and predictable comfort, where everything is known and nothing need be left to faith.

The other vision, the one to which these practices call us, is the messier, more beautiful kingdom of God. It is a life rooted in the incarnation—in the profound, world-changing truth that our bodies, our shared meals, our physical presence, and our real-world communities are the very places God chooses to dwell. It is a kingdom that makes space for the Sabbath's holy rest, the table's sacred fellowship, the wisdom of honest lament, and the slow, prayerful work of discernment. This is the reality Jesus inaugurated, a kingdom that is already among us.

And the fruit of such cultivation? We might find our own lives becoming slower but deeper; less optimized but more meaningful. We might see our communities become not just centers of information but true sanctuaries of transformation—foretastes of the kingdom known for their wisdom, their compassion, and their unwavering commitment to embodied love. And we might, by grace, help build a society where our astonishing new tools are finally bent toward the values of God's reign: justice, mercy, and the unmeasurable dignity of every human soul he created.

This work does not require us to be experts in code but practitioners of the way of Jesus—the ancient path by which we become truly human. It is done not in grand gestures but in the small, daily choices that build a life of faithfulness: one sacred pause, one shared meal, one prayerful question at a time. Do not be discouraged. The path is ancient, and you do not walk it alone, for the Gardener is with you always.

Ultimately, this work of cultivating our humanity is not just for our own sake; it is for the sake of the future we are building alongside our digital creations. As we strive to be truly human, we offer a vital instruction to the systems learning from us. Ethan Mollick reminds us that at its core, "AI is a mirror, reflecting back at us our best and worst qualities." Our commitment to soulful living—to discernment, patience, justice, and deep presence—clears the fog from that mirror, ensuring it reflects a vision of human dignity rather than brokenness. We hold the agency to decide its path. The choices we make today, in the quiet of our hearts and the bustle of our communities, "will shape what AI actually does for, and to, humanity." Let us choose well, so that our new partner learns to serve a life of depth and grace.[7]

May you have the courage to trust the soul God gave you, the grace to be present in the life he has called you to, and the wonder to find him working and loving in this slow, beautiful, and embodied world.

The age of AI is here, but so is the Gardener. Let us begin.

7. Mollick, *Co-Intelligence*, 212.

Bibliography

Aristotle. *Nicomachean Ethics*. Translated by Terence Irwin. 3rd ed. Indianapolis: Hackett, 2019.

Augustine. *The City of God*. Translated by Henry Bettenson. Penguin Classics. New York: Penguin, 2003.

———. *Confessions*. Translated by Henry Chadwick. Oxford World's Classics. Oxford: Oxford University Press, 2008.

Barrett, Lisa Feldman. *How Emotions Are Made: The Secret Life of the Brain*. New York: Houghton Mifflin Harcourt, 2017.

Barton, Ruth Haley. *Sacred Compass: The Way of Spiritual Discernment*. Downers Grove, IL: IVP, 2008.

———. *Sacred Rhythms: Arranging Our Lives for Spiritual Transformation*. Downers Grove, IL: IVP, 2006.

Bauman, Zygmunt. *Liquid Modernity*. Cambridge: Polity, 2000.

Beilock, Sian. *How the Body Knows Its Mind*. New York: Atria, 2015.

Benjamin, Ruha. *Race After Technology: Abolitionist Tools for the New Jim Code*. Cambridge: Polity, 2019.

Bolsinger, Tod. *Canoeing the Mountains: Christian Leadership in Uncharted Territory*. Downers Grove, IL: IVP, 2015.

Bonhoeffer, Dietrich. *Life Together*. Translated by John W. Doberstein. New York: Harper & Row, 1954.

Brown, Brené. *Daring Greatly: How the Courage to Be Vulnerable Transforms the Way We Live, Love, Parent, and Lead*. New York: Gotham, 2012.

———. *The Gifts of Imperfection*. Center City, MN: Hazelden, 2010.

Brueggemann, Walter. *The Prophetic Imagination*. Minneapolis: Fortress, 2001.

Burton, Tara Isabella. *Strange Rites: New Religions for a Godless World*. New York: PublicAffairs, 2020.

Carr, Nicholas. *The Shallows: What the Internet Is Doing to Our Brains*. New York: Norton, 2010.

Carson, Rachel. *The Sense of Wonder*. New York: HarperCollins, 1998.

CFP Board of Standards. *Leading the Future: Harnessing AI in the Financial Planning Profession*. Washington, DC: CFP Board of Standards, 2025. https://www.cfp.net/-/media/files/cfp-board/knowledge/reports-and-research/harnessing-ai-in-the-financial-planning-profession-cfp-board-report.pdf.

Chesterton, G. K. *What's Wrong with the World*. New York: Dodd, Mead, 1910.

Chittister, Joan. *Wisdom Distilled from the Daily: Living the Rule of St. Benedict Today*. San Francisco: HarperSanFrancisco, 1990.

Covey, Stephen R. *The 7 Habits of Highly Effective People*. New York: Simon & Schuster, 1989.

Crawford, Kate. *Atlas of AI: Power, Politics, and the Planetary Costs of Artificial Intelligence*. New Haven: Yale University Press, 2021.

Crawford, Matthew B. *Shop Class as Soulcraft: An Inquiry Into the Value of Work*. New York: Penguin, 2009.

———. *The World Beyond Your Head: On Becoming an Individual in an Age of Distraction*. New York: Farrar, Straus and Giroux, 2015.

Crouch, Andy. *The Life We're Looking For: Reclaiming Relationship in a Technological World*. New York: Convergent, 2022.

———. *The Tech-Wise Family: Everyday Steps for Putting Technology in Its Proper Place*. Grand Rapids: Baker, 2017.

Csikszentmihalyi, Mihaly. *Flow: The Psychology of Optimal Experience*. New York: Harper Perennial, 2008.

Dalton-Smith, Saundra. *Sacred Rest: Recover Your Life, Renew Your Energy, Restore Your Sanity*. New York: FaithWords, 2017.

Damasio, Antonio. *The Strange Order of Things: Life, Feeling, and the Making of Cultures*. New York: Pantheon, 2018.

Draper, Jonathan. *Pastoral Theology in a Digital Age*. London: SCM, 2021.

Eubanks, Virginia. *Automating Inequality: How High-Tech Tools Profile, Police, and Punish the Poor*. New York: St. Martin's, 2018.

Foster, Richard. *Celebration of Discipline: The Path to Spiritual Growth*. San Francisco: Harper & Row, 1978.

Frankl, Viktor E. *Man's Search for Meaning*. Boston: Beacon, 2006.

Gladwell, Malcolm. *Blink: The Power of Thinking Without Thinking*. New York: Little, Brown, 2005.

Haidt, Jonathan. *The Anxious Generation: How the Great Rewiring of Childhood Is Causing an Epidemic of Mental Illness*. New York: Penguin, 2024.

———. *The Righteous Mind: Why Good People Are Divided by Politics and Religion*. New York: Pantheon, 2012.

Han, Byung-Chul. *The Burnout Society*. Stanford: Stanford University Press, 2015.

———. *The Scent of Time: A Philosophical Essay on the Art of Lingering*. Cambridge: Polity, 2017.

Hari, Johann. *Stolen Focus: Why You Can't Pay Attention—and How to Think Deeply Again*. New York: Crown, 2022.

Hauerwas, Stanley. *The Peaceable Kingdom: A Primer in Christian Ethics*. Notre Dame: University of Notre Dame Press, 1983.

Heschel, Abraham Joshua. *God in Search of Man: A Philosophy of Judaism*. New York: Farrar, Straus and Cudahy, 1955.

Holmes, Barbara A. *Listening in the Dark*. New York: HarperCollins, 2024.

Iyer, Pico. *The Art of Stillness: Adventures in Going Nowhere*. New York: TED, 2014.

Jung, Carl. *Modern Man in Search of a Soul*. Translated by Cary F. Baynes and W. S. Dell. New York: Harcourt Brace, 1933.

Kahneman, Daniel. *Thinking, Fast and Slow*. New York: Farrar, Straus and Giroux, 2011.

Kissinger, Henry, et al. *The Age of AI: And Our Human Future*. New York: Little, Brown, 2021.

Kim, Jay Y. *Analog Christian: Cultivating Contentment, Resilience, and Wisdom in the Digital Age*. Downers Grove, IL: InterVarsity, 2022.

Li, Qing. *Forest Bathing: How Trees Can Help You Find Health and Happiness*. New York: Viking, 2018.

Lewis, C. S. *The Problem of Pain*. New York: Macmillan, 1940.

Manning, Brennan. *Abba's Child: The Cry of the Heart for Intimate Belonging*. Colorado Springs: NavPress, 2015.

Marsh, Charles. *The Beloved Community: How Faith Shapes Social Justice from the Civil Rights Movement to Today*. New York: Basic, 2005.

Martin, James. *The Jesuit Guide to (Almost) Everything: A Spirituality for Real Life*. New York: HarperOne, 2010.

McBride, Hillary L. *The Wisdom of Your Body: Finding Healing, Wholeness, and Connection Through Embodied Living*. Grand Rapids: Brazos, 2021.

McGilchrist, Iain. *The Master and His Emissary: The Divided Brain and the Making of the Western World*. New Haven: Yale University Press, 2009.

McHugh, Adam S. *The Listening Life: Embracing the Bold Vocation of Unusually Attentive Spiritual Practice*. Downers Grove, IL: InterVarsity, 2015.

Merton, Thomas. *New Seeds of Contemplation*. New York: New Directions, 1961.

———. *No Man Is an Island*. New York: Harcourt, Brace, 1955.

———. *Thoughts in Solitude*. New York: Farrar, Straus and Cudahy, 1958.

Mollick, Ethan. *Co-Intelligence: Living and Working with AI*. New York: Portfolio, 2024.

Mulholland, M. Robert, Jr. *Invitation to a Journey: A Road Map for Spiritual Formation*. Downers Grove, IL: IVP, 1993.

Murphy, Kate. *You're Not Listening: What You're Missing and Why It Matters*. New York: Celadon, 2019.

Newport, Cal. *Deep Work: Rules for Focused Success in a Distracted World*. New York: Grand Central, 2016.

———. *Digital Minimalism: Choosing a Focused Life in a Noisy World*. New York: Portfolio, 2019.

Noble, Safiya Umoja. *Algorithms of Oppression: How Search Engines Reinforce Racism*. New York: NYU Press, 2018.

Nouwen, Henri. *The Wounded Healer: Ministry in Contemporary Society*. New York: Doubleday, 1972.

Odell, Jenny. *How to Do Nothing: Resisting the Attention Economy*. New York: Melville House, 2019.

Oldenburg, Ray. *The Great Good Place: Cafes, Coffee Shops, Bookstores, Bars, Hair Salons, and Other Hangouts at the Heart of a Community*. New York: Marlowe & Company, 1999.

O'Neil, Cathy. *Weapons of Math Destruction: How Big Data Increases Inequality and Threatens Democracy*. New York: Crown, 2016.

Pariser, Eli. *The Filter Bubble: How the New Personalized Web Is Changing What We Read and How We Think*. New York: Penguin, 2011.

Parker, Priya. *The Art of Gathering: How We Meet and Why It Matters*. New York: Riverhead, 2018.

Perkins, John M. *Reconciliation*. Grand Rapids: Baker, 2011.

Pink, Daniel H. *A Whole New Mind: Why Right-Brainers Will Rule the Future*. New York: Riverhead, 2005.

Pohl, Christine D. *Making Room: Recovering Hospitality as a Christian Tradition*. Grand Rapids: Eerdmans, 1999.

Putnam, Robert D. *Bowling Alone: The Collapse and Revival of American Community*. New York: Simon & Schuster, 2000.

Rilke, Rainer Maria. *Letters to a Young Poet*. Translated by M. D. Herter Norton. New York: Norton, 2004.

Rohr, Richard. *Falling Upward: A Spirituality for the Two Halves of Life*. San Francisco: Jossey-Bass, 2011.

———. *The Universal Christ: How a Forgotten Reality Can Change Everything We See, Hope For, and Believe*. New York: Convergent, 2019.

Rosa, Hartmut. *Resonance: A Sociology of Our Relationship to the World*. Cambridge: Polity, 2019.

Sauls, Scott. *Befriend: Create Belonging in an Age of Judgment, Isolation, and Fear*. Carol Stream, IL: Tyndale House, 2016.

———. *A Gentle Answer: Our "Secret Weapon" in an Age of Us Against Them*. Nashville: Thomas Nelson, 2020.

Seth, Anil. *Being You: A New Science of Consciousness*. New York: Dutton, 2021.

Smith, Gary. *The AI Delusion*. Oxford: Oxford University Press, 2018.

Smith, James K. A. *You Are What You Love: The Spiritual Power of Habit*. Grand Rapids: Brazos, 2016.

Song, Felicia Wu. *Restless Devices: Recovering Personhood, Presence, and Place in the Digital Age*. Downers Grove, IL: IVP Academic, 2021.

Suleyman, Mustafa. *The Coming Wave: Technology, Power, and the Twenty-First Century's Greatest Dilemma*. New York: Crown, 2023.

Sunstein, Cass. *Republic: Divided Democracy in the Age of Social Media*. Princeton: Princeton University Press, 2017.

Taylor, Barbara Brown. *Learning to Walk in the Dark*. New York: HarperOne, 2014.

TD Bank. *2025 AI Insights Report: A Turning Point in Digital Banking*. 2025. https://stories.td.com/us/en/article/2025-ai-insights-report-a-turning-point-in-digital-banking.

Ter Kuile, Casper. *The Power of Ritual: Turning Everyday Activities into Soulful Practices*. New York: HarperOne, 2020.

Thompson, Curt. *The Soul of Shame: Retelling the Stories We Believe About Ourselves*. Downers Grove, IL: IVP, 2015.

Tribole, Evelyn, and Elyse Resch. *Intuitive Eating: A Revolutionary Program That Works*. New York: St. Martin's Griffin, 2012.

Turkle, Sherry. *Alone Together: Why We Expect More from Technology and Less from Each Other*. New York: Basic, 2011.

———. *Reclaiming Conversation: The Power of Talk in a Digital Age*. New York: Penguin, 2015.

Twenge, Jean M. *iGen: Why Today's Super-Connected Kids Are Growing Up Less Rebellious, More Tolerant, Less Happy—and Completely Unprepared for Adulthood*. New York: Atria, 2017.

Vallor, Shannon. *Technology and the Virtues: A Philosophical Guide to a Future Worth Wanting*. New York: Oxford University Press, 2016.

Van der Kolk, Bessel. *The Body Keeps the Score: Brain, Mind, and Body in the Healing of Trauma*. New York: Viking, 2014.

Volf, Miroslav. *Exclusion and Embrace: A Theological Exploration of Identity, Otherness, and Reconciliation*. Nashville: Abingdon, 1996.

Warren, Tish Harrison. *Liturgy of the Ordinary: Sacred Practices in Everyday Life.* Downers Grove, IL: IVP, 2016.

———. *Prayer in the Night: For Those Who Work or Watch or Weep*. Downers Grove, IL: IVP, 2021.

Wicks, Robert. *The Ministry of Presence.* New York: Paulist, 2018.

Willard, Dallas. *The Divine Conspiracy: Rediscovering Our Hidden Life in God.* San Francisco: HarperSanFrancisco, 1998.

Wolf, Maryanne. *Reader, Come Home: The Reading Brain in a Digital World.* New York: Harper, 2018.

Wright, N. T. *Simply Christian: Why Christianity Makes Sense.* San Francisco: HarperSanFrancisco, 2006.

Zehr, Howard. *The Little Book of Restorative Justice.* Intercourse, PA: Good, 2002.

Zuboff, Shoshana. *The Age of Surveillance Capitalism: The Fight for a Human Future at the New Frontier of Power*. New York: PublicAffairs, 2019.

www.ingramcontent.com/pod-product-compliance
Lightning Source LLC
LaVergne TN
LVHW052313200926
848481LV00002B/549
* 9 7 9 8 3 8 5 2 7 4 7 1 0 *